Professor Peter Greste is an award-winning foreign correspondent who spent twenty-five years working for the BBC, Reuters and Al Jazeera in some of the world's most volatile places. From Afghanistan to Latin American, Africa and the Middle East, he reported from the frontlines and beyond, although he is best known for becoming a headline himself, when he and two of his colleagues were arrested in Cairo while working for Al Jazeera, and charged with terrorism offences. He has since become a vocal campaigner and advocate for media freedom – a stance that has earned him awards from Britain's Royal Television Society, the Walkley Foundation, the RSL's ANZAC Peace Prize, the Australian Human Rights Commission's Human Rights Medal and the International Association of Press Clubs' Freedom of Speech Award. Peter is Executive Director of the advocacy group Alliance for Journalists' Freedom and Professor of Journalism at Macquarie University. He lives in Brisbane.

THE CORRESPONDENT

PETER GRESTE

UQP

First published 2025 by University of Queensland Press
PO Box 6042, St Lucia, Queensland 4067 Australia
Reprinted 2025

Originally published as *The First Casualty* in 2017
This new and revised edition published as *The Correspondent* in 2025.

University of Queensland Press (UQP) acknowledges the Traditional Owners and their custodianship of the lands on which UQP operates. We pay our respects to their Ancestors and their descendants, who continue cultural and spiritual connections to Country. We recognise their valuable contributions to Australian and global society.

uqp.com.au
reception@uqp.com.au

Cover design by Christabella Designs
Cover photo by Daniel Asher Smith
Cover image by Carnival Studio
Image copyright Pop Family Entertainment
Author photo by Louie Douvis
Typeset in 12/16 Adobe Garamond
Printed in Australia by McPherson's Printing Group

Queensland Government
University of Queensland Press is supported by the Queensland Government through Arts Queensland.

Australian Government
Creative Australia
University of Queensland Press is assisted by the Australian Government through Creative Australia, its principal arts investment and advisory body.

A catalogue record for this book is available from the National Library of Australia.

ISBN 978 0 7022 6914 1 (pbk)
ISBN 978 0 7022 7079 6 (epdf)
ISBN 978 0 7022 7080 2 (epub)

University of Queensland Press uses papers that are natural, renewable and recyclable products made from wood grown in well-managed forests and other controlled sources. The logging and manufacturing processes conform to the environmental regulations of the country of origin.

FSC www.fsc.org MIX Paper | Supporting responsible forestry FSC® C001695

According to the Committee to Protect Journalists,
between 9/11 2001 and November 2024, 1866 journalists
have been killed in the line of duty.

This book is dedicated to all media workers
who have given – or will give – their
lives in pursuit of the truth.

'The truth is always an abyss. One must – as in a swimming pool – dive from the quivering springboard of trivial, everyday experience, and sink into the depths in order to later rise again – laughing and fighting for breath to the now doubly illuminated surface of things.'

Gustav Janouch, ***Conversations with Kafka***

CONTENTS

FOREWORD

Close to midnight on 4 February 2015, I was catching a flight from Brisbane to Sydney and intercepted a former ABC colleague rushing into the airport carrying his recorder. Decades earlier, we'd both worked as journalists in Africa, reporting for the BBC World Service and CBC Canada.

'What's the story?' I asked.

'Someone's arriving,' my former colleague replied secretively.

Sure enough, a huge crowd had started gathering at Brisbane Airport.

'Is it Peter Greste?' I asked, immediately curious.

Like thousands of others around the world, I'd followed Peter's story closely and was aware that he had just been released from an Egyptian prison after four hundred days.

In the early hours of 5 February, I watched on from the arrivals lounge as Peter's family and friends waited expectantly at the gates. His face beamed as he walked into their arms – exhilarated and overwhelmed by his sudden, unexpected, but utterly justified early release from a seven-year sentence on terrorism-related charges.

Peter's experience spoke to the chilling scenario being played out all too often in global conflict zones, of journalists being criminalised for doing their job – facing trumped-up charges ranging from spying and corruption to terrorism, or any other spurious reason to 'legitimise' their arrest.

Peter's journalism had always struck a chord with viewers: it was courageous, measured and thoughtful. He embodied the best work ethos of investigative journalists working around the world in similar roles – find the story, look for evidence to back it up, maintain an open mind, remain objective and report the truth. This is the opposite of a criminal act.

Good government is directly connected to good journalism. What Peter's story attests to is the potential endangerment of his profession as an investigative journalist in territories across the globe, including some whose very stanchion is defined as democracy.

But these were thoughts for tomorrow.

On that morning at the airport, the atmosphere was one of intense relief and happiness. It was time for Peter and his family to finally exhale after four hundred fearful days of helplessness and dread. It was personal, not political.

•

Later that year, in August 2015, Peter (in absentia) and his still-imprisoned colleagues, Mohamed Fahmy and Baher Mohamed, were re-tried. Like Peter's family, thousands of others around the globe were also holding their breaths and hoping against hope for the release of their son, daughter, brother, sister, mother, father, friend, colleague – innocent captives imprisoned for writing uncomfortable truths.

Fahmy and Mohamed were pardoned by Egyptian President Abdel Fattah El-Sisi and released in September.

Peter was not pardoned and remains a convicted terrorist to this day.

I'd always maintained a deep respect for news journalists, and by this stage my work had segued into longer form documentaries and scripted series. Over the next couple of years, Peter and I spoke regularly about telling his personal story. We agreed to do 'something', and I waited patiently, confident that at some stage the time and circumstance would feel right to tell his story. I knew he needed space to process all that had happened.

I was in a hotel room in New Zealand in 2017 when I read his recently published memoir, *The First Casualty*. It left me breathless, unable to sleep, with a feeling that his story would translate into a compelling feature film.

I shared *The First Casualty* with renowned screenwriter Peter Duncan, who must have been utterly frenzied by what he was reading, as he delivered his first draft of a screenplay within a matter of days. He rang me and said, 'I've got a present for you. Check your inbox.'

It was an astonishing turnaround. Over the following months the three of us met frequently to talk over the minutiae of Peter's imprisonment, his trial and his earlier experiences as a news reporter in Africa and the Middle East. Our task was to carefully navigate the line between a factual recount of his life and the making of a creative, scripted movie.

The stars began to align when the brilliant director Kriv Stenders who, like Peter, had also grown up in Brisbane with Latvian parents, instantly wanted to be part of the project. When the masterful Richard Roxburgh took less than two days to say 'yes' to the role of Peter Greste, the project really started to take shape.

We continued to dive deeper into our character of Peter, and slowly a film was crafted on the page. After two years of development (and my slowly putting together the production elements of the film) we reached a point where Kriv declared, 'Yes, we have a film – let's go!'

The Correspondent film is fully informed by Peter's experience. At no more prescient a time than now, journalism is a craft that needs to be defended, not derided. Throughout, I wanted to honour Peter's commitment, along with the work of the thousands of other journalists across the globe who practise their craft with care and courage. But most importantly, as with this updated memoir, we all wanted simply to tell a story – a ripping yarn that has purpose and weight.

— Carmel Travers, Producer of *The Correspondent*

PREFACE

On 1 February 2015, I walked out of prison into the glare of the Egyptian sun, dazed and blinking, after exactly 400 days behind bars on terrorism charges. It was a strange anticlimax to a frustrating, frightening and at times bizarre tale.

My release was as sudden as it was unexpected. It came at a time when I was so convinced that the authorities were unwilling to bend that I was about to launch a hunger strike. When I returned to Australia a few days later, I was plunged into a whirlwind of interviews and talks, with barely enough time to process exactly what had happened. But as the attention faded away and I had more time to think, I came to see that the story of what happened to my two colleagues and me in Cairo through 2014 was, in effect, the collision of three histories.

The first two narratives were relatively straightforward. There was our own very personal yarn, of three journalists – an Australian, an Egyptian and a Canadian-Egyptian – on a journey through the Byzantine world of the Egyptian judicial system. The Egyptian government saw us as part of the second, wider historic struggle: of their corner of an existential battle with Islamic extremism that has been playing out across the Middle East since the Arab Spring erupted in 2010.

As I thought more deeply, I realised that our experience was also part of a third, more obscure conflict between journalism and belligerents on both sides of what has become known euphemistically as the 'War on Terror'. What happened to us was the consequence of a government's decision to twist and contort the definition of 'terrorism' to cover just about anybody it deems to be a threat, whether political or physical. Our experience was an extreme example of the kinds of assaults on media freedom that have been playing out around the world – not just in authoritarian regimes, but also in countries that like to think of themselves as bastions of democracy and free speech. This isn't the fault of governments alone. In this conflict over ideas, extremists everywhere have taken to attacking the agents of those ideas – the media – both rhetorically and physically.

The more I looked, the more I realised that my whole career seems to have been embedded in and shaped by both sides of that broader conflict.

We have been living with it for so long now that at times it seems as though the War on Terror is a permanent part of life, that Western liberalism has always been in open conflict with conservative Islam. And yet we forget that human ideas and ideologies are malleable, changing and evolving over time, so that what seems to be a truism today may not be the case tomorrow, and almost certainly hasn't always been so.

That is why my first experience as a young correspondent in Afghanistan in 1995 is such an important baseline for this book. It shows how before the Twin Towers attack changed everything, journalists were able to talk to and work with radical militant Islamists without being murdered or kidnapped. The fact that it is so risky now is the consequence of history – of the choices made on both sides of the conflict – rather than a hardwired fact of ideology.

The impact of those choices is being felt as much in liberal Western democracies as it is in more authoritarian regimes. That's why when I decided to write this book I wanted to make it about more than our own experience. I wanted to put it in its wider historical context, and describe both what my colleagues and I went through and the broader parallel story of the impact of the War on Terror on journalism, and what it means for press freedom – one of the most important pillars of any functioning democracy.

What follows is part memoir, part history. The memoirs are based on the notes I was able to make in prison, a handful of letters we smuggled out, and my own recollections, while the histories are accounts of key moments in the War on Terror that have targeted the media in ways that were once unimaginable.

More than a collection of stories, though, this is a reflection on two decades of reporting in some of the world's most volatile corners, as well as what happened to us in Egypt, and what it means for all of us now.

1

UNDER ARREST

28 DECEMBER 2013

It starts with a knock at the door.

The pounding is heavy, urgent, with a force that demands a response. I'm irritated by the interruption. I am getting ready to go for a swim in the Marriott Hotel's expansive heated pool. My computer is streaming Triple J – a favourite Australian alternative-rock radio station – and I am running out of time to get into the water before dinner. I'm due to meet an old colleague from the BBC who I haven't seen for years, and I'm looking forward to swapping gossip.

I'm half-dressed, wearing only my jeans, when the hammering begins again. I throw on a shirt and stride to the door just as a third round of knocking starts up. I don't bother to look through the peep-hole. It's either someone from the hotel, probably with a message of some sort, or one of the Al Jazeera News Network team keeping watch over the unfolding political crisis that I am here to report on. I'd have thought they would call first, though.

As I lever the handle down, the door flies open as if pushed by a spring. I'm shoved backwards as the room fills with heavy-set men. Five, six, seven, eight of them – too many to count. I have no choice but to back up the entrance hall to the window overlooking the hotel's leafy courtyard twelve floors below.

The men rifle through my bags, opening cupboards, searching corners, with Triple J providing the soundtrack.

'Mr Peter?' demands the one who appears to be the leader. He is clean-shaven – unusually for Egypt, where thick moustaches are the fashion. He also has no chin, and a small pot belly pushing its way through a leather jacket. He is wearing a checked shirt and jeans – standard anonymous street code for any middle-class, middle-aged Egyptian man. But there is an authority in his voice that demands it be heard.

'Yes,' I reply. 'And who are you?'

He nods, but says nothing. I am standing with my back to the window, feeling bewildered and confused; powerless to stop the raid.

The men keep searching. One unzips my grimy field bag and upends the contents onto the bed. There is a camera, my notebook, my passport, an iPod, a half-empty bottle of water, a tangle of headphones, a half-eaten packet of chocolate and a Leatherman pocketknife – the standard kit for either a tourist or a foreign correspondent. Among the group of men moving around the room, I notice one with a small hand-held video recorder. He hoses it across the equipment, pointing it at the computer, my notebook, my business cards, the mess covering the bed, and me whenever I open my mouth.

'Who are you?' I demand again, this time my voice tightening with tension as the search continues. 'Are you the police? Are you hotel security? What the hell is going on?' The questions spill out of me like the jumble of things from the bag.

Still nothing.

Even though I've been through this kind of thing before, these men show alarming seriousness and professionalism. I take my mobile phone from my hip pocket, but before I can look at the screen to dial, it's snatched from my hands. The men start sweeping up the rest of my equipment. One slams the lid of the laptop shut and the music stops. There is silence as he shovels the computer into the bag along with the rest of the equipment.

'You will come with us,' says Leather Jacket.

'Not until you tell me who you are,' I reply. 'What are you doing? Why are you here? Where is your ID?'

'We are from the Ministry of the Interior.'

'So where is your ID? How do I know? Do you have a warrant? Where are you taking me?' The cameraman now has the lens pointed at my face, pushing it within a few inches of my cheek. I can feel my face flush as I struggle to hold my composure.

Must. Not. Get. Angry.

'We are from the Ministry of the Interior,' he repeats. 'That is enough. What is in the safe? Open it.'

The safe is full of cash – about US$9000. That's not unusual: in countries with unreliable credit-card systems, cash is still the norm, and I have brought enough to pay the hotel bill and any other expenses. I'm worried that the moment I open it, they will take it. The thought of a bribe crosses my mind, but for all their shabby attire, these men move with the decisiveness of disciplined professionals. There has been no hint that this is about money, either – none of the knowing nods and winks that usually suggest a discreet few hundred dollars might solve the problem. I refuse to open the safe.

Leather Jacket turns to a man in a black suit and tie, who is wearing a name tag that labels him as hotel security. I haven't noticed him before in the melee, and after a brief conversation, he disappears out the door.

'He is getting the master key. Or you can open it now. It's your choice.'

I'm not sure if Leather Jacket is bluffing, so I cross my arms and stare at the men as they continue to search and clear the room.

The hotel security guy returns with a master key, and I realise I have no option. I open the safe and show them the block of cash, expecting Leather Jacket to make it vanish inside his coat lining. Instead, he gestures for me to put it into my own pocket and orders everyone out of the room. It is time to go.

With my heart pounding, I grab my black fleece jacket and

Akubra hat. It's midwinter and the Cairo night is surprisingly cold. I'm worried, but not panicking just yet. I've been looking for telltale bulges beneath their jackets and I can't see any concealed weapons. And I know I have done nothing wrong. I'm certain that this will get all sorted out in an hour or so, as soon as they realise they've made a mistake.

I've been in this situation before, with officious security officers from a nervous government. There is usually a lot of bluster and swagger designed to intimidate, to show who is in control, but unless you've genuinely done something wrong, it almost always ends with a couple of hours in a smoky room, some angry gestures and a few phone calls.

Almost always.

I'm escorted down the hall to the lift. We exit on the ground floor and march purposefully across the courtyard, where glamorous Egyptian couples huddle in their coats smoking shisha pipes. They chatter and giggle as we pass, happily oblivious to anything beyond their own intimate bubble and the fragrant apple-scented smoke hanging in the chilled evening air. I resist the urge to call for help, to run for it, to dash through the tables and dive through a side door to freedom. I flirt with the idea of elbowing the man on my right in the groin and swinging a right hook at the guy on my left, until I look again and realise that they are both about 15 centimetres taller than me, and twice as heavy.

And anyway, I have done nothing wrong, so there is nothing to worry about.

I am shepherded into a small ground-floor room with a desk, an armchair and a hotel couch. The air is thick with stale cigarette smoke and the table has on it nothing but an ashtray overflowing with butts and old grey powder. Behind it is a police officer with rolls of fat bulging under his chin and spilling over his belt, and I am relieved and worried at the same time. It is good news because it is immediately clear that whatever is going on has official sanction and I am not being rumbled by a gang of thugs with an audacious plan. But it is also obvious that this is going to take a while.

'Why am I here?' I demand, figuring that as long as I am asking the questions, I have a degree of control, however tiny. 'Who sent these men? Do you have a warrant?'

'Of course we do,' says the policeman. 'But can you read Arabic?'

I can't read Arabic, and nor can I speak it. I have only been in Egypt for two weeks, and while I've worked across the Middle East over the years, I've never been here for long enough to make learning the language a priority. I am feeling it now.

•

For most of the past decade I've been based in sub-Saharan Africa, covering East and Southern Africa first for the BBC and then, since 2011, for Al Jazeera. The work has focused on regional crises – the civil war in Somalia; ongoing conflict in the Democratic Republic of the Congo; the struggling, emerging new state of South Sudan.

But Egypt is new. I've been called in to cover the unfolding political crisis for three weeks over the Christmas–New Year period while my bosses in Doha keep searching for a more permanent staff correspondent.

Working in these environments always comes with a degree of risk, but foreign correspondents are generally insulated from local politics. Local reporters covering violent domestic conflicts can often be seen as players in crises that divide the country along ethnic, sectarian, cultural or linguistic lines. Simply giving your name can label you as sympathetic to one side or another, making it incredibly dangerous to work. Foreign news crews are usually seen as outsiders – if not always neutral, at least much harder to slot into one category or another. Even if we aren't welcome, that degree of detachment at least gives you half a chance to argue your way out of this kind of mess.

Egypt is different. It has come through an extraordinary period of political turmoil, and the government and its supporters often blame mysterious 'foreign powers' for their troubles, making Egyptians both deeply suspicious and openly hostile to outsiders – especially anyone linked to Qatar, which has long been accused of interfering in Egypt's internal affairs and which finances Al Jazeera.

A popular revolution toppled Hosni Mubarak from power on 25 January 2011 after having ruled Egypt for thirty years – part of the Arab Spring that had started in neighbouring Tunisia the previous year. The movement was driven by Egypt's young secular middle class, the educated, politically frustrated group of professionals and mid-level bureaucrats who dreamed of democratic freedom and faced down the government's security goons in an extraordinary and at times bloody show of defiance.

Although the Mubarak era had ended, his supporters remained hugely influential. Mubarak had been an air-force officer before he took power in a coup, and his administration helped entrench both the security services and a business elite who dominated the economy. They had a lot to lose with his departure.

When Mubarak left power, the Supreme Council of the Armed Forces (SCAF) stepped in as an interim government and to steer Egypt to the first genuinely democratic elections in its history. In those elections, a third powerful political force emerged alongside the secular middle class and the pro-Mubarak establishment: the conservative political Islamists who largely rallied behind the Muslim Brotherhood (MB).

In the parliamentary elections, Islamist figures took sixty-six of the 100 seats, with the remaining thirty-four going to secularists, leftists and old regime candidates. The last round of the all-important presidential elections pitted Mubarak-era minister Ahmed Shafik against the MB's Mohamed Morsi. That left the secular revolutionaries who had shed blood to topple Mubarak with a bitter choice: either capitulate and return to the dark days of the old military regime, or hold their noses and vote for the Islamist candidate in the hope that he would hold to the country's deep-seated secular political traditions.

It was a close-run thing. Morsi took 51.7 per cent of the vote to Shafik's 48.3 per cent.

The MB won the election, but had no experience of government. It struggled to balance its religious instincts with the realities of harnessing a vast, deeply suspicious and at times downright hostile civil service; it made promises it couldn't possibly keep (Morsi declared he would end Cairo's notorious near-permanent traffic congestion in a year); and worst of all it rushed through an Islamist version of the constitution despite a boycott by liberals, secularists and the Coptic Church, who said it failed to protect freedom of expression and religion.

By June the following year, millions of people had filled the streets, demanding the government's resignation. With the unrest and the death toll both rising, the military warned Morsi that it would intervene and impose its own 'roadmap' if he did not satisfy the public's demands within forty-eight hours and end the political crisis.

On 3 July, the military ordered its troops and armoured vehicles into the streets, declared the constitution suspended, and said the chief justice of the Constitutional Court would assume presidential powers. To Morsi's opponents, the military was simply fulfilling public opinion; to his supporters, it was a coup.

The collapse of Morsi's government was a blow to anyone who saw political Islam as a solution to the region's multiple crises. In particular it was a problem for the Qatari government, which had invested heavily in the new administration – both financially and politically – in the hope of creating an ally who could help counter the regional heavyweight, Saudi Arabia.

By the time I arrived in Egypt six months after this, another military-backed interim government was trying to draft a new constitution and organise fresh elections. Pro-Brotherhood protesters were still on the streets, while the authorities were rounding up MB officials and supporters, accusing them of supporting terrorism.

Crucially for me, Qatar and its government-funded news network, Al Jazeera, had been accused of working to undermine national security. The already-bleak political environment had turned toxic.

•

In the Marriott's police office, I slump on the couch, stretch out my legs and pull my hat low over my eyes. I want to look relaxed and unpanicked as the activity swirls around me. The men talk and smoke and I watch from beneath the brim.

A pair of badly scuffed black slip-on shoes with worn-out soles walks in and stands for a few moments accompanied by animated Arabic conversation, before turning and vanishing again. Off to one side, another portly belly in a stained shirt jiggles over a police-issue belt as its owner gestures angrily. The ashtray is so full of butts that every time someone taps his cigarette into it, a small avalanche of ash tumbles over the edge and onto the tabletop. The air is thick with the smell of stale smoke and fresh sweat.

Then, the voices rise as a new group arrives from across the courtyard. I can pick out a familiar one among them. It belongs to Mohamed Fahmy, Al Jazeera's senior bureau producer, who had been with his fiancée, Marwa, in the suite a few floors above mine that we had been using as an office.

Even in a country of loud men, Fahmy's distinctively assertive baritone rises above the others. I flip my brim up as he walks in, flanked just as I was by a couple of heavy-set men. His right arm is tucked in a black sling – he fractured his shoulder in a fall a week ago – and he winces with stiffness as he takes his place on the couch next to me.

'You okay, dude?' he inquires under his breath.

'I'm fine,' I hiss. 'I just wish I knew what the hell they want from us.'

Before we can talk any further, Leather Jacket flicks his hand at the videographer, who points his toy camera at us, and the questions begin. They are in Arabic, but I am able to follow the gist.

'Why are you hiding in the Marriott Hotel?'

'What were you doing with the Muslim Brotherhood?'

'Why don't you have press accreditation?'

'Where is your licence to operate this equipment?'

'Why are you working for Al Jazeera?'

Fahmy fields the questions with all the grace and humour he can muster. There are good answers to each of them. We are in the Marriott Hotel because police had raided the network's bureau several months earlier. We are not hiding there – a five-star hotel packed with staff, security cameras and government agents is hardly the place to work incognito – but in the increasingly hostile political environment, where Al Jazeera has been demonised as an agent of Islamic extremists, it has become too dangerous to work in an office exposed to the public, and the hotel offers several layers of security.

I don't have my press accreditation because the process usually takes a couple of weeks, and I only plan to stay in Cairo for three. And anyway, the network's relationship with the government has become so fractious that it is increasingly difficult, if not downright dangerous, to turn up at official events. Instead, we plan to cover them at a distance, using local accredited freelance cameramen to gather the footage and avoiding anything that might get us into a confrontation with officials. There is little point in the bureaucratic headache of applying for accreditation if I don't plan to use it.

Legally, Al Jazeera English staff are supposed to be fully licensed to operate from and broadcast into Egypt. The Egyptian government has withdrawn the licence for the network's Egyptian affiliate, but our bosses have insisted that we don't need to worry about our individual legal status. Our equipment – standard video cameras, lights, microphones and laptops – does not need any special documents. We have no military equipment beyond the bulletproof vests that have become standard issue for journalists working in places with bullets flying around. We are not using any special satellite equipment or banned communications gear. We are sending our material to network headquarters in Doha using the hotel's high-speed internet service.

None of this seems to satisfy our interrogators. They push on with the questions, repeating them again and again.

At first it is nothing more than an irritation. We know this will take a bit of time to resolve. There is the niggling worry that we have not been allowed to make any phone calls, but Fahmy and I don't see much to be concerned about. After all, on this assignment, my reporting has been deliberately predictable and dull. Vanilla journalism. In places I am familiar with, where my radar is more finely tuned to the limits of what the law and the authorities will tolerate, I am willing to push the boundaries. I don't mind offending officials by challenging policy or exploring more controversial subjects, such as state corruption. I've often done that in the past and half-expected the police to react. But in Egypt our relationship with the government is more fraught and my own sense of where those limits might lie is hazy with inexperience. I have made sure that within the bounds of our professional responsibility, I have been reflecting the full spectrum of any public debate by quoting the government's official position, getting hold of the opposition (the Muslim Brotherhood), and talking to an analyst to make sense of it all. My work has been predictable and flaccidly uncontroversial.

So after an hour and a half sitting in the police office with our equipment piled up in a heap in the corner, the same question keeps churning over and over in our minds like a bad pop song: why haven't they let us go?

'You're not going back to the room,' announces Leather Jacket at last. 'You're going to the police cells.'

2

AFGHANISTAN

1995

Kabul in winter is a bleak place. It has none of the prettiness of European or North American snows. There are no fir trees dusted with sugary ice; no glittering lamplit streets; no romantic forests piled high with whipped-cream snowdrifts.

Instead, dark, jagged, dun-grey mountains rise above the city like Gothic sentinels. The wind swirls around the city streets, driving frozen air down from the heights of the Hindu Kush mountains and deep into your bones. The alleys that run between the squat brown homes are clogged with icy mud, and people pick their way around the slosh under thin woollen cloaks pulled tightly under their chins in a futile attempt to ward off the cold. You wouldn't put a picture of a wintry Afghanistan on a Christmas card.

The Kabul I drove into early in 1995 was a shattered city largely forgotten by the rest of the world. I had been appointed as the BBC's Afghanistan correspondent – my first major assignment with the corporation – and made the overland journey from neighbouring Pakistan with my colleague Dan Lak, who was the correspondent based in Islamabad.

Afghanistan has since become a byword for Islamic extremism, alongside Iraq and Syria, where journalists serious about covering the conflict risk kidnap, torture and beheading if they venture too close to the Islamists.

Too often, commentators talk of an age-old conflict between the Islamic Middle East and Judeo-Christian West, as though there has been such a 'clash of civilisations' since Islam's inception 1400 years ago. They speak of it as a given, an inevitability, as if there has never been a time of accommodation between the religious communities, and that the current conflict is simply an extension of the wars that Mohammed first launched.

In that narrative, if you are Christian and mad enough to venture into the Islamist heartland, you are bound to literally lose your head. If that were the case, as we drove towards a city being fought over by rival mujahedin factions and with the Taliban newly emergent in the far south, Dan and I were on a suicide mission.

And yet it wasn't suicide. Through the 1990s, Afghanistan was a very different place, with an understanding of the media and war that was a world away from what it would later become. For Afghans who had been largely ignored since the Soviets abandoned their occupation of the country in 1989, journalists brought attention that validated their suffering. We were reminding the rest of the world that Afghanistan was still struggling to shake off more than a decade of violence in the wake of the withdrawal.

There was hostility, to be sure, but mainly from warlords who wanted to keep their plundering and murdering hidden. For the rest, we were independent observers with all the legitimacy of aid workers, and had every right to be there.

Although I didn't know it at the time, the Afghan civil war would become something of a baseline for me, defining the role of journalists in wars across the Islamic world before 9/11 turned the relationship on its head and made the media not so much observers as unwilling participants.

•

We began our journey on a local bus from Peshawar in Pakistan – now an unimaginably dangerous undertaking, but at the time safe enough for two BBC journalists with a local guide to steer us through the checkpoints. Armed with visas issued by the Afghanistan Embassy in London, we travelled by bus up through the Khyber Pass to the border crossing in Torkham and on into a civil war. Eight hours later, the bus stopped just before the town of Surobi, with its local gang of thugs who had a reputation for robbing and raping passing travellers.

There we joined some former British Royal Marines from the HALO Trust – an aid agency set up to clear landmines laid during the previous sixteen years of non-stop fighting. Their convoy of ex-army Land Rovers was ideal for the trip, partly because the vehicles were perfect for Afghanistan's rutted, boggy highways, but also because the Afghan militia were so devoted to their Toyota Hiluxes that none of them were interested in nicking a car that was impossible to find spare parts for.

As we drove the last few kilometres towards Kabul across the high plains, the clouds lay over the city like a lead blanket. The mountain peaks had vanished, and the wet, cold air held a promise of sloshy snow. The city was little more than a crooked muddy smudge on the horizon, and in the late-evening light it was hard to tell where the grey of the sky ended and the dun-brown skyline began.

As the fields began to give way to outlying suburbs, we pulled up at a checkpoint. Shivering militiamen – it would be too much to describe them as mujahedin, or 'holy warriors' – breathed hashish smoke into our open window and demanded the usual road tax. Our driver flipped them a few small notes and they opened the crooked iron boom gate to let us pass.

The highway took us past the long-abandoned industrial area and through the Mikroraion district – a neighbourhood built by the communists in classic Soviet style with high-rise concrete apartments standing like ranks of ragged, faceless soldiers in long, exhausted rows. Every building had been scarred by artillery and small-arms fire. A corner of one had been blown away at the third storey to expose the stairwell as if it were a broken bone in a gashed thigh. A tank round had blasted open the front room of another apartment to show the ripped-up remains of family life within.

In those days, the front lines drifted around the city as though pushed by the wind. Sometimes they would snag on a stubborn bit of geography and the fighting between rival militias would get stuck for months or even years. At other times they would lurch suddenly across large sections of the city before catching on another ridge or a line of buildings and the attrition would start all over again.

The BBC bureau was a house in the more up-market district of Wazir Akbar Khan. It was a relatively modern three-storey stone building, someone's stab at 1970s modernist architecture. Usefully, it had a basement with its own well where you could hide for a few weeks if need be. (We stockpiled dozens of cans of fish down there, just in case.) Sandbags protected the doors and the low-level windows. All the windowpanes had either been blown out or removed and replaced with sheets of plastic to keep anyone inside from getting covered with shards of glass every time a bomb landed close by.

As we pulled into the driveway, the bureau staff lined up to welcome the newest resident reporter: Hajji, the tall, dignified driver from Ghazni whose haughty bearing would save us at countless checkpoints; Faramouch, the toothless, grizzled cook who somehow managed to conjure up Afghan classics like kabuli palaw on a single smelly kerosene burner; Sultan, the cleaner whose ethnic Hazara roots would have had him killed if he moved into the wrong part of town; and the brilliantly astute translator and fixer Sayed Salahuddin, who would become my eyes, ears and, more often than not, my brain over the coming year.

•

At the time, the war in Afghanistan was one that few people outside the country cared about or were even aware of.

The violence had been unrelenting since 1978, when a group of left-wing military officers seized power in a coup and the following year 'invited' the Soviet Union to send troops to prop up the government. The West regarded this as an invasion, and poured millions of dollars into military aid to support the mujahedin rebels who fought to oust the Soviet troops and their unpopular puppet government.

Afghan society is highly fractured, a product as much of its splintered geography as of its tribal traditions. People's loyalties are first to their family or clan, and then to the local community with its leaders and militias. Then comes the district, then the ethnic group and finally the nation. In fact, the only time Afghanistan tends to behave as a country is when it is being invaded. That sense of loyalty – from the local to the national – helps explain the multitude of mujahedin forces that often popped up as self-defence units. It is hard to be precise about the number of groups that emerged during the Soviet occupation through the 1980s – they formed and dissolved with dizzying frequency – but the more established factions numbered close to a dozen.

As the conflict developed, the factions coalesced into two broad and constantly evolving alliances: one behind the charismatic Jamiat-e Islami commander Ahmad Shah Massoud, and the other behind Gulbuddin Hekmatyar, who led the Hezb-e Islami movement. Both were conservative Islamists who used their religion as a kind of organising force, providing the ideological framework to justify their actions and hold their militias together in their struggle for political power. In the absence of any functioning state, militant political Islam filled the need for structure in Afghanistan's instinctively conservative society.

Massoud was an enigmatic figure who understood the value of the media. He brought many Western reporters onto the battlefield, charming them with his wit and feeding their appetite for drama. He was a relatively moderate Islamist, and although Tajiks dominated his Jamiat-e Islami party, it had a policy of building a broad base of support from across the national ethnic spectrum. He was a favourite of

Western powers, such as the United States, Britain and France, who channelled millions of dollars in arms and ammunition to his group. Jamiat became the main proxy in the West's attempt to drive the Soviets out of Afghanistan without having to commit troops itself.

Hekmatyar, by contrast, was a much more conservative, uncompromising figure. He had begun his career as a member of Jamiat and a compatriot of Massoud's, but broke away in 1976 to form his own Hezb-e Islami party with a much narrower ethnic base, mainly recruiting Ghilzai Pashtun from the south of Afghanistan.

We met Hekmatyar on several occasions, the last time at his base in Charasyab, a ragged little satellite town just outside Kabul from where he directed his fight to win control of the capital from his old rival. Austere, straight-backed and soft-spoken, he was nonetheless as welcoming as any Afghan traditionally must be, greeting us with sweet tea, dried fruit and nuts. It was hard to reconcile the slightly built figure dressed in a spotless and perfectly pressed formal shalwar khameez with his ruthless reputation.

Hekmatyar developed close ties with like-minded groups across the Middle East, receiving finance and military aid principally from the Pakistani government, Saudi Arabia and the Muslim Brotherhood. That's why he had little interest in Western reporters, who sometimes brought unwelcome attention. He gave us access only when he felt he needed to.

The Soviets fought to crush the insurgency for almost a decade, but after losing almost 15 000 troops, with a further 53 000 wounded, they finally withdrew through the freezing February of 1989. They left behind a client government led by Mohammad Najibullah, a former secret-police chief, who held on to an ever-shrinking patch of territory until the city fell in April 1992. The two mujahedin factions then turned their guns on one another in a violent dispute over who should claim the right to run the country.

•

The Kabul I entered almost three years later was still a battle zone. Jamiat-e Islami controlled the northern and eastern neighbourhoods, including most of the government buildings. The movement's political leader, Burhanuddin Rabbani, was now president of Afghanistan, and Massoud, as the military commander, had been named defence minister. Crucially, Massoud's troops also held a prominent ridge that runs like a hunchback's spine through the middle of Kabul. From there they could shoot down into the south-western sector held by a rival militia, Hizb-e Wahdat, which was allied to Hekmatyar's Hezb-e Islami party.

As a newly arrived correspondent, my first job was to establish contacts with all the rival groups, regardless of their politics or ethnic make-up. That was so axiomatic as to go without saying: to report the news, we needed to hear from as many sources as we could. Seeing Jamiat officials was relatively easy – we lived in territory they controlled and routinely visited their offices for tea and updates – but we also needed to build a relationship with the opposition, and that was a much riskier proposition.

As well as following our natural journalistic instincts, clearly we had a responsibility to uphold the BBC's reputation for accuracy, impartiality and fairness. The corporation had an extraordinary position in Afghanistan at the time. The country had no television networks beyond the capital (and even then none but a handful of the very wealthy could afford both a TV and a generator), and no distribution network for newspapers. Radio was the only medium that counted.

The few local stations that did manage to stay on air were run by warlords and pumped out barely concealed propaganda. The only credible networks that broadcast into Afghanistan in local languages were the BBC and Voice of America, and the BBC had a deep-rooted historical respect. You could walk down the streets of Kabul as the sun set around five o'clock and hear the BBC news jingle filter through the windows of almost every house. The BBC's managers estimated that about 70 per cent of Afghans tuned into the Pashto and Farsi broadcasts each week. The locals only half-jokingly referred to the BBC as 'the Big Mullah'. Failing to be fair and balanced in our reporting would have been an abrogation of a heavy responsibility.

Covering all sides in the conflict was not just a matter of professional ethics, though. For me, it was also a question of survival. In a war like Afghanistan's the last thing we wanted was to be seen as hostile to one side or another, and so wind up being regarded as a legitimate target. We were often on the front line – sometimes on a daily basis – and as a clean-shaven white guy among heavily bearded Afghanis, I was relatively easy to spot from the opposition trenches. If we failed to make contact and win the trust of both the government *and* its opponents, you could guarantee that at some point someone would start shooting at us.

In a functioning state, contact would simply involve picking up the phone and calling the opposition, but in the Afghanistan of 1995, telephone networks were hopelessly broken. The landline system was so dysfunctional that we almost never used it (I can still remember the three times our office phone actually rang), and mobile-phone networks were still years away. A handful of militia leaders had satellite phones, but they worked only when their owners switched them on, and that was for such brief periods that we could never rely on them. The only viable solution was the old-fashioned one: crossing the front lines to visit in person.

Our first trip was to meet Abdul Ali Mazari, the Hizb-e Wahdat leader huddled among his notoriously tenacious Hazara tribesmen in the ruins of the Kart-e Sey district. This neighbourhood lay in the direct line of fire of Massoud's tanks parked on the hills above, and had been so badly smashed up by artillery that when I looked down at it through a tank commander's binoculars, it seemed impossible for anybody to live in the piles of rubble. But the Hazaras had built hidden networks of trenches and barricades so effective that they managed to hold Kart-e Sey for years.

Within days of my arrival, we heard that a British diplomat, Steven Evans, had flown in from Pakistan for a routine visit to the otherwise-abandoned embassy, and a round of meetings with government officials. Purely by coincidence, he received word that Hizb-e Wahdat was holding a British spy and was ready to release him.

This was puzzling for a number of reasons. None of us, including Evans, had heard of a British national who had been captured by the opposition, much less a spy. Indeed, it was hard to imagine that the British government would even risk sending a spy into a war it had only a passing interest in.

'You need to be careful,' my translator, Salahuddin, told me with a frown when we discussed the story. 'Maybe they want to get some foreign journalists and officials across the front lines so they can use you as hostages.' Then his face cracked. 'But maybe they also want you to see the sights. It could be fun.'

There were only two other foreign correspondents based in Kabul at the time: Terence White, who worked for the French news agency AFP, and freelance reporter Tim Johnston, who worked mainly for the Associated Press and Voice of America. Both of them had a lot more experience of Afghanistan than me. They were convinced it was a legitimate story, and that the risk wasn't too serious. We decided to go.

The following morning, our office driver, Hajji, checked the old Land Rover and loaded it with bulletproof vests, helmets and a first-aid kit so extensive that we could almost have performed emergency open-heart surgery. Salahuddin and I climbed in and we drove to Jamiat's forward positions.

Our greatest guides were the locals who lived around the front lines. After a period of calm, and if they sensed no growing tension, they would slowly venture out, the braver ones occasionally scurrying across no-man's-land to visit relatives or to trade.

We talked to a few who had crossed, asking about any tension or violence on the other side, and questioned the front-line commanders about any plans for attack. Finally, when we were as confident as we could be that nobody was about to start another round of fighting, on the back of the car Hajji mounted a huge white homemade flag that said 'BBC' in both English and Persian script. We slipped on our flak jackets and clenched our buttocks before he manoeuvred our car around the barricades and we crossed into opposition territory.

•

Like most Afghanis, the Hazaras are deeply conservative Muslims. Their faith gives meaning to the suffering they have endured through decades of almost constant conflict. It provides form and structure to their lives, measured out with the five daily prayers and an unshakeable belief that whatever fate imposes and however hard one tries to avoid it, only Allah can choose the time and manner of one's death. They are also extraordinarily welcoming, with a deep-rooted culture – almost a cult – of hospitality. It is virtually impossible to arrive at a Hazara's house without being greeted by a cup of sweet peppermint tea and bowls of dried fruit and nuts – one of the reasons their region in central Afghanistan became the high point of the hippy trail through the 1960s and 1970s.

Still, we were nervous as we approached Hizb-e Wahdat's forward positions. We could see the barrels of the PK light machine guns aimed directly at us from behind the sandbagged barriers on either side of the road.

But we were expected. At the boom gate that marked their side of the lines, they waved us through and we drove down the narrow streets towards the heavily barricaded hotel they had commandeered as a headquarters.

We took our place in a room crowded with local journalists, Hizb-e Wahdat fighters and Steven Evans. We waited expectantly, and then a hush fell across the crowd as Mazari entered with his bodyguards and, shuffling behind them, a cowed, bearded prisoner in a threadbare sweater and black shalwar kameez.

With his grey beard and tanned, leathery face, Mazari commanded the respect of his men. As much religious leader as military commander, he dominated the room, silencing it with his mere presence. Once the hubbub had settled and in the measured voice of a man in no hurry, he said that his prisoner, Eden Paul Fernandez from St Ives in Cambridgeshire, was a spy who had produced seven reports for British intelligence.

'But we have decided that in light of Britain's past support for the Afghan mujahedin forces during the Soviet occupation, we are releasing him as a gesture of goodwill,' he announced.

In truth, Fernandez was nothing more than an unemployed printer with an idealistic and overactive sense of adventure. He had travelled to Afghanistan five years earlier to join the mujahedin after watching a story about them on an evening news bulletin. Jamiat-e Islami had taken him in and he had found what he was looking for – the thrill of battle and the camaraderie of his fellow fighters – until Hizb-e Wahdat captured him. Fernandez told me later that he had invented the spy story eight months after he was taken, when he realised he would be released only if he gave his captors what they wanted.

The fact that an Islamist militia caught someone they believed was a British spy and released him as a goodwill gesture with no ransom or obvious concessions now seems incomprehensible. The idea of a 'war on terror' and an age-old clash of civilisations is so embedded in our minds that it is hard to imagine anything different. We tend to assume that the phrase 'Islamist militia' is just another way of saying 'bloodthirsty terrorists'.

But in 1995, the war was between rival Islamist factions, not with the West, and even a Western agent was regarded less as a protagonist and more as an observer. To Hizb-e Wahdat, Fernandez was keeping watch over events in Afghanistan on behalf of his government, but they had no particular interest in him and were not concerned about his intentions or even the British government's motives. And if that was the way they saw Fernandez, it was also how they viewed us, the foreign media. We too were observers, watching and reporting on the unfolding conflict for the rest of the world. We were taking serious risks to bring attention to what they knew was a conflict that very few people outside the country had more than a passing interest in, if they were aware of it at all. And for that, they even seemed grateful.

•

Once we had established contact with Mazari, his forward commanders and their militiamen, we routinely made the journey across the front lines. Sometimes it was for a specific story, to get their views on the latest peace initiative or an update on the constantly shifting alliances, but at other times, it was just to make the crossing for its own sake. If we didn't have a particular story to chase and the front lines were quiet, we would simply head over for tea and conversation. We figured that the risks of getting caught in crossfire were worth taking if it meant avoiding the greater danger of being seen as partial.

By early February, though, what was already a complex multiparty conflict was about to get even messier. Not only was there the struggle between the two rival mujahedin alliances, with no less than nine separate factions between them who were constantly doing deals with one another; now, the newly emergent Taliban had seized control of the strategically vital garrison town of Maidan Shahr from Hekmatyar's troops, and posed a serious threat to both groups.

Back in 1995, the Taliban was just another militia in an already overcrowded and over-armed landscape. It seemed unlikely that it would ever be a significant player, but its members were a little different: they refused to align themselves with any other group.

They also had a strong story to tell about how they had formed. Although there was some uncertainty, it is now widely accepted that the movement came out of madrasahs (religious schools) in the refugee camps of neighbouring Pakistan as a reaction to the corruption and lawlessness of the factions that had ground down the country for years. 'Taliban' literally means 'student', and the Qur'an was the movement's inspiration. In the absence of any functioning legal system, like other mujahedin factions it used sharia law as its organising principle, except that Taliban took their religious devotion and piety to a fanatical level.

The Taliban's own foundation myth tells how Mullah Omar first mobilised his followers in the spring of 1994 when he learned that the local governor in the southern district of Singesar had abducted and systematically raped two teenage girls. Mullah Omar organised a relatively small force of thirty Taliban and freed the girls before executing the governor. Some weeks later, two militia commanders in the Mullah's home town of Kandahar killed civilians while fighting for their right to sodomise a young boy. Once more Mullah Omar moved in. He freed the boy and executed the two commanders, but this time he stayed.

Over the following months supporters flooded in from Pakistan, and the Taliban quickly took control of the nearest border crossing, at Spin Boldak. Neighbouring districts fell as locals fed up with the anarchy of the warlords joined the movement, and the new force began advancing north towards Kabul, declaring that its ultimate goal was to destroy all the mujahedin factions, restore law and order, and establish an Islamic state based on sharia law across all Afghanistan.

These goals were noble enough, but there were other agendas. Some analysts believe the Taliban was a creation of Pakistan's Inter-Services Intelligence agency. Certainly, if the ISI didn't invent the movement it took advantage of the opportunity that Mullah Omar presented, supporting him with money, arms, ammunition and a near-endless supply of recruits.[1] Pakistan saw the Taliban as a way of exerting control over its neighbour, and opening up trade routes to Central Asian countries such as Uzbekistan.

So when Maidan Shahr, on the south-western approach to Kabul, fell to the Taliban after a brief but fierce battle with Hekmatyar's troops, it became clear that they were a significant force in their own right and we needed to go and see them.

•

Maidan Shahr sits at the southern end of a long valley. Whoever controls the town controls all the traffic into Kabul's southern flank, about 30 kilometres away.

Countless tanks had broken up the road out of the capital, hollowing out vast potholes, and as we drove along it, our Land Rover rose and fell like a ship in a heavy swell, disappearing completely in the troughs before cresting and then vanishing once more. Finally the road flattened out as we rounded a bend at the head of a broad, U-shaped valley. The road was brown, barren and dead straight, with government trenches and tanks in defensive positions at our end, and the Taliban trenches just visible at the opposite end about 4 kilometres away.

On the day we arrived there was no shooting – local villagers told us it had been quiet for hours – and we watched as a few civilian trucks bounced their way across the battlefield. Once they'd made it safely through, I turned to Salahuddin and Hajji with a question in my eyes. Without answering, Hajji shrugged and started the engine.

As we approached the Taliban trenches, I struggled to control the sweat that had beaded on my forehead despite the winter chill. I could see black turbans rising above the Kalashnikov barrels that poked through the sandbagged barrier, and couldn't help but think of the stories we'd heard of the ruthless executions of anybody the Taliban disagreed with. It was always risky approaching a line without prior warning, but in capturing Maidan Shahr, the Taliban had just won a significant victory, and we hoped they'd be feeling confident and relaxed.

We stopped at the checkpoint, safely out of range of the government trenches, and the Taliban commander approached our car. His weathered Pashtun eyes widened as soon as he saw me – a white man on an Afghan battlefield – and he broke into a huge grin.

'BBC?' he asked, glancing up at the flag hanging from the mast at the back of the car. 'Welcome, welcome.'

•

The Taliban's headquarters were in a school we'd visited just a few days earlier. It was strewn with the detritus of battle – empty artillery-shell casings, the scars of countless rounds of AK-47 fire, abandoned bedrolls left by fleeing fighters, and a liberal sprinkling of bloodstained bandages – but the concrete building had survived largely intact. As we pulled up outside, the new arrivals were cleaning captured tanks, rocket launchers and anti-aircraft guns.

The Taliban's regional leader was Mullah Rabbani (no relation to President Burhanuddin Rabbani), a huge man with a thick black beard and a chest like a bull's. When he shook my hand, my fingers disappeared in his massive fist and it looked as though he was shaking the branch of a skinny sapling. When we arrived he was busy meeting local leaders, but he set aside his work and, without asking if we were thirsty, ordered a round of tea.

'Why don't you come to Islam?' he asked in a booming voice when I introduced myself. 'It is the religion of peace.'

'Ah, Mullah Rabbani,' I replied. 'When Allah considers me worthy, I'm sure he will show me a sign.'

The mullah burst out laughing, his belly jiggling beneath his waistcoat, and for a moment he looked more like an Afghan Santa Claus than one of the most powerful military and political figures in the Taliban. It was an exchange we would repeat every time we met over the coming months.

Rabbani was committed to the strictest interpretation of the Qur'an, even refusing to be photographed because he said it was 'un-Islamic'. (The most conservative Muslims believe that if God created man in his own image, any attempt to produce an image of a man is therefore akin to creating an image of God, which is an act of blasphemy.) Later, when the Taliban finally captured Kabul, Rabbani would become the city's mayor and earn a reputation for brutality by enforcing sharia law, with public floggings, amputations and even executions. But on that first visit, while he was unwilling to let us bring out our cameras, he was more than happy to answer our questions.

We knew he had already met a delegation from one of the mujahedin factions allied to Jamiat-e Islami, who had been hoping to negotiate a deal, so I asked what he had said to them.

'I told them that we don't have any specific differences with any of the parties, but that we are against anything that damages our religion and that we are against insurrection,' he said without irony. 'We will disarm them all.'

That was as close as we could ever get to a coherent political policy from the Taliban. Despite continued probing, Mullah Rabbani – and indeed all the commanders we met – refused to give any more detail, and I came to believe that it really was the extent of their plan.

Of course, it was a simple and supremely attractive message for Afghans who by then were utterly sick and tired of the infighting that had destroyed both their lives and their country. The Taliban's refusal to soil their hands with the messy detail of politics wrapped them in a fog of pious idealism. That same idealism made them fearsome and often successful opponents on the battlefield. For most of the factions, sending village boys to fight for no obvious cause other than loyalty to a commander was a tough case to make, and movements in the front lines often had more to do with cash deals between rival commanders than any pitched battle. (I remember one frank conversation in a bunker in the Salang Pass when a fighter quite openly told me that the price for a position on that particular front line was half a million Afghanis, or about US$5000.)

The Taliban were different. The only leader they claimed to follow was Allah, and as the NATO forces discovered to their cost after the invasion of Afghanistan in 2001, that can make for a formidably committed enemy.

In 1995, it meant that our long discussions were theological rather than political, curious but never hostile.

'I don't understand your Christian beliefs,' one young Talib admitted as we squatted in a freezing trench over another cup of tea. 'You say that Christ was the son of God. But how can that be? To us he is a prophet, but nobody can be the child of Allah. And how are the Father, the Son and the Holy Ghost all supposed to be the same thing? What does that mean?'

Even for committed Christians the Holy Trinity can be a tricky thing to get your head around, and I was as stumped as he was for answers.

'But don't worry,' he continued, as he fingered his AK-47. 'You are safe with us. You are the people of the Book – we are all children of Abraham, and the Qur'an says we must protect you.'

The Jewish Torah and the Christian Gospels were part of God's legacy, and even if they might not have understood the other two Abrahamic faiths and believed that Islam was the highest expression of the word of God, the Taliban fighters we encountered in 1995 accepted that we all followed the same deity, whether he was named Jehovah or God or Allah, and so they had a responsibility to protect us.

Finally the Talib stood, stretched, and scratched his beard. 'Allah is like a mountain that we are all trying to climb. It is just that we follow different paths to the summit,' he said.

It was a saying I would hear often through that year.

•

Within a matter of weeks, the Taliban had radically shifted the military and political landscape of Afghanistan. After capturing Maidan Shahr they turned west, and in an attack that scrapped any previous deals, they ousted Hekmatyar from his command post on the outskirts of Kabul. Then they forced other Hizb-e Wahdat fighters out of their front-line positions in the city and murdered the group's leader, Abdul Ali Mazari. Suddenly, in a series of well-organised and strategically astute attacks, the Taliban had become the single most powerful force in Afghanistan, controlling more than half of the country and laying siege to the capital. Instead of having to drive 30 bone-jarring kilometres from Kabul to see them, now we would only have to do the front-line dash a few suburbs away.

•

Regardless of what they thought of the Taliban's approach to women and human rights, the West and in particular the United Nations had no choice but to take them seriously and include them in peace negotiations that had floundered for years.

The Taliban never saw itself as just another armed militia. Instead, it presented itself as a kind of independent national peacekeeping force, above the fray of the mujahedin factions. Time and again, its leaders, like Mullah Rabbani, said they had no particular argument with any of their rivals as long as they were willing to lay down their arms and submit to the Taliban's edicts.

Importantly, the group wanted to be accepted by the outside world, including the United Nations and Western powers such as the United States and Britain, as the only truly legitimate Afghan force. If they bargained with the other factions they would be stooping to the same level, and that was something they could never countenance. When they met foreign diplomats and UN envoys, Taliban commanders continually tried to present themselves as the only force with any legitimacy, and they struggled to understand the Western obsession with their treatment of women or their human-rights record.

'How else do we bring peace to our country?' one exasperated front-line commander, Mullah Borjan, said when I pushed him on the subject. 'Sharia law is all we have. And we have stopped the extortion and killing and made the people safe in whatever territory we have captured. Why do they think the old mujahedin parties are a better option than us? It is madness to include them as equals in any peace process.'

Through the 1990s, neighbouring states – Pakistan, India, Iran and Russia – were often accused of meddling in this essentially domestic conflict, of trying to use it as a foreign-policy tool in a continuation of the regional squabbles that had plagued Central Asia for centuries. But most Afghans, including the Taliban, just wanted support to help sort out the mess and deal with their country's crushing poverty. Most importantly of all, they craved recognition of the suffering they were enduring.

•

I left Kabul early in 1996 at the end of my year-long assignment, with the Taliban still trying to fight their way into the capital. The siege ebbed and flowed, with several attempts by the UN to broker a ceasefire and some kind of power-sharing agreement. But the Taliban consistently refused to share anything with Rabbani's 'government'. Outside the capital, they continued to advance across Afghanistan, defeating mujahedin factions one by one until they controlled about 70 per cent of the country. Defence Minister Massoud and his allies fought hard to maintain a tenuous grip on the capital and an ever-diminishing region in the north.

As the Taliban established their dominance, rumours began to circulate that they had a new foreign sponsor who was bringing troops, weapons, money, and a far more radical ideology than anything the Taliban had preached. He was a Saudi militant called Osama bin Laden.

Under the influence of bin Laden and the foreign Al Qaeda fighters he brought in to train with the Taliban, the already-austere brand of Islam evolved into something so intolerant that even conservative rural Afghans began to despise their edicts. And with that came a change in the attitude towards the media. It was as if a curtain slid across Afghanistan. Local newspapers were forbidden from printing commentary, photographs or readers' letters. They were reduced to propaganda sheets praising the latest Taliban victory. The few television stations that had survived the war were shut down, while local radio became little more than an electronic pulpit, broadcasting religious sermons unbroken by music.

Most foreign reporters abandoned the country under intense pressure from the Taliban. They couldn't work without a minder or strict censorship. Both of my colleagues – Mark Lavine from AFP and freelancer Tim Johnston – eventually pulled out (Mark replaced Terence White who was wounded in a mortar blast), leaving the BBC's tenacious Kate Clark as the only Western reporter based in Kabul until she too was expelled in March 2001.

Under Al Qaeda's influence, the Taliban launched a kind of cold war on news, freezing the flow of all information apart from the most pious religious sermons and trite gossip. Nobody could have seen it coming, but their attacks on the media were a kind of prelude to the crisis that would unfold just five years later.

3

INTERROGATION

30 DECEMBER 2013 – 5 JANUARY 2014

The police station is an old colonial-era building, with a grand staircase leading through an arched doorway decorated with what once must have been ornate filigree but is now chipped and faded. It's a single-storey limestone building that looks strong and squat and completely out of place in the tiny alley crowded with crumbling concrete apartments.

By the time we arrive it is almost midnight, and the lights cast a dim, sulphurous glow over the building's entrance. Fahmy and I are cuffed together as we are led inside – his good left arm chained to my right, while his right arm hangs in its sling.

Inside, the rooms are bare and filthy. The police office is dank and dimly lit by a single, naked bulb hanging from the ceiling. As always, it smells of stale cigarette smoke and there are butts and ash littering the floor, but the officer in charge is disarmingly friendly. He and Fahmy know each other and the two exchange greetings. They met when Fahmy worked on a story for CNN about a year ago.

For a moment, I begin to hope that the first friendly face of the evening might actually give us a way out. Instead, he confiscates our wallets, belts and shoes (leaving me with my Akubra). But he is surprisingly sloppy with his search, and although I'm still worried, I have to suppress a grin when he misses the thick wad of hundred-dollar bills tucked inside my fleece. Then he leads us to a large arched-steel door with detailed decorative welding. As he fiddles with the lock, I can hear people shuffling inside.

The door swings open. Hands unlock our cuffs from behind and push us inside.

The cell is a tall, bare limestone room with no windows and an alcove set into the opposite end. It isn't big – one-and-a-half body-lengths wide and only slightly longer – and has no water or toilet. The ceiling is decorated with a plaster rosette. The room looks as though it was designed as an office for a colonial official rather than a holding cell for suspected criminals, and it is already overcrowded with nine men, most of them sitting on thin blankets spread across the floor. I stare down at them and wonder where Fahmy and I will fit.

I needn't have worried. A massive Egyptian who reminds me of Mullah Rabbani with his thick black beard and wide neck stands in the alcove and orders his cellmates to make space for us. He is clearly the cell leader, and they shuffle over without complaint.

The men are unexpectedly welcoming, offering us leftover bread and fried chicken that one of the prisoners' families brought in earlier that night. They tell us they've all been locked in the tiny room for weeks. In a small but extraordinary act of generosity, one man sees how much pain Fahmy's arm is causing him and hands him a small pillow, a precious commodity on the cold concrete floor.

The big man introduces himself as Mohammed. He tells us he ran a gym – for bodybuilders, unsurprisingly – and that he's been accused of training Muslim Brotherhood militants. Another of our cellmates says he is a clothing retailer, without explaining how he wound up in the cell. He is well dressed in a tailored shirt and pants, and has a close-cropped beard. In broken, friendly English, he asks how much my hat cost. (I lie.) A third looks like a heroin addict struggling to cope with withdrawal symptoms, face the colour of cigarette ash and eyes vacant. He has a bulbous hooked nose and a misshapen head, and eats in sullen silence. Mohammed says this man is a Syrian with mental problems who was arrested after he murdered three people at a pro-government demonstration, apparently for money.

Mohammed tells us he has a mobile phone hidden in the cell. We don't ask how he smuggled it in. He offers to let us make a quick call or send an SMS, but in a moment of supreme frustration, I realise that I can't remember a single phone number apart from my ex-wife's. It was a difficult break-up, and in my sleep-deprived mind, I imagine that she'd be quite delighted to hear I've been locked up. I decide to let Fahmy make the call.

He manages to get through to his uncle, a retired cop who has already heard of our arrest – apparently it is all over the news and social media. It's not just the two of us who have been picked up. Another producer, Baher Mohamed, has also been arrested. The police apparently raided his home in New Cairo, and shot his dog in the process, terrifying his wife and two children. Baher is a soft-hearted charming man with an extraordinary knack for talking the most recalcitrant person into giving interviews. He and I went horseriding in the desert a few nights ago, and I can't believe he too has been locked up somewhere. And then there is cameraman Mohamed Fawzy, another gentle giant who was also arrested in a raid on his home. I worked with Fawzy once on the frontlines of Somalia where I came to respect both his enormous compassion and his courage. Four of us, all under arrest.

I can't make up my mind whether the fact that the story is in the media is a good thing or not. If it is now public knowledge, our chances of having this resolved quickly and quietly has probably gone. But if everybody already knows we're in the cells, it will be much harder for us to disappear.

As the night deepens, the atmosphere in the cell becomes surprisingly jovial. Everyone talks and laughs constantly, giggling at their own jokes, singing songs, telling stories, but because I can't understand Arabic or take part in the banter, it just becomes noise.

I try to sleep on the blanket fully clothed, with my fleece for a pillow and my hat pulled down over my eyes, but the cold keeps seeping into my hips and shoulder and the ache becomes impossible to ease as I turn and roll, trying to find a comfortable position. I can't imagine how Fahmy is managing on the floor with his bad shoulder.

The incessant chatter, once amusing, is now infuriating. I am stressed and tired and I can't think straight. I know I will need all my mental faculties if we are to get through this intact, and I badly need some rest. Finally, around 4 a.m., they stop talking and I settle into a light sleep, nose-to-tail with my neighbours across the cell, and with the Syrian's feet digging into my ribs.

•

I am the first to wake. Everyone else is exhausted by the party and still sleeping fitfully when I hear movement in the police office outside the cell door. A voice calls for Fahmy, and I nudge him awake.

'You two get ready to go.'

'Where are you taking us?' Fahmy asks.

'Can't say,' comes the reply.

Fahmy asks to go to the toilet. It is in another part of the police station, and you can't go without being escorted out. When he returns, he looks pale.

'I just paid a cop to tell me what they're going to do with us,' he says. 'They're going to hood us and give us to the National Security for interrogation. Those guys are bastards. Once you go in there, you can disappear for a very long time.'

He looks scared and in pain, and it doesn't help my own composure. But there is nothing we can do except sit and wait.

Eventually, after an hour or so of anxious fretting, there is a rattle of keys and the clanking of the lock, and the door swings open. Fahmy and I are ordered to our feet and once again we are cuffed together. We are led outside, and with profound relief I see that there are no hoods, just a line of prisoners from another holding cell squatting together in the dust, waiting for their transport.

We are ushered into a cage in the back of a small van with three other prisoners. None of us has any clue as to where we are going, and we sit in silence as the driver ploughs his way through Cairo's morning traffic jam.

•

I've never been arrested before. The only other time I have been in the back of a police van was when some helpful Sydney cops gave my cousin and me a ride home after a particularly raucous New Year's Eve in Kings Cross. But this is an entirely new experience. Surprisingly, as we duck and weave through the traffic, I don't feel worried. Whenever I've imagined this in the past, I've only ever seen myself panicking. I've pictured myself sweating, wide-eyed and panting with stress, terrified of what might happen. I've rehearsed it often enough, especially when we have broadcast something we know will upset someone official or have crossed a border illegally to chase a story we know a government wants to keep hidden. I always thought my insides would stew in a cocktail of adrenaline and bile.

And I always expected to feel guilty. Whenever I walk into a police station, even if it is only to sign a document, the stress rises as I feel the cops' eyes on me, searching for the things I must have done wrong. I know that whenever I've seen a prison van pass in the street, I've always assumed, with an inbuilt prejudice that I suddenly find quite shocking, that whoever is inside must have done some unspeakable crime.

But now that I'm on the inside, staring out through the bars trying to figure out where we are headed, I want to shout at everyone glancing up with a sneer in their eyes that we are innocent men. All of us. I don't feel angry, or even scared. I am anxious, of course, as anyone facing an uncertain future would be, but I don't feel the mix of emotions that I expected. This isn't out of any misplaced courage; it comes from a deeply comforting conviction that we are guilty of nothing, and that whatever happens next is utterly out of my control.

Growing up, we are constantly told that justice will prevail, and that as long as we do nothing wrong, we will live safe, comfortable lives. It is a profoundly Christian, Western view of the world that our fates are largely in our own hands – that if we succeed it is because we have worked hard or are particularly talented, or if we get into trouble we have failed in some way, or done something wrong to incur God's punishment.

As a reporter, I have covered enough misery to know that this is nonsense. Life is shaped far more by accident of birth – whether you are lucky enough to be born into a well-educated family with access to opportunity, or happen to find yourself growing up in a South Sudanese village where a gun is thrust into your hand before you have a chance to pick up a pencil. And if it isn't birth, it is chance encounters that decide whether you are introduced to the CEO of a company, who just happens to be looking for someone like you, or a guy at a party, who introduces you to drugs.

In the Islamic world, 'inshallah', or 'God willing', expresses this. Muslims believe that it is impossible to know the mind of God and that we must simply accept whatever fate – or God – dishes out to us. In the back of an Egyptian prison van on my way to be interrogated, it is an oddly comforting thought.

•

After a forty-minute journey, we arrive. Through the bars of the van I recognise New Cairo – an up-market district of expensive restaurants, shops and huge air-conditioned villas. I was here just a week ago, when we came to film a relatively bland story about an entrepreneur who saw the local traffic as an opportunity to set up an executive commuter service – a fleet of luxury minibuses with onboard wi-fi so that passengers could start their working day from the moment they stepped on board. Surely *that* can't be the story that has upset the authorities.

We pull up inside the compound of an imposing building, and a line of police takes us one by one, still in cuffs, into a reception area with all the grime and bored security guards that are now a familiar feature of Egyptian bureaucracy. We are in the National Security building, and Fahmy is taken off in a different direction while I'm hustled up to the fourth floor into a waiting room.

The room is sparsely furnished and freezing cold – the clothes I have from tropical Kenya are hopelessly inadequate for an Egyptian winter. The chairs are all broken, and the one window faces onto a brick wall that lets only a weak light filter through. Two guards, each with a heavy coat and a cigarette permanently hanging off their bottom lips, prop themselves up on rickety chairs. They gesture for me to do the same, but I choose to stand with my arms crossed and stare at the tiled floor instead.

Waiting is the killer. In the empty space, my mind loses the composure it had in the van and starts a dialogue.

'This isn't serious,' I say. 'We've done nothing wrong, and it'll all be over in a matter of hours. A day or two, max.'

'Who are you kidding?' my mind responds. 'You are in deep trouble. This is the National Security Directorate. These are the guys who handle terrorism cases, and you've heard the stories of torture and disappearances. If you don't get out of this soon it could become very painful, and you know how terrified you get every time a nurse approaches you with a needle.'

Still I wait.

'We are Al Jazeera, and I'm a foreigner,' I reason. 'Surely that's got to make a difference. We are respected journalists. Maybe once they realise it's been a terrible mistake, they'll say sorry and let us go with a handshake.'

'Ha! A foreigner?' retorts my mind. 'They've been calling foreign journalists spies and throwing rocks at them. If you don't get out today, you're spending a lot of long nights on cold concrete.'

'But surely Doha knows what's happened to us and they're working the phones right now. Maybe that's why I've been waiting so long. Maybe they're trying to work out a solution to whatever the problem is.'

'Nobody knows where you are. Even if they know you've been taken – and that's doubtful – they don't know which of Egypt's labyrinthine security agencies has you or even where to start looking. Remember the stories of families who spend weeks going from cop shop to cop shop trying to find their boys who've been arrested?'

Hours pass as I struggle to suppress the mind-chatter. There are no lawyers, no phone calls and no questioning. Nothing. I still can't decide if that's good or bad.

Eventually two short, round women walk in together with an air of official purpose. One is fair-skinned and dark-haired – clearly a Westerner – and the other is her Egyptian negative, with a brown face and salon-blonde hair.

The Westerner extends her hand and introduces herself as Erika Tolano, the Australian consul. The Egyptian is the embassy's translator, Amani. They heard about our arrest within an hour or so of it happening. Somebody in Al Jazeera called the Australian Foreign Ministry's emergency number in Canberra, and the ministry alerted the embassy staff. Apparently our detention is all over the press in both Australia and Egypt.

Erika is formal and stiff with procedure. I am sure she's had to deal with far too many Australians who have got into trouble for drinking and groping local women, and I am just another consular headache. She gives me the standard advice for detained Australians, explaining the limits of what the embassy can do for me (they *can* advise my family of my situation; they *can't* provide or even recommend lawyers). After our initial conversation, it is clear that I can't slip her the cash I've stashed away, so I ask for the toilet and, once inside, I break the wad into two and slip them into the soles of my socks.

Erika is invited to stay during the questioning, and suddenly I feel relieved. With a consular official listening in, they will have to play by the rules. But she tells me it is against departmental policy to attend interrogations, and she'll seek advice from the ambassador. She leaves with a promise to return tomorrow if I am still under arrest.

Finally, after almost six hours of waiting, the prosecutor arrives and I am ushered into his office. It is cavernous, with a vast desk facing the door and threadbare couches lining the walls. A smaller desk stretches out from the centre of his into the middle of the room, forming a 'T'.

The prosecutor is called Mansour. Even in this plush room it is so cold that he wears a heavy coat over his navy-blue suit, which shines as it catches the light from the neon bulbs overhead.

Mansour is clearly young – in his thirties, I guess – and he has slicked-back hair and clear brown eyes. Unusually for Egyptian men, he is clean-shaven, and he addresses me in the polite, formal but slightly halting English taught in the elite schools of Cairo.

Before we can begin, we have to wait for the court translator. Even though Mansour's English appears good enough, according to the rules the transcript of the interrogation has to be in Arabic. We also can't begin without a lawyer to represent me. I decline the first court-appointed lawyer who shows up – he can't speak English and looks as though he's struggling to pay for dry-cleaning. I am confident that if Al Jazeera knows we are under arrest, they will be looking for good legal representation. I just need to hold out until someone arrives who I know is acting in my best interests rather than the state's.

And so, without lawyers or a formal translator, we make small talk as I try to get my head around the mess I've found myself in.

•

Egypt's legal system is an awkward blend of British common law, Islamic sharia law and Napoleonic codes that reflects the country's history of occupation. In our case, the prosecutor is acting under the Napoleonic, inquisitorial part of the system that deals with serious crimes. He is responsible for carrying out interrogations, examining the evidence and deciding if there is a case to answer. If it ever comes to a trial, he will act as an assistant to a panel of three judges who become inquisitors-in-chief.

I am still convinced we won't ever go that far. After all, once the prosecutor realises that there has been a huge mistake and there is absolutely no evidence to support the allegations, he'll have no option but to release us, probably with an apology. I just can't imagine what grounds anybody could have for taking our case to court. And anyway, the law demands that anyone who has been detained must be brought before a magistrate and formally charged within forty-eight hours, or released. It has been twenty-four hours since we were arrested, so we've only got another day to endure.

But I also know that political activists and suspected MB members are still disappearing off the streets, often for months at a time, and re-emerging with stories of torture and abuse. Nobody seems sure of what laws the authorities are using to detain them. If any.

If it all seems rather confusing, that's because it is. Part of my university degree involved studying the Australian legal system, and I spent the early years of my career covering the courts. I thought I was pretty comfortable with legal concepts, but what I'm learning about the Egyptian system has me baffled.

Prosecutor Mansour himself is not responsible for any decisions. He reports to the enormously powerful prosecutor general, who will make the final adjudication on what to do with our case.

Eventually Mansour asks about my career and what I am doing in Egypt, taking notes as I answer. He is relaxed and friendly, but by 9 p.m., with no sign of either a lawyer or a translator, we give up.

•

In the prison van that takes us back to the cells, Fahmy and I exchange notes. It seems that while I'm struggling to get legal representation, he has an oversupply. Two lawyers sent by Al Jazeera appeared, his family sent two more, and a couple of human-rights lawyers who'd heard about our arrest also came to offer support. I get lawyer envy.

Fahmy is just as baffled as I am about why we have been arrested. 'Whatever you do, don't tell them I am bureau chief,' he says. 'I am just another producer. If they think I am in charge of everything, I'll be held responsible for whatever we are supposed to have done.'

I'm not convinced this is the best approach. It won't take long for the investigators to work out that Fahmy is running the Al Jazeera operation – there is plenty of evidence from emails to our editors in Doha, along with bills that he's been paying, that make it clear he is running the bureau – and when they do, they will wonder what he is trying to hide.

'Trust me,' he says. 'I know how the system works here. I know how they think, and the best thing is to keep telling them that I am nothing more than a producer.'

The van bounces its way across dimly lit potholed streets, and we eventually pull up outside an imposing facade with a massive timber and iron door. It is clearly not the police station we were held in last night. As we rise to get out, a guard orders me to stay seated. This is Fahmy's accommodation – I'm going somewhere else.

This is alarming. I don't like being separated from the one person I know I can trust, and who speaks perfect English, but I have no choice. As we drive off into the night, I can feel the anxiety rise once more in a tide of bile at the back of my throat.

Eventually we pull up at another broken building – this one much less intimidating – and I am led inside. It is another police station, and this time the guards take my belt, my wallet and my watch before taking me to a cell.

The cell itself is a freestanding concrete box in the middle of a courtyard. From the outside it looks tiny, and apart from a small hatch in the door, I can't see any windows. I can't imagine that it can hold more than two or three people at the most.

The guard unlatches the door, and once again I hear a rustling of bodies and murmuring of voices. When the door swings open I am staggered. Inside, nine or ten prisoners are standing to attention in neat ranks, and I can't believe how they manage to exist in there.

The prisoners make space as I'm shoved inside. They jostle and nudge one another, giving up precious centimetres here and there until they create a tiny square I can squat in, knees under my chin, with elbows, knees and feet jabbing me from all sides. In one corner a sink drips constantly, and in the other a squat toilet emits the ammonia stench of stale urine. Under the sink, the prisoners have placed a few plastic bags of fast food that their relatives have brought. But, either because nobody is willing to throw out food or there is no way of getting rid of the rubbish, old chewed-up chicken bones are lying alongside bags of stale bread. Next to the food is a small, chaotic pile of shoes, and with a gesture, the cell leader orders me to add mine.

His nickname is Otno (Arabic for 'cotton') and at seventeen, he is paradoxically one of the smallest and youngest of all the prisoners. He has dark olive skin, an intelligent but lopsided grin, and a mop of curly black hair. He looks terribly thin, and his left leg bows outward at an alarming angle, as though it could snap like a dry twig if he leant too heavily on it. He has an energy about him that refuses to be contained within his scrawny body. Once the prisoners have created a bit of space for me, he wriggles and talks almost non-stop, the words tumbling out of him, sometimes with hysterical laughter, sometimes with melancholy. I can't understand any of it, of course. One of the others, who introduces himself as a university student, tells me that even he struggles to make sense of anything Otno says.

Through the student, I ask Otno how he came to be in prison. He suddenly turns sullen, refusing to answer my questions. He says his story is too long and too sad to relay. The others fill in the gaps.

Otno's father was a drug dealer and abandoned the family about five years ago, and Otno, as the oldest boy, turned to petty crime to help feed his brothers and sisters. He started out stealing the occasional bag of apples and bread, then began taking things he could sell on the black market. Finally, he graduated to carjacking. Once, drunk on back-street whisky and with a joint clamped between his teeth, he took off in his latest acquisition. None of the prisoners know exactly what make the car was, but the consensus is that it must have had a powerful engine, because somehow Otno got into a high-speed chase and crashed, mangling his leg. (I was not entirely convinced – it is hard to imagine anybody driving fast through Cairo's 24-hour traffic jams – but everyone insists it is true.) After a year in prison it became clear that his leg badly needed an operation. While he was in hospital Otno escaped, dropping from a second-storey window onto his good leg and hobbling off into the night. He evaded the police for another year before he was rearrested and thrown into the tiny cell we are now in, waiting for another trial. That was six months ago, and he hasn't left the concrete box since.

The others have more prosaic stories. Four of them survived on the streets for years as a loose gang, collecting and selling scrap metal. The police found them with a few lumps of old iron and arrested them for stealing. The youngest looks to be about twelve, and I am staggered when he says he is sixteen. He used to work as an assistant at a metal workshop but was paid only about 50 dirhams a week – less than a dollar a day – and quit when he realised that on the street he could do much better. On a good day, they tell me, they could earn up to 30 dirhams each, though on most days it was nothing. None of them are literate, and all but one wishes they were back at school.

Another four are students who were leaders of various political groups. With others, they met at a cafe about three weeks ago to discuss their strategy after a big day of protests – nothing seemed to be working, the interim government had been steadily rolling back all the reforms won in the 2011 revolution and, most alarmingly of all for the students, more and more of them were being killed, injured or locked up with no obvious political gain. Just as their meeting was getting underway, the police burst in with weapons drawn. The group scattered, but these four were grabbed and pinned to the floor before they could escape. The police accused them of plotting to burn down their station next door, and said they found police weapons on them.

Of course it is impossible to know if the students are telling the truth, but they're convincing. They seem earnest and idealistic if naive in their politics, and their arrest is consistent with the ruthless crackdowns on dissent we've been seeing across the country over the previous months. The interim government has arrested the secular leaders of the 2011 revolution and rounded up the leaders of the MB and anybody suspected of being a member. And on 25 December – four days before our arrest – it declared the Brotherhood to be a terrorist organisation. By the time we were picked up, some human-rights groups estimated that at least 20 000 people had been thrown in prison.

Given their situation, the students are surprisingly cheerful, and excited by the prospect of having someone to practise their English with. As we continue our discussion of local politics, there is a commotion outside the cell. Everyone springs to attention as the lock churns and the door swings open. The police shove a wiry old man forward; he grabs one of the students for support, dragging one bad leg painfully behind him. As we once more shuffle up to make space for him to lie down, I can see urine stains down the front of his trousers.

At first I guess he is an incontinent old drunk who the police have picked up off the street. But then one of the students wipes away a tear. 'He's my father,' he explains. The father came to try to get his son out of prison, and had an argument with the police. One of them kicked him and dislocated his hip. The student weeps with rage and frustration.

The room falls silent as the old man groans on the floor. We all try to make room for him, but that is hard in a box barely wider than a man's body-length that now has eleven people in it.

Soon, there is another round of shouting from outside. Once more we all spring to attention, and once more the police push bodies inside the cell. Five more. We are sixteen now, including the student's injured father. It is impossible for us all to lie down at once.

I am exhausted and filthy and once more needing sleep. But soon enough the chatter starts up again, and Otno begins joking and singing and performing like some crazed vaudeville act. At one point he begins an improvised rap song, rhyming to the names of people in our cell. He has a razor-sharp wit that betrays an intelligence honed on the street, but he is bordering on manic and I wonder how much more of being in this cell he can take before he – or any of us – finally goes mad.

I try to put it out of my head, and pull my hat over my eyes hoping that sleep will find me. But I am sitting against a cold wall with my knees pulled up against my chest because that is all the space I have, and on every side my neighbours move and bump and nudge me as they join in the conversation, giggling at Otno's antics.

'Hey, you . . . Mr Peter. I love you.'

Everybody laughs as I push my hat up.

'I want to kiss you,' Otno says with a leer. He comes over and tries to hug me, and as I shove him away, he whispers into my ear, 'I want to fuck you.'

I come very close to slapping him, but there is something pathetically endearing about him. He is too small to be a threat, and I am not sure if his advances are genuine or part of the joke. I dismiss his behaviour as a kind of prison psychosis.

Just as exhaustion takes over and I finally lose consciousness, another commotion erupts, this time inside the cell. As my eyes snap open, bodies are churning and limbs flailing. Two of the men are fighting, throwing punches and kicking, and in the tiny space some of the blows miss their mark and land on others as they try to pull the pair apart. Someone steps on the old man, who is trying to shield his leg, and he groans and grits his teeth in pain.

I lose my temper. 'Fucking stop it!' I bellow, until I realise it is stupid when neither of the fighters understands a word I am saying.

I turn to the student who was translating earlier. 'Fucking translate this!' I shout. 'And you can translate "fucking". I don't know who started it, and I don't fucking care. We can't afford to fight. If we fight in this space, we all lose and they win.'

I jab the air, pointing at the door. 'What do you think those cops are thinking right now? I think they're happy we're beating the shit out of each other – it saves them from doing the job. So whatever the other one did to you, suck it up, shut up and sit the fuck down!'

The room finally settles, and as we fall asleep in a tangle of limbs, I realise that we are so tightly packed that wherever I turn I can feel the pulse of at least one other person.

•

The following day, the interrogation gets underway. We have an official court translator and a scribe for the statement, and while we wait for a lawyer, Erika and Amani arrive from the embassy.

We have a chance to talk in the corner of Mansour's office about how the media is covering the case back in Australia. Apparently my mother has been talking about my arrest, along with the foreign minister, Julie Bishop. Although the minister isn't saying much beyond the fact that she's aware of the case and they are offering consular support, I am relieved that it is being taken seriously at the most senior level.

'So in the ministry, is this just another case of an Australian on criminal charges, or am I being seen as a political prisoner?' I ask.

'The fact that I'm here ought to tell you that we don't see this as a routine detention,' Erika replies.

Eventually a lawyer and his associate turn up. He introduces himself as Mohammed Mughlis, a lawyer hired by Al Jazeera to represent me. He is sharply dressed in a crisp white shirt and well-tailored suit, and I heave a huge sigh of relief. (When Mansour leaves the room to go to the toilet, Mughlis and I go into a brief huddle. I slip him the wads of cash, and his eyebrows rise an inch. 'Give it to Al Jazeera,' I hiss, and he nods with a conspiratorial wink.)

Relieved of the money, and with a team behind me, at last we can get on with the questions.

With everyone in place, we turn to face Mansour as he reads out the charges against me: being a member of a terrorist organisation;

financing a terrorist organisation; supporting a terrorist organisation; knowingly broadcasting false information to spread fear and discontent with intent to destabilise Egypt and defame the government; broadcasting without a licence; possessing broadcasting equipment without a licence; and working as a journalist without a permit.

For a moment I am stunned. I sit in silence while I digest the allegations. These are terrorism charges, and as ridiculous as they are, I slowly begin to understand just how serious the situation is. But I also know there is no evidence to back up any of the allegations, except perhaps working without a permit, though that is a misdemeanour and certainly not a criminal offence. On that charge, the most they can do is give me a fine and kick me out of the country. The rest are nonsense, and I am at a complete loss to understand where they could possibly have come from. Being a *member* of a terrorist organisation? I don't even know what group they're referring to. And where on earth did they come up with the charge of *financing* a terrorist organisation? Surely they'd need some kind of money trail to justify that one, and I know I have only spent money on food, Christmas presents and a few souvenirs.

Broadcasting false news should be an easy one to deal with. By definition everything we have produced is on the public record, and although there is a small chance we got some detail wrong, I sincerely doubt it. Both Fahmy and Baher scrutinise every word of every script, and their experience is so deep that any errors will stand out like flies on a bedsheet. Anything we aren't sure of, they check. We also have script editors back in Doha go through our stories line by line. It's possible I said something wrong in a live interview, but again, I don't think so. We went through all the details with Baher and Fahmy before each live shot, and they listened in to every word I broadcast. And anyway, even if we got something wrong, the prosecutor would need to show it 'spread fear and discontent with intent to destabilise Egypt and defame the government'. Without clear documentary evidence, showing intent is surely impossible.

Mansour snaps me out of my thoughts with a question: 'How do you respond to the charges?'

This is my opportunity to tell my story, from my early career through to how I came to be in Egypt and what exactly I am doing here. I draw a deep breath and we begin.

4

AFGHANISTAN

2001

Once more, Afghanistan was locked in winter. But this Afghanistan was a very different place from the one I left almost six years earlier.

It *looked* much the same, of course. The plains that flank the Amu Darya river, which forms the northern border with Tajikistan, had the same dun-brown dustiness that I had seen on my last trip. The distant Hindu Kush mountains from which the river flows had all their familiar white-capped hoariness. And I smiled at the old bearded Tajiks with their tightly wound turbans and shalwar kameezes that I remembered from years gone by.

Superficially, very little had changed. But it was now November 2001, just two months after Al Qaeda brought down the Twin Towers, and *everything* had changed.

Afghanistan used to be the high point, both literally and figuratively, on the hippy trail in the 1970s. Afghans have always been deeply traditional and fiercely conservative, but back then they tolerated the crazy Western visitors with a kind of bemused detachment, watching as they came searching for carpets, enlightenment and hashish. As long as you didn't try to change their ways, Afghans were happy to welcome guests.

But war, the Taliban and Al Qaeda had made them exhausted, cynical and small-minded – or, more specifically, Al Qaeda had. The outsiders had imported and imposed their austere, puritanical brand of Wahhabi Islam, which sat uncomfortably with Afghanis' traditional sense of tolerance and hospitality.

The shift began soon after I left in 1996, when the Taliban finally captured Kabul. They spread their influence across the south and then advanced north into all but a relatively narrow wedge of territory that runs from the mouth of the Panjshir Valley just north of the capital, through the impossibly hostile mountains bordering China further to the north-east, and north-west towards the Uzbek city of Mazar-i-Sharif. Eventually, even that city would fall.

The Taliban argued that they should be treated as the legitimate government – perhaps not unreasonably, given that the government they had driven out of Kabul had also claimed legitimacy through conquest and never controlled more than half of Afghanistan. But the rest of the world, apart from the Taliban's kin in Pakistan, refused to have anything to do with them, offering neither political nor material support. This left a gap that Al Qaeda gleefully filled.

Towards the end of my time in Kabul in early 1996, rumours had begun circulating about an Al Qaeda camp that had been set up to help train and equip the Taliban's troops. We were never able to pin it down (and anyway, I was never going to make a close-up inspection – even then, Al Qaeda had a reputation), but by late that year it became clear that Osama bin Laden had become the Taliban's new best friend. He had a safe haven where he could operate out of sight of the Western agents who already suspected him of links to the first attempted bombing of the World Trade Center in 1993, as well as space to train and blood his recruits. Along with the weapons, ammunition and ambush drills came the ideology. Bin Laden brought in a patchwork of extremists from across his sphere of influence: Saudis, Egyptians and Yemenis from the Middle East, of course, but also Chechens from the north, Uighurs from China to the east, and Kashmiris from northern India. It became a kind of jihadi university, and together, they drove the already conservative Talib ideology even further to the fringe.

By 2001, the once-welcoming Afghans had become anxious and scared. Where we used to encounter curious grins from behind women's veils, now there was fear and hostility. The kids who in the past had always been delightful irritants, leaping in front of our cameras, were sullen and wary. Afghanistan felt a much darker place.

I was back in the northern region as a part of the BBC's team covering the West-backed push by the Northern Alliance to overthrow the Taliban in the wake of 9/11. An advance guard of BBC camera operators, producers, correspondents, engineers and security experts had established a base in the dusty frontier town of Khoja Bahauddin along with hundreds of other journalists and chancers, who'd arrived mostly so they could plant a foot south of the river and claim to be reporting from Afghanistan.

It was a long way from the actual fighting, and even further from the truth.

•

Covering the conflict was profoundly different, too. Extremely limited access to the front lines and almost no access to the Taliban made it virtually impossible to check the details of official stories or the overactive rumour mill.

One of the most seductive reasons for becoming a reporter is the privilege of having a ringside seat to history. Nobody looks forward to sitting through news conferences – we'd all much rather be in the field, talking to people who have seen and experienced the key events or, even better, seeing and experiencing them for ourselves. Now all we had was propaganda: briefings by the Taliban's associates in distant Pakistan, and the occasional satellite telephone call to their commanders; press conferences with Northern Alliance officers with their own agendas to spin. We urgently needed to get closer to the fighting to cover it ourselves, ideally from both sides of the lines.

In flying their hijacked planes into the Twin Towers, Al Qaeda had announced unequivocally that they were hostile to all things Western, and American in particular. By hosting and protecting Al Qaeda, the Taliban had effectively adopted the same policy. George W. Bush had responded in kind when soon after the attacks he declared before a joint session of Congress: 'You are either with us, or you are with the terrorists.'[2]

Bush's speech was aimed explicitly at other nations to force them into backing the United States' plans for an invasion of Afghanistan (and later Iraq) rather than make the politically impossible alternative declaration of support for Al Qaeda. But this binarism had deeply disturbing implications for the media. In Journalism 101 courses, students everywhere are told that they are to be friends of nobody, that their job is to question and challenge all sides in any given story, and that the moment you become too close to any particular group is the moment you lose that vital neutral, independent voice.

The incomparable Middle East-based journalist and commentator Robert Fisk wrote in 2016 that more than being witnesses to history, the primary responsibility for journalists – and indeed the main reason reporters exist – is to hold those in power to account on behalf of those over whom the powerful have dominion. That philosophy has underpinned news reporting in the West since the Second World War. It has been a linchpin of Western democracy, informing public debate, allowing a free flow of ideas, and holding governments responsible for the decisions and policies they enact in the name of voters. Regardless of whether you support or oppose a particular government, your job as a reporter must always be to question and challenge.

Times of national crisis put enormous strain on that role. Even at the best of times, democratic governments generally only tolerate media scrutiny through gritted teeth, knowing that in an established democracy, attempting to muzzle the press will be political suicide. But when a nation goes to war, the media come under huge pressure to do their 'patriotic duty' and support the government of the day. Questioning or challenging policy is suddenly seen as sowing doubt and discord and therefore deeply unpatriotic. At worst, it is equated with treason.

In wars over tangible things – whether land, water or ethnicity – there are clear front lines, or at least clearly understood lines of conflict between rival political forces, even if the battlefields aren't defined by sandbags, trenches and firing zones. The media, and the foreign media in particular, are spectators – often inconvenient ones to be sure, but still regarded as separate from the conflict itself – with the same neutrality as humanitarian workers. They are observers rather than participants. Of course, if a reporter stumbles on something a soldier wants to keep hidden, there is a good chance the reporter will be shot, but that is an occupational hazard.

On a superficial level at least, this was true in Afghanistan. It was very much a battle over turf and politics. The Northern Alliance was a highly unstable grouping of warlords and militias with only one thing in common: their desire to destroy the Taliban Islamists, who were a product of the Pashtun tribes in the far south. The Northern Alliance had been bolstered by special forces sent by sympathetic governments, and by enormous US air support, and was rolling back the Taliban's zones of control on its way to restoring a government acceptable to its US allies.

Journalists died in that battle. On 11 November, just a few weeks into the war, Johanne Sutton, Pierre Billaud and Volker Handloik became the first reporters to be killed. They were riding on a Northern Alliance armoured personnel carrier when the Taliban attacked it with rocket-propelled grenades.[3] But as tragic as that attack was, theirs were incidental deaths, the consequences of working in a dangerous environment with explosives and bits of metal flying around at supersonic speeds. They were not the targets of the attack – their convoy was.

Crucially though, as well as the physical war, the struggle for control of Afghanistan was a proxy for a much more poorly defined conflict over ideas. It was a battle between Al Qaeda's millennial view of Western imperialism, decadence and corruption on the one hand,

and Western ideas of liberalism, democracy and personal liberty on the other.

In that war there are no front lines and no clear battlegrounds, and the very ideas themselves are spongy, mutable, and constantly open to debate. It is impossible to draw a clear distinction between one side and the other, either on a map or on surveys of sectarian affiliation. A good friend once quipped, with a glass of whisky in hand, that the War on Terror is a war on an abstract noun. It means whatever anyone wants it to mean and, as you will see later in this book, governments are exploiting that sponginess by redefining it in ever-broader terms.

The problem for journalists is that in the war of ideas, the battlefield extends to the place where ideas themselves are tested – in other words, the media. We are no longer simply witnesses to the struggle. We are, by definition, a means by which the war itself is waged.

This is not an abstract concept.

•

On 13 November, Al Jazeera Arabic's correspondent, Tayseer Allouni, locked his office in the network's bureau and headed home. He'd been covering the war since the beginning and was the only foreign reporter to be working in Kabul, behind the Taliban's lines, while the Northern Alliance advanced south. A month earlier, he'd secured the first interview with Osama bin Laden – a hugely controversial exclusive that the network's critics said effectively made it a propaganda machine for Al Qaeda. Several Western television channels later broadcast portions of the tapes.

Although Al Jazeera Arabic had been on air since its launch in 1996, it had gone largely unnoticed in the West until it began airing the messages from Al Qaeda and the Taliban in the wake of 9/11.

Allouni had also been criticised for broadcasting images of civilians killed and wounded during the US bombardment. The then US secretary of state, Colin Powell, even asked the Qatari government to rein in Al Jazeera (though he later told a news conference that he viewed the request as 'advice'as opposed to an 'order'.).[4] The network insisted it was only doing what any responsible news organisation should: covering the conflict from both sides of the lines, using all its contacts and resources to provide balanced reporting, and questioning and challenging all of the forces involved, including the Americans.

However, as the Northern Alliance pushed closer to Kabul and the Taliban defences began to crumble, the network managers in Doha ordered Allouni and his staff to leave. They were concerned about their team's welfare in the chaos of the city's fall. But Allouni's own contacts in the Northern Alliance assured him that he'd be safe, so he decided to defy the order and stay.

As Allouni settled into his apartment a few blocks away from the bureau, the recently arrived BBC correspondent William Reeve went on BBC News to report on the day's developments. Reeve was an old Afghan hand and knew the country and its people well. He had volunteered to use his experience to report from inside Kabul along with another seasoned front-line correspondent, Rageh Omaar. As Reeve began his live TV broadcast, a massive explosion interrupted the transmission and he could be seen, on air, diving under his desk to escape the blast of dust and rubble.

The US bombs landed directly on the Al Jazeera bureau next door, causing no casualties but destroying its offices and equipment and damaging not only the BBC bureau but the nearby Associated Press office as well.

In a terse letter to Al Jazeera the following month, the assistant to the US secretary of defence for public affairs, Victoria Clarke, said, 'The building we struck was a known Al Qaeda facility in central Kabul . . . There were no indications that this or any nearby facility was used by Al Jazeera.'[5] Al Jazeera's chief editor, Ibrahim Hilal, said the bureau's location was well known to all the forces involved. The network had given the location of its Kabul office to the authorities in Washington long before the fighting began.

Regardless of anyone's opinion of whether Al Jazeera was behaving ethically, the attack was seen as an attempt to silence a media organisation that had been interviewing and broadcasting the voices of 'the enemy'. BBC presenter Nik Gowing raised the bombing at a journalists' conference in Barcelona soon after, arguing that Al Jazeera's only crime was that it had been 'bearing witness' to events that the US would rather it did not see. Others, like Matt Wells from *The Guardian*, said there was 'no clear evidence that Al Jazeera directly supported the Taliban – simply that it enjoyed greater access than other stations'.[6]

Al Jazeera kept an open mind on the issue and called for an official inquiry,[7] but at the time of writing – more than twenty years on – there has been no investigation. Even if we never learn whether the bombing was a deliberate attack on a news organisation, what matters is the chilling impact it had on news agencies that might otherwise have tried to cross the lines to report from the other side of the battle.

•

It wasn't just the US government that appeared to shift gears. In agreeing to let the BBC into Kabul to report on the battle alongside Al Jazeera, the Taliban seemed to recognise the value of having Western media attention. But any glimmer of hope for a softening of their attitude was dramatically snuffed out less than a week after the city's fall in November 2001.

By that stage, the BBC team travelling from the north had made it into the capital, beating even the Northern Alliance troops. The advancing militias had paused on the fringes of the city to avoid the house-to-house fighting that would have made a mess of the already badly damaged suburbs and would have caused large numbers of civilian casualties.

With reports that the Taliban had fled their positions around Kabul, the BBC's John Simpson and his colleagues decided to push past the Northern Alliance checkpoint on the fringes and go into the centre to witness the crowds who'd filled the streets in celebration. I followed a few hours later, driving through the euphoric city to join the BBC team at the Intercontinental Hotel, a battle-scarred Soviet-era lump of concrete and glass that stood on what was once a prominent front-line ridge.

There, we set up a fully-fledged broadcast centre, with satellite dishes on the roof and a view across the city that made a perfect backdrop for reporters going live into the network's news bulletins. We hired several connecting suites and rearranged the furniture to create a newsroom. Then we organised a small army of drivers, fixers and translators to help ferry teams around the country to cover the unfolding conflict and its aftermath. I spent hours broadcasting from the roof in the freezing winter air, drawing on my time in the country five years earlier to help make sense of the war and its consequences.

In the days that followed, the Taliban troops beat a disorderly retreat, fleeing through the hostile valleys to the east of the city. That network of valleys partly explains why the town of Surobi, which I had encountered on that first drive into Kabul, is such a notorious place for smugglers and bandits. The valleys are deep and hostile. They've been the back door to the city for millennia, offering an alternative passage for anyone game enough to negotiate their way past the local tribes and navigate through the mountain passes. Smugglers have always used them to shuffle contraband between the capital and Pakistan, and armies have traversed them as a way of both attacking and fleeing the city. Crucially, Surobi is the place where that mountain route intersects with the main east–west road to Jalalabad and Pakistan beyond.

On 17 November, four days after the fall of Kabul, the BBC team gathered for a meeting in one of the rooms at the Intercontinental. Some of them had been working non-stop under extraordinarily tough conditions for well over six weeks; they were utterly exhausted and badly needed a break. The question on the table was: with the first civilian trucks arriving from Pakistan, was it worth trying to drive out over the border?

Some of the team were prepared to take the risk. 'Surely the locals will know if it's okay to make the drive. They're not suicidal, and they've got much better radars than us,' one producer argued.

'Absolutely not,' I said. 'Surobi is notorious for trouble at times like this. Taliban stragglers are still probably moving down through the valleys towards Kandahar. They'll be angry and looking for heads to kick. We need to see at least a week of safe civilian traffic through there before it'll be safe enough for any white guys like us.'

In the end, the team reluctantly agreed to wait.

In Jalalabad, though, another group of journalists was having a similar debate that had a tragically different outcome. Julio Fuentes of the Spanish paper *El Mundo*, Maria Grazia Cutulli from the Italian paper *Corriere della Sera*, and two Reuters staffers, Australian cameraman Harry Burton and Afghan photojournalist Aziz Ullah Haidari, were all desperate to get to Kabul and catch up with those of us who had come down to the city from the north. Like all good journalists, they weren't interested in watching from the sidelines. After a long discussion, they agreed to make the journey in a convoy with seven other cars. With an early start they'd reach the capital in a day. They left two days later, on 19 November.

Maria was an old friend whom I first came to know when she began covering Afghanistan in 1995. She was an outstanding reporter, fiercely devoted to stories she believed in and remarkably courageous. I knew she was in the region and was looking forward to seeing her again over a drink at the Intercontinental.

Accounts of what happened in Surobi vary, but we know that a group of eleven Taliban fighters stopped the convoy as it approached a bridge. Four vehicles at the back of the group sped off and escaped the ambush, but the four journalists were dragged out of their cars and into the dusty hills out of sight.

The Australian war correspondent Michael Ware knew Burton well and investigated the incident. He likes to believe that the four had reason to hope they'd only be robbed and perhaps knocked around a little,[8] but to me their treatment makes it clear that they were in a situation far more serious than a standard robbery. Their driver and translator, who were allowed to flee, said the gang began to stone their victims before firing full magazines of bullets into them. The autopsy indicates that Maria was raped before she was murdered.

After the invasion, Afghan investigators eventually arrested three men for the murders – two brothers, Mahmood Zar Jan and Abdul Wahid, and the third, who was the 'leader', Reza Khan. All were executed for the killings. Crucially, in his trial, Khan admitted he was involved but said he was following a general order to kill journalists, issued by a Taliban leader called Maulawi Latif.[9]

The Surobi murders marked a crucial turning point in the War on Terror. It was the moment when the Taliban came to see journalists as representatives of a world they had rejected, one that was antithetical to their beliefs. It wasn't enough to simply refuse to engage with journalists, though. To the Taliban in that post-9/11 world, journalists had become agents of the liberal Western thought that they saw as antithetical to the fundamentalism they were fighting for. Journalists were suddenly *the* enemy, and therefore legitimate targets to be attacked and murdered with impunity.

•

If this change wasn't immediately apparent at the time, it was because most of us were still consumed in reporting on – and surviving – the chaos of the war. The Taliban had been ousted from Kabul but the fighting had moved further east, towards Jalalabad and the mountains of Tora Bora, where Osama bin Laden was believed to be hiding out with his most loyal fighters. I headed down there to cover what most of us thought would be the coup de grâce for Al Qaeda – the final battle in those splintered mountains that would see the death of bin Laden, his movement and, most importantly, his ideas. We watched from a camp at the foot of the mountains as US aircraft dropped huge, sarcastically named 'daisy cutter' bombs on bin Laden's suspected hideout, shaking the earth in deep, groaning waves that you felt long before you heard.

Bin Laden famously escaped, of course, crossing the frozen mountains into Pakistan. Then, in February the following year, Al Qaeda brutally articulated its war on Western liberalism and freedom of speech with a trick that has proven to be shockingly effective time and again.

The story of what happened to Daniel Pearl involves a complex mix of politics and motivations, but it underlined the period when the Islamic radicals came to reject old media and instead coopted the still relatively new social media as one of its principal weapons.

Pearl was one of the *Wall Street Journal*'s most outstanding reporters, committed to understanding and explaining the Islamic world with intelligence and nuance to his readers in the United States.[10] As we covered the fighting in Afghanistan, Pearl was mining his own contacts for a greater understanding of what drove the extremists.

He was never one to take a story at face value. In 1998, for example, he investigated the US bombing of a Sudanese drug factory in August the previous year – it had been bombed because the CIA suspected it was producing chemical weapons. 'Some US allies and Washington officials still doubt the US hit a legitimate target, and the full truth of El Shifa, wrapped in the divisive politics of antiterrorism, may never be known,' he wrote. 'The hardest evidence is a scoop of soil, taken near the plant and judged by the US to contain a chemical used to make nerve gas. But other evidence becomes murkier the closer you look.'[11]

It was classic Pearl, revealing an almost obsessive urge to dig deeper and get to the less obvious truth hidden beneath the easy clichés, the propaganda and, in this case literally, the dirt that inevitably surround conflict.

As Islamabad correspondent, Pearl worked on stories that explored the background to the 9/11 attacks and the ongoing conflict they had launched.[12] In an email in September 2001 he indicated he was following his instincts once again: 'I'm writing a story about how everybody here thinks the Jews did it [9/11]. Bound to piss everybody off, but I think people should know what people in other parts of the world REALLY think, and why. Right?'

On the day he was kidnapped, Pearl was investigating the background to Al Qaeda's failed 'shoe bomber', Richard Reid, who tried to blow up an aeroplane over the Atlantic. One of his contacts was Omar Sheikh, a young British-educated radical who had met Pearl two weeks earlier in a hotel outside Islamabad and offered to connect him with the man suspected of being behind the attack – something Sheikh knew would draw the *Wall Street Journal* reporter like a bee to honey.

On 23 January 2002, Pearl went to another hotel for the promised meeting, but instead Sheikh and three accomplices abducted him and took him to a 'safe house' where they kept him in chains. The kidnappers appeared to be uncertain about their ultimate goals, issuing several ransom demands. In their second email, they threatened to abduct more US journalists and vaguely threatened other Americans as well.[13]

Although the connection between the kidnappers and Al Qaeda is unclear, it appears that Al Qaeda was not involved in the kidnapping itself. Instead, the man considered by the US to be the mastermind behind 9/11, Khaled Sheikh Mohammed, learned about it through another Al Qaeda colleague. In testimony to his FBI interrogators, Mohammed said he took a phone call from the colleague, who told him the kidnappers 'don't know what to do with him [Pearl]. They want to know if we want him.'

According to Mohammed's statement, his colleague thought this was an opportunity: 'We can take advantage of it. We should make sure it's an Al Qaeda thing.' Mohammed went on to tell the FBI that they decided to execute Pearl by beheading him and exploit the murder for its propaganda value.

Over the following weeks, Al Qaeda released several harrowing images of their hostage, one with him seated against a blue curtain and holding a copy of a newspaper to confirm the latest date that he was alive; another with him in the same position but staring sullenly at the camera with his hands bound in chains; and a third with his head bowed between his knees and an anonymous hand poking into the frame, pointing a pistol at his temple.

Predictably, the photographs made it onto the front pages of countless newspapers around the world, doing precisely the job the kidnappers had hoped for: terrifying those who saw Al Qaeda as the enemy, and sending an unequivocal message to journalists who might have been considering investigating their side of the conflict.

Finally, Pearl's captors released a video that showed him denouncing American foreign policy and then being gruesomely beheaded. Most news organisations chose not to show the knife sawing at his throat, but the video still circulated widely online. It was a brutally crude piece of propaganda that predated most social media, so it did not have anywhere near the kind of impact that later Islamic State videos would have, but it still taught Al Qaeda the extraordinary power of the internet to amplify its messages.

It was also the moment when the extremist movement began to understand how to use the Western media against itself. By supplying such shockingly compelling images, it could force the media to do what the extremists had wanted all along. The extremists could terrorise an entire population while at the same time intimidating journalists out of their professional obligation for aggressive inquiry.

The Pearl Project, which provides the most comprehensive publicly available investigation into the case, points out that up until Daniel's execution, journalists had routinely relied on their independence to give them access to underworld figures: 'Pearl thought he was about to have an interview like so many he had had in the past with dodgy characters in Pakistan. Even in the early days after 9/11, it was common for reporters to go in the vehicles of suspicious strangers to interview known extremists. It was a calculated risk. At the time, most journalists felt they had certain immunity with even the most hardened criminals or radicals because they gave voice to the disenfranchised and dispossessed.'[14]

I had worked that way as a matter of routine during my earlier stint in Afghanistan, and until Pearl's execution, had been searching for ways of doing similar work to get a deeper understanding of the culture and ideology behind Islamic extremism.

Suddenly, chillingly, that door had slammed shut. The Surobi murders underlined known dangers, and showed that fundamentalist groups wanted to silence Western reporters. The Pearl kidnap and murder made it clear that journalists were being specifically targeted and then used as tools of propaganda. And with its bombing of the Al Jazeera bureau in Kabul, there was the chilling suggestion that the US government's tolerance for independent reporting had reached its limits.

Journalists everywhere were forced to face a confronting truth: in the wake of 9/11, the world had become a very different and much more dangerous place.

5

TORA LIMEN PRISON

2 JANUARY – 8 FEBRUARY 2014

It is late evening when my prison van pulls up at another imposing old colonial-era door. I am still struggling to make sense of the interrogation when I am ordered into the dust outside a place I am not expecting.

It looks like a medieval portcullis, with massive timbers reinforced with iron straps and studded with bolts. It is illuminated with spotlights, and in the sulphurous yellow light I can see a date carved into the lintel: 1889.

'Welcome to our museum,' says one of the guards. He yanks me out of the van and I stagger for balance, my hands cuffed as he shoves me through a small hatch in the outer door. I have no idea why I am being moved to a new prison. Very little of what has happened makes sense, and I doubt that even if the guards spoke English they'd be able to give me any answers.

In the corridor behind the hatch, I pass through a dusty old metal detector that screeches at my handcuffs. I am ushered into a courtyard with perhaps a dozen guards standing idly in a semicircle, watching as I am led to a table beneath a large fig tree.

'Strip,' one of them demands.

'What?'

'Strip. Take off clothes. All.'

It is still cold, even with my fleece, but I have no choice. I remove my jacket, my shirt, my shoes and socks, my jeans. I hesitate at my underwear, and one of the guards gestures that I've gone far enough. In the freezing cold, I'm feeling more exposed than I've ever been. I am a prisoner in a place I do not know, with a language I do not speak and a system I do not understand, and for the first time I realise something deeply unsettling: I am utterly powerless. What happens from here is completely out of my hands. I don't know what's coming, where I am going, or what will happen there. Nor do I have a say in any of it.

The guards hand me my prison uniform – thin, rough cotton pyjamas with Arabic script in shabby blue letters printed across the back of the shirt and down one leg of the pants; I find out later that it means 'accused prisoner'.

They shove my clothes, watch, wallet and hat into a plastic bag and gesture me forward. I am shivering in the winter-evening chill, as much from nerves as from the cold.

The prison is a large complex of cellblocks that radiate from the central courtyard. I can see high brick walls studded with rows of tiny barred windows, but the guards don't lead me anywhere near those. Instead, they take me through a small door in a blank wall that leads to another courtyard, sectioned off with a chain-link fence topped with barbed wire. We pass through a low gate towards a freestanding cellblock that is well isolated from all the others. Its inmates are clearly people the authorities don't want mixing with any other prisoners.

I'm scared now. I don't want to be somewhere I can't communicate with anyone, and none of the guards seem to speak English. I doubt any of the other inmates will, either. I don't want to be with violent prisoners as a foreigner accused of spying on Egypt. I don't want to be in a place where I have to fight to survive. Suddenly, for all its discomforts, I yearn for the crowded community of the police cell I've just left behind.

The block is a long, single-storeyed set of cells with a corridor running down the middle. There are perhaps half a dozen cells down each side, marked with dark-blue steel doors and small barred windows. There is no heating.

The guards search for an empty cell. It seems they weren't expecting me, and none is ready. They find one about two-thirds of the way along, but it is filthy with the detritus of the last inmate – a few rags, food scraps under the bed, bits of notebook, and at least a month of dust. In the weak prison light, two young inmates dressed in blue appear with mops and a bucket and sluice out the concrete floor, wipe down the bunk, and lay a thin mattress and blanket on the steel frame.

The cell is about 2.5 metres square and is lit by a single bulb dangling from the high ceiling. There is a double bunk welded together out of angle iron, and a tiny bathroom that includes a sink, a toilet and a dripping pipe for a shower. There is no other furniture, but compared to the last few nights' accommodation it is generously roomy. From the top bunk I guess that at a stretch I might be able to see out the window, but it is clear there will be very little daylight. The paint on the walls is flaking with rising damp, and I shiver once again.

The guards order me back into the corridor to let the inmates finish cleaning out the cell.

'Are you Mr Peter?'

The voice comes from one of the neighbouring cells. 'Australian? Al Jazeera?'

I can't quite believe that this person has already heard of our arrest, much less knows who I am.

'Do you need anything?' the voice asks, and hands start thrusting through the bars of the cells up and down the block as voices call out. Someone waves long underwear at me; another hand clutches a blanket. A thin pillow lands on the floor with a soft thud as somebody else waves a bar of soap, and soon there is a minor avalanche. Food, bottles of water, clothing, another blanket – everything I could possibly need clatters and thuds to the ground, and I am overwhelmed with gratitude for my new neighbours.

I shovel all the things into my cell, and the door bangs shut as the guards turn the lock and march out of the block.

I take a deep breath and do an inventory. Tissues, three packs. Two plastic bags of Egyptian flatbread, about sixteen foil packs of date biscuits (5 centimetres each). A box of halva (an Egyptian sweet made from sugar and ground sesame seeds), a dozen small assorted fruit-juice packs, a large bottle of water, six rolls of toilet paper, a plastic bag of fruit, a set of thermal underwear (long-sleeved top and long pants); a white tracksuit (XXL – far too big, but right now I don't care), white socks, two sets of prison whites, two blankets, a pair of flip-flops, a bar of soap and a bottle of Dettol.

The generosity is staggering. For prisoners, even a bar of soap or warm clothing is precious, and yet I have everything I need – more, even – and none of my neighbours will take anything back.

As I am going through the gifts, the voice that first spoke to me calls out once again. I can't see where it is coming from, but it sounds as though he is two cells away. 'Hello, Peter, and welcome to Tora Limen. My name is Alaa Abd El-Fattah, and you are in the political wing of our prison.'

Alaa's voice echoes up and down the corridor and is clear, deep and comforting. He has an accent, but his English is practised and articulate.

'You are being held in solitary confinement,' he tells me. 'That is standard practice for any new prisoner. You won't be allowed out of your cell until the warden decides you've had enough. We are not supposed to talk to you, so you will be on your own for a while. It isn't going to be easy, but all of us have gone through it before, and we know you will make it too.'

'Thanks for the news,' I reply. 'By the way, how do you know who I am?'

Alaa chuckles. 'It is very hard to keep anything secret in here. News travels fast. We knew the next day that you had been arrested, and we wondered if you would be joining us.'

'So why am I here?' I ask.

'That, I am afraid, I can't say. Only the prosecutor knows that. But what I can tell you is that all of us here are either leaders or members of political parties, activist groups or trade unions. We are here because of our political activities, although of course the government won't ever say that. It says we are guilty of crimes like inciting violence or attacking the police.

'It is good that you are here with us, because at least you know that they regard you as another political prisoner rather than as a common criminal, and although it might not feel like it, that is good news. It means they know your case is going to be watched very closely, so they will make sure your conditions are better than most prisoners. You don't want them to treat you like all the other criminals.

'But that doesn't mean this is going to be easy. They are going to leave you in the cell for a period of solitary confinement – usually about ten days – so you are not going out except when they want you for interrogations or visits from the embassy. You're not going to get exercise and there will be no social time. Nothing. So you'd better get used to living inside your own head for a while.'

I thank Alaa for his advice, but it is late, I am exhausted after four almost-sleepless nights, and I need time to sit and take in the news. I stare at the most obvious things in front of my face: the wide, featureless slabs of concrete that form the cell. The gifts from the other prisoners are comforting, but as the block swiftly settles back to sleep and the darkness closes in, for the first time since our arrest I feel profoundly alone.

Soon, the walls start to creep in. I blink at first, wondering if it is just exhaustion that is messing with my head. But then I see it, so real that I can almost hear the concrete groaning with the effort. The cell is shrinking. The bars are growing thick. And I begin to shake. It starts with my fingers, and a fluttering in the middle of my chest. The fluttering expands like a balloon, displacing my lungs until I am struggling to breathe, and spreads until it feels as though my body has been taken over by a giant demented butterfly.

Until now I've been busy. I've had things to think about and work to do. There have been interrogators with questions, and my own physical comfort and safety to manage. I've had to work out how to defend our team and come up with strategies to get us out of this mess. There has been a mad psychological busy-ness amid all the distractions of the new. I've allowed my professional journalistic curiosity to take over, observing the weirdness of all that has been taking place around me, almost as if it has been happening to somebody else. And suddenly there is no way of avoiding the truth of what is happening.

I am in prison, and I am utterly powerless to change that one hard, simple fact. Whatever I might try to do, ultimately the decision about whether to keep me locked up is somebody else's to make, and that person is both nameless and faceless to me. I have no point of contact. No way of directly influencing them. No way of extending an arm, much less an argument, beyond the walls to make them give the order to release me.

As I sit and stare at the door, I become aware of a surreal contradiction between time and space. There is a vast, empty, formless blob of time stretching out in front of me with no edges to it. There are no deadlines, no dates, no particular time for anything.

Time, such as it is, becomes meaningless without markers. The need to get up, eat breakfast, catch the train to work, meet a deadline, get to the shops before they close or to the weekend for a bit of rest – all lay down waypoints that help keep this thing we call time on some kind of leash. Time is vast, but that vastness poses no threat or discomfort if the view is obscured by things-that-must-be-done. Without any of those flags, a minute, an hour, a day, a year becomes the same thing: unfilled space. And the sheer emptiness of that expanse is terrifying.

And yet, in this tiny concrete box, physical space is so terribly limited. It is three short paces long by one and a half paces wide – certainly no more than 3 metres. No matter how you do the calculations, the numbers are small and inflexible. The walls are thick, the bars are cold, and neither will give way.

Einstein might have been technically right when he said that time and space are different aspects of the same thing, but here in the cell, reconciling hard-edged space with limitless time seems simply impossible.

As I sit, struggling to bring my rising panic under control, I understand something fundamental. My greatest challenge – indeed, my only challenge – is to manage my own sanity. Railing and screaming and shouting mean nothing in here. They bounce off the walls and echo back into my own head. I have to trust those outside the prison – the ones with access to lawyers and diplomats and the media – to fight the legal and political battles. They have the power to be informed, to make choices and to act on my behalf. The idea that I can do any of that is an illusion that will only end up driving me mad if I hold on to it.

And so, I sit. It's the only thing I know how to do in this empty hole.

•

Years ago, my marriage collapsed. I had let my wife down badly and caused a lot of pain to both of us. Battered and bruised from the break-up, I knew I needed to do something radical to steady myself, so I enrolled in a Vipassanā meditation course.

Vipassanā is a form of meditation from the Indian Buddhist tradition. The word means 'clear sight', 'to see into' or 'to see in a special way'. The literature says it focuses on an 'insight into the true nature of reality'. That is a rather grand statement, of course, but in practice it means watching yourself as an objective observer with the same neutral curiosity as a scientist studying a bug or the cosmos. It is a way of setting aside the emotional baggage we often bring to a situation.

Vipassanā has its roots in pre-Buddhist Indian philosophy that dates back more than 2600 years, and it involves austere practices of self-denial and periods of weeks or even months of almost continuous mediation. Modern introductory Vipassanā courses are a little less brutal than that, but are still fairly serious undertakings. They start with a ten-day course of silent meditation. Throughout the ten days there is no reading material, no writing material, no communication with anybody other than the teacher – not even eye contact – and up to eight hours a day of sitting with eyes closed, focusing on yourself.

In the silence of my cell, it occurs to me that I have been in such a situation before. Vipassanā has given me the tools to deal with solitary confinement.

•

I wake early, determined to set in place a strong ritual of physical exercise, meditation and intellectual activity. I have no idea how long I will be here, or when the next stage in the investigation might unfold, so I focus on the job at hand. It will take a few days to settle into the routine, but I need to make sure I can survive this. The solitary confinement won't be easy, but plenty of others have done it before and I will too, as long as I am prepared mentally.

First things first: the cell is filthy. I start working with water and tissues, wiping down the top bunk and all the surfaces.

Halfway through this job, I get a visit from an officer dressed in a crisp white uniform with gold-embroidered epaulets, accompanied by an entourage of guards. In rough, thickly accented and broken English, he asks my name and demands to know why I've been imprisoned. 'I'm a journalist,' I reply. 'Beyond that, I don't know what I'm supposed to have done wrong or why they've put me here. You look like you're important. Can't you tell me?'

The officer draws a deep breath and sighs. 'Okay then. What have you been charged with?'

'I've been charged with being a member of a terrorist organisation, financing a terrorist organisation, broadcasting false news to undermine national security.' I have recited the charges so many times that the allegations have lost their ability to shock or intimidate me. They are simply words.

'Were you working without a licence?'

'I'm not in prison because someone thinks I failed to fill out a few government forms,' I reply.

The conversation continues for a few minutes, with the officer parrying and me fending, before he finally departs, his entourage trailing after him like leaves.

As soon as they're gone, I finish cleaning the cell and begin a workout. First there is a warm-up, and I spend what I guess to be about twenty minutes jogging on the spot, going for as long as it takes to drive the cold from my bones and get my chest heaving.

Then I do some push-ups. I guess that fifteen will be an easy number to aim for first off, and I'm startled when my arms begin to shake after just eight. By number twelve, I'm barely able to lift my body off the ground, and I realise with a grimace that this experience might actually turn out to be good for me.

So, day one is about testing my physical limits. How many sit-ups, squats and dips can I do? How long can I hold my body rigid in a plank? How long can I sit in silent meditation before I have to move? Once I have the answers to those questions, I'll know what targets to set each day.

Without a watch, working out the time is a little more complicated, but not impossible. Each day, the muezzin calls the five Islamic prayers – shortly after 5 a.m., at dawn a little over an hour later, at 12 noon, at sunset around 5.30 p.m., and finally around 7 p.m. The precise times vary with the sun, but I can hear them and use them to set my daily program. My neighbours are also allowed out for two hours of exercise each day, in two shifts – from 10 a.m. to noon, and again from noon to 2 p.m.

None of it is precise, but it is enough to mark out a little over an hour for meditation at either end of the day between the calls to prayer, and times to begin my workout and creative period. The days begin to take on structure.

•

Shortly before noon, I hear a voice just outside my cell door calling my name. It is Alaa again, and he has come to talk quietly while the guards are busy elsewhere. He is a 'blogger, coder and activist' by his own description, from a politically active family. He tells me a little more of his story.

He grew up in a family of activists. His father, Ahmed Seif El-Islam Hamad, is a human-rights lawyer who was arrested, tortured and imprisoned for five years under the Mubarak regime. Alaa's mother, aunt and two sisters are all prominent activists, and as a child he was immersed in debates over human rights, politics and social justice. Political activism is in his DNA.

He trained as a software coder and used his skills to develop open-source programs that support freedom of expression and protect digital privacy. He also launched the first Arabic news aggregation websites that refused to censor contributors, making them hugely popular, particularly among wired young Egyptians.

Alaa is so outspoken that he has been imprisoned by every regime in Egypt. Hosni Mubarak's administration locked him up for demanding an independent judiciary. He was arrested again when he protested crackdowns by the short-lived SCAF government that stepped in after Mubarak's fall, and then by the Muslim Brotherhood that followed. Now, it's the turn of Adly Mansour's interim government, which arrested him two days after it passed a law prohibiting any protest that wasn't officially sanctioned. (Alaa would be released on bail, tried, convicted and sentenced to five years in Abdel Fattah el-Sisi's crackdown on dissent, keeping his record intact.)

As he stands talking softly outside my cell door, I sense intelligence and good humour that refuse to be smothered. His voice is as calming as it is inspiring, but his experience is sobering. Egypt's authorities, whatever their stripe, have a disturbing tendency to crush freedom of expression, and a chronic intolerance of any form of criticism, whether it is in the media or on the streets. As Alaa does a quick rollcall of the cellblock, I realise that our arrest is part of a pattern and I am surrounded by the evidence.

In the cell to my right is Dr Gamal Abdel Salam, a member of the board of the Egyptian Doctors Syndicate who has been imprisoned for criticising the interim government's crackdowns. Then there is Alaa's cell, followed by those of Fareed and Yasser, the only two prisoners who've been convicted of a relatively normal crime (theft). They are in the closing stages of their sentences and have been assigned to our block to help manage the rest of us.

Ahmed Douma is in the last cell on my side of the block. He is a charismatic, much-loved youth activist and poet who has been imprisoned for his very public role in pro-democracy protests. I recognise him from the graffiti portraits I have seen spray-painted on the walls of the American University in protest at his imprisonment.

Essam Sultan is in the first cell on the opposite side of the block. He is the co-founder and vice-president of the Al-Wasat Party, a group of moderate Islamists who split from the Muslim Brotherhood in 1996.

Ahmed Maher is next, the founder of the April 6 Youth Movement that is credited with using social media to inspire and galvanise the protests that eventually toppled Mubarak in 2011. His deputy, Mohammed Adel, is in the cell next door. Both have been convicted of inciting street violence under the anti-protest laws.

The frail, ageing former Supreme Court judge Mahmoud Al-Khudairi is next door to Adel. He is on trial along with eight others for his alleged role in torturing a lawyer in Tahrir Square in 2011, though it seems more likely that he is here because of his outspoken demands for an independent judiciary.

There is Adl Adli, whose only crime seems to be that his son was an aide to Mohamed Morsi; Ahmed Mosalim, who has been accused of being an Islamist; Ahmed Hillel, who owned a flat that he rented to a

Muslim Brotherhood leader; and finally Dr Mahdi Abdul Hadi, a former aide to the minister of aviation and a labour organiser. (Mahdi had helped organise a series of strikes by air traffic controllers that were predictably successful. They also helped land him in prison.)

The only common denominator – indeed, the very obvious common denominator – is that all of them have been either accused or convicted of political crimes; each in his own way has posed a very public challenge to the military-backed regime that is trying to tighten its grip on power in Egypt.

Alaa and I have to cut our conversation short when I'm called to the warden's office.

•

The warden is at once both pleasant and hostile. His manner is relaxed enough – unthreatening and easy – but his questions are aggressive and loaded with assumptions.

'Why were you broadcasting lies about Egypt?' he says as he taps the ash off the end of his cigarette.

'Why did you say our country is in a state of war and falling apart?' He drags deeply. 'Why did you interview terrorists who are determined to destroy Egypt?'

'I didn't tell any lies, and I didn't say the country is falling apart,' I reply. 'I stand by my work. Everything we produced is on the public record, and it's out there on the internet, so I'd like you to show me what we said that was wrong, or a lie, or suggests the country is falling apart, or promotes terrorism.'

One of the warden's deputies then accuses me of working undercover. 'Why didn't you have accreditation? That must be because you were trying to hide from the government. No country in the world allows journalists to work without official accreditation.'

'It depends on what you are covering,' I tell him. 'In Australia if you don't go to official events, you don't need accreditation. Nor in Britain, or in most of the ninety or so countries I have worked in over the years. In fact, in my experience the only ones that do require accreditation are those that are afraid of a free, uncontrolled press.'

Once again I remind the warden that I am not in prison because they think I failed to apply for media accreditation. I am in prison on terrorism charges, with no evidence that I can see.

It is not an interrogation, but nor is it a particularly friendly conversation, and I begin to feel like a curiosity – a strange and slightly dangerous zoo creature, wheeled out of his cage and prodded so the senior prison staff can get a little thrill.

Eventually I'm returned to my cell. When the door swings open I am overjoyed to see lunch set neatly on the bed. In Egypt's prison culture, it is the prisoners' families who are expected to look after them. There is prison food, of course – mainly flatbread and fūl, a bland staple of mashed fava beans – but it is hardly nutritious. If that is all you eat, scurvy will be a constant companion. But families are allowed to bring in food (and even clothing as long as it fits the prison regulations). Although they are only allowed to visit once a week for accused prisoners (and once every two weeks for convicts), in communal cells like ours, families often coordinate their deliveries to bring in enough food for all.

Today, somebody's family has brought in grilled fish with tomato, cucumber, preserved lemons and olives, and somebody else has sent over a box of feta cheese. It is simple, rustic food, but after three days of stress and very little nutrition, the meal tastes extraordinary. I am not sure if the new isolation has sharpened my tastebuds, but I am acutely aware of how each mouthful tastes and feels: the rich, salty fish with a slightly bitter charred edge to it and the texture of soft, flaky flesh against crisp skin; the intense salty sourness of the lemons; the fresh, cool, sweet tomatoes and crisp cucumbers with their shiny, almost plastic skin. Alone in the cell, surrounded by silence, I can't recall ever being so intently focused on or appreciative of food.

•

Over the next ten days I try to build my routines so that they become deeply ingrained habits: morning meditation, exercise, eating, memory games. Blissfully for me, Alaa manages to slip me a few books in English, and suddenly I have another way of soaking up time and filling mental space. One of them is *The Book of Disquiet* by the Portuguese poet Fernando Pessoa. It's an extraordinary meditation on boredom and solitude, on the tedium of a clerk's life in a dull Lisbon office. Its lingering, meandering reflections on the diners in a restaurant or the way the light filters into his office, offer a form of liberation and clarity.

I focus intently on each little development in the cell, and realise that I am living more mindfully than I imagined possible. It isn't out of any pious commitment to Buddhist teachings, just that the focused awareness of each moment – whether it is the noises outside the cell, or the smells that waft in from time to time – helps to fill the time. It also helps keep my mind in the present and stops it from drifting off into imagined conversations in the prosecutor's office about how they plan to use me, or fears that my friends, family and colleagues have got bored with the story and given up on getting me out.

A couple of hours meditating, one hour of exercise, one hour of pacing, a couple of hours of reading – and that's six gone, just like that. But the discipline must remain. There must be order to the day so it doesn't become homogeneous, formless, soupy time.

I even begin to appreciate the rough simplicity of the prison food. It's a peasant's breakfast, but no less perfect for that. Once more, I pay close attention to the plate before me. The bread is unrefined, earthy, coarse. The flour looks to have been stone-ground, but not in the trendy Western middle-class way that the term implies. It has been ground with stones, simply, cheaply, unromantically. It is what the Vaucluse set, the King Street Rangers, the Upper East Siders all look for, but without the pompousness or the fake idealism.

The eggs are greasy and salty, and farmy, with a faint hint of the fish meal the farmer must have used to feed his chooks. The fūl is deeply unappetising to look at – mashed brown beans in oily brown liquid – and there is always a fine line between earthy deliciousness and just plain earth, but it has a bitterness that, this time, is pleasing. Slightly peppery.

Against the odds, I'm learning to appreciate this experience. Like at the Vipassanā course, here, when you dial down the noise, you start to see and appreciate things that would normally disappear in the hubbub. Food tastes better, clearer, more defined. The sounds that drift in from around the cell say so much when you listen. Soft, rubber flip-flops belong to prisoners – depressed ones drag their heels along the ground (and in time I'll be able to tell a heavy-set prisoner from a skinny one). Leather slapping on the concrete means guards are approaching, and if it comes with the sharp click of new soles, the shoes probably belong to an officer. Wind blowing from the south brings the oily odour of the prison workshops; from the west it's the tang of cows. There is no need to rush. There is time to experience it all, with each sense.

With my back to the wall, I can look up at the window high above the bed to see leaves from a tree waving in the breeze, and for an hour or so in the morning, the sun hits the wall and I can stand there with it warming my chest. I'm tempted to drift away. The tree thrashing in the breeze reminds me of watching the trees in Argentina while I was on a hang-gliding course, and brings back an odd cocktail of emotions – happiness at the memory of the course itself and the people I was with, including the almost self-consciously heroic trainer. I feel a surge of contentment at the memory of the experience: the freedom of the air, the thrill of the lift-off and the glide.

One day, there is a commotion at the end of the block. Three of the prisoners are on a hunger strike and they are throwing food and possessions out of the cell, demanding basic rights: four hours a day of exercise rather than just two; visiting rights for families; access to reading and writing material. The prison officers say they are weighing the food and know that the trio – Ahmed Maher, Ahmed Douma and Mohammed Adl – are eating, but after a week the authorities finally relent. We all get the rights the three have fought so hard for. It is a small victory but also a powerful lesson in the impact of a carefully calibrated protest.

Whenever they can, the neighbours who speak English stop outside my cell for whispered conversation. Maher, the leader of the April 6 Youth Movement, comes past. He is highly intelligent, charismatic in an understated kind of way, instantly likeable, rational and moderate. He opposed the old dictator Hosni Mubarak and helped draft the Muslim Brotherhood's new constitution, but publicly condemned the Brotherhood government when it broke its election promises. Now he's opposed to the interim government, which he believes seized power in an undemocratic military coup.

We talk about his movement, which is named after the general strike of 6 April 2008, from which it grew. He helped launch that strike with a Facebook page that unexpectedly drew enormous support. The strike was hugely successful and, through it, he and his cohorts formed a moderate, secular, leftist pro-democracy group. Over the years they worked with Poland's Solidarity union movement and Serbian social groups, among others, to work out how to organise popular resistance and build effective pressure.

Young, dynamic and socially wired, April 6 is the kind of movement governments fear. It is nimble, with its messages spreading like wildfire among like-minded, politically motivated youth who would otherwise struggle to organise without social media. The internet is part of its DNA, and although it can't claim full responsibility for filling the streets with the protesters who eventually toppled Mubarak, it is hard to see how that could have happened without April 6. And yet, while April 6 hasn't gone away and its members are just as angry as ever, Maher's and Adl's arrests have sent a very old-fashioned message: for all your digital sophistication and virtual messaging, we the government can still put you in a very analogue, very real-world prison. Of course, as social media evolves and encryption improves, activists such as April 6 will in all probability figure out ways of outwitting the authorities, but right now, in the early days of 2014 and as the prisons swell with tens of thousands of angry young men, they look disturbingly disconnected and impotent.

The situation of April 6 also explains the enduring influence of old-world media in helping to undo all that the digital youth achieved in the Arab Spring. Just as social media was crucial to chopping out the old regime's leaders, so traditional physical newspapers and analogue television stations were central to uprooting the new MB government and restoring the old networks of power. Anybody who owned a licence to broadcast television or print a newspaper by definition had to have close connections with the Mubarak regime; a few independent papers were allowed to operate, but they acted more as safety valves for dissent than posing any serious challenge to the authorities. The media organisations tended to be staffed by well-educated middle-class professionals who were physically and ideologically a long way from the slums where the MB had most of its influence, and were instinctively suspicious of, if not downright hostile to, conservative Islam. That made it almost impossible for the MB to win the support of the deeply sceptical political centre for the year they were in government, and easy for the interim administration to demonise them as terrorists after they were ousted from power.

And so there came to be two narratives: an underground debate among angry regime opponents, carried out on their mobile phones, about democracy, human rights and social justice; and another debate above ground about national security and the need to stamp out terrorism.

My case has become part of the official case against the Muslim Brotherhood – and although I can't see it, I know that the Egyptian media are being deployed against us.

•

After a week of solitary confinement, I struggle to maintain a sense of balance and composure. I finish a meal and settle down to meditate and suddenly, uncontrollably, I'm overcome by a sense of darkness as I remember my ex-wife, the pain I caused her, and the pain for both of us through our separation.

In the space of a few fleeting seconds I go from joy to despair, regret and recrimination, without having moved an inch. I wonder if God, karma, the universe, whatever, has somehow decided to punish me for sins of the past, and that perhaps somehow my imprisonment is deserved, if not for the crimes I'm accused of then perhaps for the sins I've actually committed.

It's ridiculous, of course, but I can't shake the shadow that settles over me. Alaa comes past for one of his whispered conversations through the cell door and I gratefully shuffle up to the metal grille to offload my sense of guilt, to try to work out what's going on in my head.

Even before I can begin the story of my failed marriage, he interrupts. 'I don't know what happened,' he says, 'and to be honest, it really doesn't matter. What you did or didn't do in your relationships has nothing to do with why you are here – certainly not as far as the government is concerned, and I can't believe that the universe has any opinion on it, either.

'In the time I've been in prison, I've learned a few things about getting through it, and the biggest lesson is this: you cannot make it through prison – you will not survive, certainly not with your sanity intact – unless you are able to make peace with yourself.'

It would become the most powerful piece of advice I received in Egypt.

•

It would be easy to lose myself in fantasy, to escape the walls with imagined fancies about what was, what might have been, or what could still come. But as the Buddhists repeatedly tell us, none of that is real. The only reality is here, now.

As it is, here and now isn't all that bad and, looking around, I'm surprised by how contented I am at this moment. My neighbours keep asking if I have all that I need, as if I'm somehow suffering. In truth, when I think about it, there is nothing I lack – not a jot. I have a bed. It's not made of feathers, fancy springs or therma-foam curves, but it's soft enough not to disturb my sleep. My blankets are warm (even if the fibres seem to get up my nose or into my mouth). I have a flush toilet that is clean, a sink with running water, a shower and soap to wash myself with, and although in the mornings I would kill for warm water, I don't need it. The cell seems dry (I haven't tested it in the rain) and, while it is damp and cold and the walls are flaking, I am sheltered from the elements. I have food – more than enough, in fact, and the biggest danger seems to be that I'll get fat. Other prisoners keep sending little gifts around – fruit, juice, tins of tuna, boxes of feta – and the dinners that the families have organised are simply delicious and nutritious. (The best is the moussaka – wide slices of roasted eggplant and big, fat, mild chillies in a rich, oily paprika sauce.)

And, against all expectations, I don't feel lonely or alone.

Mahdi comes past to see how I am doing. We talk a little and then I tell him I know it could be a lot worse, and that while I know we need to fight for improvements, I am still grateful. He misunderstands me in a delightfully perceptive way. 'All of us,' he says, stirring the air with his finger, 'are grateful for the chance to reflect and think and write. It is a gift.'

Indeed it is.

•

I now know what it is to be a baby again, utterly devoid of both power and responsibility. I have no say over my movements beyond bed and toilet. I have no control over when I leave my cell, and if I do leave my cell, where I go or what I can do. Others decide when and what I eat, what I can read, who I can see and when. In short, I am just like a toddler who has no choices and no control, including over my own fate.

I am allowed no calls to lawyers, and only the occasional call at the prosecutor's office to my parents. I can't offer any help with the legal strategy they are adopting in my defence. I have no input and no say at all. Their discussions are unknown to me. The only part of my fate that I have any influence over is the way I answer the prosecutor's questions. And even then, I can only respond to what he asks. It feels pathetically impotent in the face of such a big threat to my future.

But if I am stripped of control, I also have no responsibility. I can issue no orders, and I can't make decisions that affect anything beyond whether to read or sleep, to lie this way or that, to do sit-ups or push-ups.

Even the news comes filtered through layers of intermediaries – snippets of information shared through the prison grapevine and then translated for me, rumours heard and headlines half forgotten, passed on amid other conversations. Stripped of their detail and context, they lose their relevance and vitality, their connection to reality. I try to make them real in my head, but it is a struggle I seem to be losing. Even that is a form of lost responsibility – I no longer need to respond to events taking place in the world around me, professionally or personally.

As the hours in solitary slip into days and I start to lose count (has it been one week or two?), odd random memories bubble up from the depths of my past. For reasons I can't explain (for surely I wasn't digging around for them), my old BBC staff number pushes its way into my consciousness – 312260X; then my ex-ex-ex-girlfriend's favourite perfume (Chanel No. 5), the numberplate on my father's temperamental old Fiat 124 sports car that he drove in the late 1970s (JG 771), and the meal I ordered at the Nautilus restaurant in Port Douglas at the end of a long family camping trip more than thirty-five years ago (scallops in a garlicky cream sauce – even better, I can still taste them).

Eventually, after ten days of being locked in the cell, I am allowed out, blinking in the sunlight that fills the exercise yard behind the block. It feels slightly discombobulating, almost as if walking around the yard is somehow a guilty treat rather than a right I deserve under countless human-rights conventions. I feel like one of those animals that is released into the wild after a prolonged period in captivity, more afraid of the unknowns that freedom brings than the false security of the cage.

I feel scruffy. I haven't had a shave since we were first picked up, and my beard is a loose tangle of thin grey wires. It should hardly matter – neither the guards nor the other inmates give a damn – and yet I feel strangely self-conscious.

With a scratch of my chin, I set off, striding with a length that feels utterly luxurious, kicking out one foot after the other knowing that no wall is there to get in the way. I find myself giggling at the sheer silly joy of it.

•

Later that day, an uncharacteristically grim Alaa walks over to me in the exercise yard, after a visit from his sister.

'I've got some news,' he says. 'Last night, on one of the biggest national TV talk shows, they broadcast the video of your arrest. Someone in the interior ministry must have leaked it to make you look like terrorists. It means they are trying to turn public opinion against you. It's pretty bad.'

'Bad?' I say. 'What do you mean? Bad as in bloody awful TV? Or bad in that it really does look like we are part of a big conspiracy?'

'Both,' he replies. 'My sister says it was so awfully done that it actually makes them look like incompetent fools, but there will be plenty of people here who think it proves the government's case against you.'

The video was broadcast on Al Tahrir TV, a private network close to the military, and widely circulated on social media. In the film, the presenter explains that they have exclusive footage of a police raid that conclusively proves that the Al Jazeera team were actually a cell of spies. 'Just relax. Take it easy. Close the matter,' he says smugly before sitting back in his chair, slapping his hands together and declaring, 'Send them to prison.'

The shaky video is set to the thumping, sinister score of the superhero movie *Thor: The Dark World*. It follows the plain-clothed officers into our hotel rooms and hoses around our equipment, zooming in on cameras, laptops, studio lights and microphones – all standard tools for a team of reporters working in the field – before panning up to my confused, contorted face filled with questions about who and why.

Neither the video nor the charges makes any sense to me. I struggle with the gulf between what we are accused of doing and the clear evidence of what we were *actually* doing – the allegations of spying and the reality of reporting.

After talking it over with Alaa, I suddenly realise something fundamental. It smacks me in the face like a slap. This has nothing to do with us and everything to do with press freedom. It is not about anything we have done, but about what we represent; it is about intimidating every journalist working in Egypt, whether foreign or local, and the fact that the authorities have come after us because, as Al Jazeera staffers, we are politically convenient.

With his background as an activist, Alaa suggests I write a letter and get it out of the prison secretly. It will not be just a cranky letter to the editor by 'Angry of Tora Prison.' A note smuggled from prison carries a moral authority that elevates it above the ordinary. It is also likely to be widely published and will help us take control of the story. While the government has accused us of personally being involved with terrorism, I need to frame our case as a struggle between an authoritarian government and the democratic principles of freedom of speech and the public's right to know.

It is hugely risky, of course. I have no idea how the authorities will react once the letter is published. They will probably clamp down and deprive me of privileges, such as exercise time and visits. There is a real prospect of some kind of physical abuse. I also have no idea whether a letter will have any impact on the campaign to get us out, or on the wider debate about democracy in Egypt. Either way, I don't feel I have much choice. Now that I have realised that this is not about me but about the media in general, I have a moral obligation to fight on behalf of my professional colleagues. An estimated 2665 people have been killed, almost 16 000 injured and 21 000 arrested in the five months since Morsi's ouster on 30 June, and failing to speak out against this war on free speech suddenly seems unconscionable.

In secret, I draft two open letters outlining our position. We smuggle them out of the prison hidden in a basket of laundry. The first letter says:

> *I am nervous as I write this. I am in my cold prison cell after my first official exercise session – four glorious hours in the grass yard behind our block – and I don't want that right to be snatched away.*
>
> *I've been locked in my cell 24 hours a day for the past 10 days, allowed out only for visits to the prosecutor for questioning, so the chance for a walk in the weak winter sunshine is precious.*
>
> *So too are the books on history, Arabic and fiction that my neighbours have passed to me, and the pad and pen I now write with.*
>
> *I want to cling to these tiny joys and avoid anything that might move the prison authorities to punitively withdraw them. I want to protect them almost as much as I want my freedom back.*
>
> *That is why I have sought, until now, to fight my imprisonment quietly from within, to make the authorities understand that this is all a terrible mistake, that I've been caught in the middle of a political struggle that is not my own. But after 2 weeks in prison it is now clear that this is a dangerous decision. It validates an attack not just on me and my two colleagues but on freedom of speech across Egypt. All of a sudden, my books seem rather petty . . .*
>
> *Fahmy and Baher have been accused of being MB members, so they are being held in the far more draconian 'Scorpion prison'*

built for convicted terrorists. Fahmy has been denied the hospital treatment he badly needs for a shoulder injury he sustained shortly before our arrest. Both men spend 24 hours a day in their mosquito-infested cells, sleeping on the floor with no books or writing materials to break the soul-destroying tedium. Remember we have not been formally charged, much less convicted, of any crime. But this is not just about three Al Jazeera journalists. Our arrest and continued detention send a clear and unequivocal message to all journalists covering Egypt, both foreign and local.

The state will not tolerate hearing from the MB or any other critical voices. The prisons are overflowing with anyone who opposes or challenges the government. Secular activists are sentenced to 3 years with hard labour for violating protest laws after declining an invitation to openly support the government; campaigners putting up 'No' banners ahead of the constitutional referendum are summarily detained. Anyone, in short, who refuses to applaud the institution.

So our arrest is not a mistake, and as a journalist this IS my battle. I can no longer pretend it'll go away by keeping quiet and crossing my fingers. I have no particular fight with the Egyptian government, just as I have no interest in supporting the MB or any other group here. But as a journalist I am committed to defending a fundamental freedom of the press that no one in my profession can credibly work without; one that is deemed vital to the proper functioning of any open democracy, including Egypt's with its new constitution.

Of course we will continue to fight this from inside prison and through the judicial system here. But our freedom, and more importantly the freedom of the press here, will not come without loud sustained pressure from human rights and civil society groups, individuals and governments who understand that Egypt's stability depends as much as on its ability to hold open honest conversations among its people and the world as it does on its ability to crush violence.

We know it is already happening, and all of us are both moved and strengthened by the extraordinary support we have already had, but it needs to continue.

Peter Greste
Tora Prison

My second letter begins:

Tora Prison, 21/1/2014
Journalists are never supposed to become the story. Apart from the print reporter's byline or the broadcaster's signoff, we are supposed to remain in the background as witnesses to or agents for the news; never as its subject.

[I make the point that the very mundanity of our reporting, which nevertheless seems to have attracted the authorities' ire, shows how far 'normal' or the middle ground has shifted in Egypt, and that if my cellmates can be arrested by each of three successful, opposed governments, this has become not about policies but about power.]

Our arrest doesn't seem to be about our work at all. It seems to be about staking out what the government here considers to be normal and acceptable. Anyone who applauds the state is seen as safe and deserving of liberty. Anything else is a threat that needs to be crushed.

•

Once, years ago, after an arduous day covering massive floods and elections in Venezuela (which hit coincidentally on the same day and with the same kind of cataclysmic force), an exhausted colleague flopped down in a chair in our hotel, ordered a beer and said, 'I shot a piece into the air; it fell to earth I know not where.'

It was an apt corruption of the Henry Wadsworth Longfellow poem 'The Arrow and the Song', and as I lie in bed now, wondering what has happened to my letters, the end of the verse floats through the mist of rising sleep.

Long, long afterward, in an oak
I found the arrow, still unbroke;
And the song, from beginning to end,
I found again in the heart of a friend.

A week passes, then two, and we hear nothing. There is no change to the prison routine, no denial of privileges (as limited as they are), no extra searches or sanctions. Nothing.

It's as if the letters have disappeared with the laundry and gurgled down somebody's drain. I'm puzzled and, in a way that I didn't expect, I also feel disappointed. The rants were my first timid attempts at being a revolutionary, a nervous shot at joining the hallowed tradition of inspired prison letters. I didn't expect to be on the same plane as Mandela or Gandhi, but I hoped to cause some ripples.

I have.

Unknown to us, the letters are slowly seeping through social networks and into newspapers. They are being passed around on email and Facebook and eventually work their way up into political offices in a kind of social capillary action, until they finally land on desks in the White House and the UN Secretary General's office.

•

One day, after I have been in the cells for almost a month, we settle down to listen to the radio. The authorities have relented under pressure from human-rights groups and allowed one of the prisoners, Dr Mahdi, to have a small, scratchy AM radio. Each evening after lockdown since then, the cellblock has hushed while we sit with our ears pressed to the grille on our doors and listen to a news broadcast played out through the bars of Mahdi's cell.

As usual, once it is over, Alaa gives me a translated summary, but this time his voice carries an unfamiliar tone of alarm. 'There was a news conference today by the interior minister. He announced that the journalists in the Marriott Cell have been formally charged with terrorism offences, and that the trial is going to begin in a few weeks.'

I laugh. I can't help it. It is ridiculous; a joke. Our lawyers, my colleagues, my cellmates – no one we've spoken to has thought they'll try to take this to trial. Everyone has assumed that with no evidence they'll rather want to avoid the embarrassment of trying to prove the unprovable; that if they want to intimidate journalists they've done enough by throwing us in the cells for a month, and it is high time to let us go and relieve the international pressure.

But Alaa isn't laughing, and I twist my face into a grimace. 'This is serious, isn't it,' I say.

'Yes. It's serious. They didn't mention any names in the news conference, but if you're a part of that group, then you're going to trial.'

6

SOMALIA

In 2009, journalist Jeffrey Gettleman wrote a feature for *Foreign Policy* magazine in which he described Mogadishu, Somalia, as 'the most dangerous place in the world'.[15]

'(You) can get kidnapped or shot in the head faster than you can wipe the sweat off your brow,' he wrote. The line was more colourful journalistic prose than a statement of objective fact, but it nonetheless gave a sense of the place as it was around the end of the first decade of the twenty-first century.

Even by Africa's grim standards, Somalia has been a blood-coloured stain on the continent. It started out as a hot extension of the Cold War – an unstable place at the best of times that had the misfortune to occupy a strategically vital peninsula that juts out into the Arabian Sea like a broken thumb jabbing into some of the world's most important shipping lanes.

From the 1960s until the country's complete collapse in 1991, the United States and the Soviet Union both found proxies and primed them with ammunition and money to win influence in the Horn of Africa and stop their rival from gaining the upper hand. There was enough weaponry to fuel the civil war for the next decade as clan militias fought for control of anything they could use to make a buck – ports, telecommunications towers, even intersections where they could set up checkpoints to extort passing motorists. Somalia became the closest thing the modern world has seen to a nationwide experiment in anarchy.

When the Cold War faded and the War on Terror became the dominant struggle, the front lines remained but, crucially for this story, the motive for the fighting shifted from politics to theology. Instead of a proxy battle between the giants of communism and capitalism, it became a fight between militant Islamists and Western-backed militias, and journalists once again wound up as unwitting, un-enlisted foot soldiers in an often deadly struggle over ideas as much as territory.

•

I arrived in Mogadishu with my BBC producer, Kate Peyton, in early 2005. At the time of that assignment, Western visitors could still drive around the Somali capital, but only with an escort of a pick-up truck full of armed bodyguards and a 50mm-calibre machine gun mounted on the back. In most of the world's cities nobody less than president would get that kind of security, but in Mogadishu it hardly drew a second glance. Politicians, visiting foreigners and even businessmen all routinely moved across town with armed escorts to fend off would-be kidnappers. We were there covering what to us was clearly a legitimate story: the return of the Somali government after years in exile and a decade of civil war.

The 'government' had been formed from a council of clan delegates. Some Somalis considered it to be nothing more than a gang of thugs running Somalia from neighbouring Kenya – or rather, holding token parliamentary sessions in the ballroom of a Nairobi hotel to claim fat stipends, that often ended in acrimonious if comical bouts of chair tossing. Its critics accused the government of being merely a club of warlords growing fat on donations and doing nothing to bring stability to the country.

Meanwhile, in Somalia itself, an unlikely alliance of Islamists and businessmen had been quietly filling the power vacuum. With no police or judiciary to speak of, a collection of conservative and radical Islamists had begun establishing local courts using sharia law to investigate and punish crimes and adjudicate disputes. They were disparate local responses to the anarchy that was tearing Somalia's social and physical structures apart. Some were run by relatively moderate, pragmatic groups who saw sharia law as a practical tool in the absence of any other state-run legal system. Others were far more extreme, using the courts as a way of imposing strict Islamist ideology on society, and one of these was an obscure and little-known group called Al Shabaab, or 'The Youth'.

Eventually, in 2004, the courts came together to form a coalition called the Islamic Courts Union (ICU) to organise and coordinate their work. At their first meeting, the delegates elected a full-lipped, soft-spoken, politically astute cleric called Sharif Sheikh Ahmed as their president. The ICU wasn't a government, but it had its own governing council, its own judiciary and its own heavily armed enforcers, and it fast became one of the most powerful groups in the country. By the following year, Mogadishu was beginning to show a degree of stability, and the government announced it was returning home.

The emergence of the ICU was one of the stories Kate and I planned to cover. So was the impressively cheap and efficient telecommunications system, and the state of government infrastructure that the new administration would have to manage – all the buildings were full of displaced people who'd fled the fighting and taken shelter in government offices.

For our own security, we hired a 'technical' – one of the pick-up trucks made famous during the abortive UN interventions in the 1990s, with the top sawn off, a machine gun mounted on the back and seating for eight armed bodyguards to protect us from the kidnappers. Gettleman colourfully described this as the 'threat du jour'.

We never got beyond the first day.

•

We landed at what was only half-jokingly called the Baledogle International Airport, about 50 kilometres outside the capital. The runway was a dusty airstrip, the arrivals hall a rusting tin shed too hot to actually sit in, and immigration was an old school desk propped up in the shade of an acacia tree where an official with a dirty uniform, a stamp and his own armed guard processed new arrivals.

Our local fixer was Ajoos, a talkative, well-connected man from the Shamo Hotel who had a knack for charming the grumpiest of warlords. He was there to meet us with our contingent of bodyguards, also from the Shamo. With the precious entry stamp in our passports, we climbed into a beaten-up Toyota with tinted windows and sped across the broken highway into town with the technical trailing in the dust behind us.

Kate and I had a plan, of course. One of our first stops was to be at a cafe that had been taking advantage of the state-of-the-art internet access provided by some of the mobile-phone companies. We were interested in the way the phone companies had thrived in the absence of government regulation, providing some of the fastest and cheapest internet on the continent, and we thought the cafe would be a great way of telling the story.

The cafe managers were delighted to see us, but told us to return in a few hours when customers would start to come out in the cool of the evening. So, with a few hours to fill, we decided to drop past the Sahafi Hotel, where a delegation of parliamentarians had been staying while they worked out the logistics around the formal return of the government. We had no particular interviews lined up – it was just a last-minute decision to make use of the time and see what we could find out.

The Sahafi is just off what Mogadishu locals call 'K4', a roundabout 4 kilometres from the city centre, and one of the most strategically important intersections in the city. The hotel has witnessed much of Mogadishu's bloodshed from behind its high concrete perimeter wall.

When we arrived, we found the hotel compound jam-packed with cars waiting to ferry the parliamentarians to their next meeting. With no space behind the barrier, we decided to park in the street. I wasn't particularly comfortable with the idea – being exposed to public view was something we had been warned against. But the street itself was heavily guarded, with at least sixteen militiamen fiddling with their Kalashnikovs in the shade of the trees that arched over the wall. Our guards would bring that number to twenty-four.

We were inside for only a short time – fifteen minutes at the most – before we realised that anybody who had anything useful to say had already gone. We decided to move on. As we walked out of the hotel into the muggy tropical-afternoon heat, Kate adjusted her head-scarf to cover her blonde hair and walked to the side of the car facing the street while I stood by the kerb. I called for our driver, and our guards rattled their Kalashnikovs as they moved to their technical and began climbing aboard.

Without warning, without commotion, I heard the single sharp crack of a gunshot echo up and down the street. I ducked down behind the vehicle, unsure of where the sound had come from. There were a few seconds of silence while everybody tried to work out what had happened, and then the street erupted with engine noises and the guttural staccato of Somalis shouting, but no more shooting.

I stood cautiously to see Kate slumped across the back of the car, groaning softly. I thought she had been frightened by the commotion and went around to comfort her. She put her head on my chest, and I patted her on the back in reassurance. When I lifted my hand, I saw a crimson smear across my palm and a stain slowly spreading down Kate's white shirt.

She'd been hit in a drive-by, but there was no time to ask who was responsible, or why. Kate needed medical attention, and we all needed to get somewhere safe. I pushed her onto the back seat while the driver and Ajoos climbed into the front. I grabbed a plastic bag from my kit and clamped it over the wound, trying to keep air from getting into her chest cavity and blood from getting out.

We sprinted through the broken streets, swerving like a dodgem car through the traffic to the Medina Hospital, run by the Red Cross, while I tried to hold Kate steady and the wound sealed.

The Medina was the best of a dismal collection of medical facilities in Mogadishu. With no reliable power, it fired up its generator only when it needed lights for surgery. Its stores of drugs and dressings were acutely low, and it had no reserves of blood for transfusions. What it lacked in facilities, though, it made up for in experience.

'Nobody in the world knows as much about treating gunshot wounds as these surgeons,' I told Kate, who was still conscious as we wheeled her into the operating theatre with its chipped walls and stench of fresh blood.

She nodded weakly as I told her of a friend who got a gut full of shrapnel in Kabul, and how the local doctors had operated before we got him evacuated. He had to have follow-up operations in France, but the surgeons said the Afghan doctors did some of the best work they'd seen.

'I am pretty sure these guys will have just as much experience,' I said gently. 'They know what they're doing.'

Kate nodded again as the anaesthetist injected drugs to knock her out. 'I'm scared,' she said in a hoarse whisper.

'Don't worry,' I replied, trying to convince myself as much as her. 'I will be here when you wake up.'

•

Kate survived the operation but never woke from the anaesthetic. She died in the recovery ward, in part because the doctors couldn't find enough donors to give her all the relatively rare O-negative blood she needed.

For years I assumed the shooting was an opportunistic killing intended to send a clear message to the incoming government that outsiders were not welcome in Mogadishu. Nobody could have known that we were going to be at the hotel. We dropped in with no warning, so it couldn't have been a planned assassination. I always guessed that the shooter was simply hanging around outside looking for a target of opportunity, and when Kate walked into the street and turned her back, she unwittingly provided one.

But if it had simply been a random attack, Kate's story wouldn't have a place in this book. Now, more than a decade later, I suspect it was much more calculated: a targeted assassination aimed specifically at a foreign journalist.

Over the previous week, a group of journalists had been following the government delegation, working on a similar set of stories to Kate and me. Among them were reporter Alexandra Zavis and photographer Karel Prinsloo, both from the American news agency Associated Press.

Several days before we arrived, Alex and Karel went to talk to the leadership of the ICU. The man they most wanted to interview was the ICU's president, Sharif Sheikh Ahmed. By the standards of Somalia's Islamists, Sheikh Sharif was a moderate and a pragmatist who was more interested in governance than in enforcing radical Islamic ideals. (In 2009 he became Somalia's internationally recognised president, winning an election among clan elders who were searching for a leader who hadn't been sullied by years as a warlord.)

Alex says her meeting went well, with no particular incident to make it notable. 'There was nothing in the interview that made me feel uncomfortable at the time,' she said. Sheikh Sharif was articulate and intelligent, though in the end Alex decided it wasn't worth a story in its own right. Instead, she used several quotes for a much broader piece about a week later.

Crucially, the president wasn't the only ICU figure there. Alex told me that according to her notes, among the men listening in was Aden Hashi Ayro. Ayro was an anonymous figure at the time, but his name would become synonymous with some of the most extreme acts of terror in a country already overloaded with violence. His uncle Hassan Dahir Aweys, another hard-line militant and a senior ICU leader, reportedly sent Ayro to Afghanistan to train with Al Qaeda and the Taliban before 2001.[16] When he returned, Ayro took over command of Al Shabaab. US intelligence agencies have since linked him to the murder of four Western aid workers, the desecration of a cemetery for Italian Catholics, and a string of suicide bombings.

According to Alex, several days after the interview her translator told them there were rumours that a hit had been ordered. The team didn't take it too seriously – the threat was unspecific, with no details about who had allegedly issued the order or why, and it was in line with a generalised sense of tension around the government's return. So she and Karel kept their heads low, finished their work and left Mogadishu soon after.

But Alex said she and Karel *had* established a routine. 'Each day we would go and visit the Sahafi Hotel,' she explained. 'We wanted to talk to government officials, and that's where they were staying. We were also using security guards from the Shamo Hotel.'

A white Western male/female team, visiting the Sahafi Hotel, with an escort from the Shamo Hotel – exactly as we were doing on the day Kate was shot. 'Hostile Zone 101 is that you don't set up a pattern, and we set up a pattern that you walked into,' Alex told me.

One of the most experienced and astute analysts of Somali affairs is Matt Bryden. He runs his own consultancy (though at this time he was working for the International Crisis Group) and when I asked him to use his contacts to see if he could find out who was responsible for the shooting, he did the most thorough investigation of Kate's murder ever conducted.

'When I started asking my contacts who were close to the Islamist groups, it became clear that there were a number of killings with the same pattern: three men in a nondescript white or grey Toyota murdering people with a 9mm pistol,' he told me. 'And there were two names that kept coming up – Salah Tafey, who was the shooter, and

Aden Hashi Ayro, who was the guy ordering the killings. In all, there were twelve to fourteen killings that fitted the pattern, but Kate's murder was different for two reasons: she was the only Westerner and the only woman.'

According to Matt, all the other victims had been working for warlords who'd been accused of collaborating with the US in some way.

In Alex Zavis's view, 'Having a government return to Mogadishu would have undermined their [Al Shabaab's] authority, so if they were trying to frighten off outsiders, send a message about insecurity in the city, *and* keep foreign reporters from covering the story, a Western journalist would have been the perfect target.'

The evidence is purely circumstantial, of course, and we will never get a chance to ask Ayro about his role in the incident. He was killed in a US airstrike on the town of Dhusamareb on 1 May 2008.[17] American military officials said Ayro was close to the top of their list of 'most wanted', because of his roles as an Al Shabaab commander and in a series of terror attacks.

•

Kate was the first Western journalist to be killed in Somalia for almost a decade, so at the time it was hard to see it as anything other than the tragic consequence of working in a place full of people brutalised by war who thought nothing of murder as a political tool. But when the assassin put the 9mm bullet into Kate's back, he also fired the starting gun on one of the most dangerous periods in one of the deadliest countries for journalists.

Later that year, local radio journalist Duniya Muhyadin Nur was shot dead while he was covering a protest near the capital.[18] The following year, in 2006, an award-winning Swedish freelance cameraman, Martin Adler, who was working for the British TV news service ITN, was shot at close range in the back of the head while he was filming a political rally in Mogadishu.[19] Then in 2007 eight died, including seven who the Committee to Protect Journalists found were murdered specifically for their work.

According to the CPJ, the worst year was 2012, when fourteen were killed. In all but two of those cases the motives were clearly connected to their journalism.

By the CPJ's count, eighty-one journalists have lost their lives in Somalia between 1992 and November 2024. There was a bad period during the generalised violence of Operation Restore Hope through the early 1990s, including a tragic incident in 1993 in which four foreign reporters died at the hands of a mob, but it stayed at a relatively low ebb from 1995 until Kate's killing a decade later, when the numbers took off.[20]

The key question is why. Was it simply the consequence of living in one of the world's most dangerous environments, where Kalashnikovs are as ubiquitous as shoulder bags? Or were journalists targeted specifically to silence critical reporting? One of the biggest problems in answering the question is that few of the murders have ever been properly investigated, and even fewer of those investigations have resulted in anybody being held to account.

Iraq, Syria, the Philippines and Algeria all have higher totals than Somalia, but in 2015 the CPJ put Somalia at the top of its annual Impunity Index, which tracks not only the overall numbers but also those places where there have been few or no convictions.[21] According to the report:

> Not one year has passed over the last decade without a journalist being murdered in civil war-wracked Somalia, which first appeared on the index in 2008. At least 30 journalists have been murdered without any consequence for the perpetrators in this index period, the majority targeted by Al-Shabaab militants who for years have threatened and assaulted journalists in relation to their coverage of the group's activities. While the government has pinned its impunity problem on the political instability and shortage of resources

> inflicted by 20 years of civil war, journalists say authorities fail to conduct even minimal investigations when journalists are killed.

The CPJ found that in only 2 per cent of cases was there full justice. In 84 per cent of cases, there was complete impunity.

Without proper investigation, once again it is hard to say with certainty what has been going on in Somalia, but according to the CPJ's statistics, the majority of shootings were by 'political groups', while in at least a quarter of all cases – 28 per cent – the perpetrators are unknown.

A huge part of the blame rests squarely with the Islamist extremists Al Shabaab. A breakthrough came in 2016 when Hassan Hanafi – a former journalist who had joined Al Shabaab – was convicted of being involved in the murders of no less than five of his ex-colleagues. In his role as a liaison officer with the militant rebels, Hanafi would often call journalists and radio stations and threaten them over reports that weren't supportive of the rebel group. His threats forced a lot of local media outlets to censor their work.

Hanafi later led Al Shabaab's media unit, inviting journalists to press conferences and hosting battlefield tours. He would urge journalists to follow Al Shabaab's media rules, which were essentially 'Report what we say and ignore everything else.'

'Al Shabaab killed many journalists, but personally I killed only one,' Hanafi said after he was convicted. 'But I am indifferent if you kill me. You will see if killings will stop even after my death.'[22] Hanafi was executed by firing squad in April 2016.

Few will admit to self-censorship as a result of the threats, but Mohamed Ibrahim, who leads the National Union of Somali Journalists (NUSOJ), said everybody feels intimidated. To their usual kit of pen, notebook and camera, some reporters have even added a pistol. 'This absolutely targets the independence of the news. It's unlikely that the public receives balanced and independent information, because of the fear that journalists are feeling,' he told me a few years after Kate's killing.

Matt Bryden agrees: 'There's no doubt that they've also been targeting anybody who challenges their view of the world and the way that Somalia should be. Often that means civil society activists and politicians, but it also means journalists.'

•

As in Afghanistan, the assault on the media in Somalia hasn't been from extremists alone. While the Islamists have brutally underlined their intolerance for anything resembling a free exchange of ideas or a press that asks challenging questions, the government has used national security as an excuse to go after any media that tries to hold it to account.

When he was elected Somali president in 2012 at the height of the killings, Hassan Sheikh Mohamud offered great promise. He had long been one of the most astute observers of national affairs and a champion of human rights, including freedom of speech and freedom of the media. Before his election, he was dean of the Somali Institute of Management and Administration (SIMSAD) and we often interviewed him for Al Jazeera when we needed a rational, clear-headed analysis of his country's byzantine politics. Articulate in both Somali and English, he seemed committed and principled – the perfect antidote to the corruption and cynicism of previous administrations.

Just a few days after he was elected, Hassan Sheikh held his first news conference as president at the Jazeera Hotel, a few hundred metres from the heavily fortified airport zone. Because of its proximity to the airport, the district itself was closely watched and heavily defended. The hotel also had several rings of security: an outer cordon of African Union troops who had been deployed to help support the government, and inside the compound a group of the hotel's own guards as well as a contingent of the president's bodyguard.

The news conference took place on the top floor of the eight-storey building. My Al Jazeera crew and I were there, along with several other international journalists and almost twenty local reporters and cameramen. Just a few minutes into the president's opening remarks, an explosion rocked the building, followed by a heavy burst of gunfire.

Nobody quite knew how to respond. Was it a controlled blast somewhere close to the hotel? Was it an attack of some sort? And if it was an attack, what was our escape route? Down the stairwell?

A few minutes later there was a second explosion and yet more gunfire, and almost everyone in the news conference dived to the floor looking for cover. I peeped over the windowsill to find out what was going on in the compound below.

Two suicide bombers from Al Shabaab (as we later found out) had detonated their vests in an attempt to blast their way inside. Their remains lay scattered across the road along with the bodies of four Somali government troops and one African Union soldier, who were all killed in the assault. A third attacker had made it through the outer cordon and into the compound itself, where the hotel guards had shot and killed him. He lay on the ground face down with an undetonated suicide vest still strapped on.

Even before the dust from the explosions had settled, President Hassan Sheikh calmly told his audience that the attack underscored two things: first, the urgent need to sort out security, and second, the vital need to defend and uphold the democratic principles of rule of law, freedom of speech and freedom of the press.

•

One of Hassan Sheikh's first acts after the attack was to order a special commission to investigate journalist murders. Such an open, articulate, principled figure in power seemed to offer a genuine change from the brutal, cynical and corrupt regimes of the past, and journalists who covered the country were excited by what appeared to lie ahead.

But Somalia is a place that eats optimism for breakfast. The commission failed to come up with either plausible theories about who was responsible for the killings or ideas about how to stop them. However, determined to give the appearance of action, the Somali parliament passed a media bill in December 2015 and the president signed it into law the following month.

At first reading, the law seems benign enough. Article 4 prohibits the media from disseminating 'false news', 'inciting hatred', 'encouraging tribalism', 'defamation of persons or institutions', 'hate speech' and 'news based on extremist views'. But it is disturbingly similar to those used against us in Egypt, which turned the act of reporting on current events into a crime against the state. As NUSOJ pointed out in its annual report that year, 'these are vaguely worded terms that could be used to prosecute independent media and censor journalists, who are committing no crime other than telling an inconvenient truth'.[23]

In fact, all Hassan Sheikh did was codify in law arguments that had already been routinely used to shut down legitimate reporting. In the eleven months before the president's signature, the authorities raided, arrested and silenced news agencies, on largely trumped-up charges, at an average of just over one per month.

On 1 March 2015, for example, a court in Mogadishu found three journalists working for the popular Radio Shabelle guilty of a series of crimes collectively described as 'attack(s) on the integrity, independence or the unity of the Somali State'. In the eyes of the law, that was considered to be 'high treason' and carried the death penalty – though the trio were sentenced to time served (seven months) and the network was fined US$10 000. The deputy news editor was also sentenced to time served and was fined an extra $500.

On 23 March, the court finally released Radio Shabelle editor Mohamed Bashir Hashi on bail after 198 days in detention. NUSOJ said he'd been held on 'trumped-up charges of "terrorism" and "assassination" designed to silence both him and Radio Shabelle'.

And on 3 April, five heavily armed technicals from the National Intelligence and Security Agency (NISA) raided Shabelle's offices, once again shutting down both Radio Shabelle and its sister station SkyFM. The NISA agents confiscated all the network's computers and arrested twenty-five people, including twenty-three journalists and media workers. The agents took their prisoners to the NISA regional headquarters for interrogation. Most were released later that night, but three senior managers were held in detention for almost two weeks before being freed. Security officials said they launched their raid after Radio Shabelle violated an order prohibiting Somali media from broadcasting anything from Al Shabaab. The journalists freely admitted that they broke the rule, but argued that they had a responsibility to publish the statement claiming responsibility for an attack on Garissa University College in neighbouring Kenya that killed 148 students and staff – one of the bloodiest assaults in Kenya's history.

The NUSOJ report goes on to catalogue dozens of arrests and detentions, many for reasons that have never been explained, and plenty of others that it regards as utterly unjustified. But more than the imprisonments, killings and beatings, impunity is the thing NUSOJ believes is most serious of all:

> Not only are the perpetrators of violations of media freedom not held to account, but those who work to prosecute those perpetrators, including witnesses, union activists, defenders of press freedom and families of victims, are threatened with violence and coercion.
>
> The Federal Government has failed to respond adequately to crimes against journalists, including murders, physical attacks and threats, creating a climate of impunity that only encourages more severe violations.

Of all the journalist murders in the decade from 2006, only 4 per cent resulted in a court case. And while the NISA has arrested suspects in journalist killings, of all the cases documented by NUSOJ in that time, not one was solved through the work of the Somali Federal Police and its Crimes Investigation Department, the primary law enforcement agency in Somalia.

This is obviously concerning to the journalists' union. But as it points out, when politicians and businessmen are intimately connected in a deeply corrupt set of networks, the press is often the only institution able to expose those links. If the press is not protected by the courts or the police, those corrupt and often violent groups are able to expand and consolidate:

> Impunity has led to a climate of self-censorship among the media. Journalists, fearing for their own lives or for the lives of their families, do not cover certain stories, and these are often the ones that need to be told the most.
>
> Self-censorship is especially destructive in Somalia because it is an undetectable, often unnoticeable phenomenon. The number of media killings has fallen since 2012, when 18 media professionals were killed. The reason is not that the killers do not want to kill any more, but because high levels of self-censorship that fear of the killers has instilled in journalists in Somalia has meant there is less reason to.

7

MULHAQ PRISON

8 – 20 FEBRUARY 2014

Routine is a wonderful thing. Even in the direst of circumstances (*especially* in the direst of circumstances), it gives form and structure – a kind of temporal scaffolding that offers the illusion of stability. When everything is collapsing around you, when your survival is no longer guaranteed, or at least when you have no way of knowing what tomorrow will bring, doing the same thing today that you did yesterday, and the day before that, implies that tomorrow you'll be doing it again. It's that steady drumbeat rhythm that gives an almost hypnotic sense of security.

The French composer Maurice Ravel understood that when he wrote *Boléro* – a piece that relentlessly repeats a theme so simple that he could play it with one finger. ('Don't you think it has an insistent quality?' he asked a friend.[24]) As the orchestration slowly builds, the audience becomes mesmerised by the endlessly repeated sequence, comfortable in that rhythmic sense of predictability: the future is going to be exactly as the past.

But fifteen minutes in, just as the audience is lulled into a trance, Ravel shatters the peace with a screeching gear change that, to anybody who hasn't heard it before, can be utterly shocking. At the composition's first performance, a woman in the audience reportedly leapt to her feet shouting, 'Au fou, au fou!' ("The madman! The madman!') When Ravel was told of this, he apparently replied: 'That lady . . . she understood.'[25]

In prison, I take refuge in routines. They give me a sense of control that belongs to me and not the authorities. *I* decide when to exercise in my cell. (Six a.m. every day, followed by running whenever we are allowed out.) *I* decide how many push-ups (fifty, eventually) and how many sit-ups I'm going to do (100). *I* decide when to meditate (always after waking, after exercise and before sleep), when to play mind games (after meditation) and when to sleep (10 p.m.). The patterns and routines and rhythms are as comforting as they are illusory.

One day, about a month after my arrest, I know something is out of place when well after lockdown I hear the guards' keys rattling in the outer doors of our block and their feet clattering down the corridor. The effect is as electrifying for me as it was for that startled lady listening to *Boléro*.

There is an urgent conversation between the guards and Alaa next door before he shouts a translation of what they've told him. 'Pack your things,' he says. 'They're moving you. I don't know where or why – could even be they're about to let you go.'

His words are hopeful, but his tone is heavy with doubt. 'You have five minutes.'

Without ceremony, the guards help me shovel my few possessions – some books, clothes and toiletries – into a couple of plastic bags before marching me out of the block. I grasp at the hands thrust through the bars of my neighbours' cells in farewell as we leave.

'Go well, my friend,' says Alaa. 'We will miss you here. Stay strong, whatever happens.'

•

The drive in a small caged wagon is short. I can't tell much about where we are going, but through the bars I catch glimpses of a rutted dirt road and old walls of chipped concrete bathed in sulphurous yellow light. It seems as though it is a back road, if not into hell itself, at least into somewhere on the way.

We finally pull up outside another, clearly newer and much more serious prison. The main entrance is unimpressive – there is a large metal gate topped with razor wire for vehicles, and a small metal portal with a padlock on it – but inside it is intimidatingly well organised. A path leads us past a few low, functional office buildings to a large caged vestibule with another big metal door behind it. The concrete building looks industrial, more like a warehouse storing coal for Hades' furnaces than anything intended for humans.

Inside the cage, once again I am ordered to strip. The guards thoroughly search both me and my possessions. I am photographed and my things are catalogued before the guards return only my clothes.

'You are allowed none of these here,' one says, waving a hand dismissively at my books. 'Only the Qur'an. Do you have a Qur'an? You might need it.'

I am shoved forward, through the steel door and yet another inner cage into a cavernous, brightly lit cellblock. The sound of the lock clacking shut behind me echoes up and down the vast inner hall. It is two storeys high, but each level on its own seems big enough for another couple of storeys. There are rows of anonymous cell doors – perhaps half a dozen on either side – with a metal staircase leading to the upper level.

The guards push me towards a door on the left, halfway along, and turn the lock. As it swings open, I see Mohamed Fahmy standing inside.

•

My heart sinks. Fahmy is a powerful, uncompromising character. I have enormous respect for his professional skills as a producer, and for his depth of understanding of Egypt's politics. He has a sharp eye for detail and can spot an error in a story in the same way a hawk zeroes in on a fieldmouse.

But Fahmy and I are two very different characters. His obsession is control – a very useful thing to have in a senior producer steering a news bureau through a political crisis – but he is also utterly uncompromising, and that is likely to be a difficult thing to live with in the hard-edged confines of a prison cell where you need to be malleable, flexing around one another's quirks without getting caught on the corners and burrs. Outside prison, before our arrest, we knew each other's roles, and we understood the way our professional relationship had to work. But from the moment we met, I knew we would never be friends. Now, the idea of being locked together in a concrete box for an indeterminate amount of time makes my guts tighten.

Fahmy gives me his lopsided grin and winces as he opens his arms in greeting. His injured shoulder is still clearly painful, and he doesn't seem to have had any treatment. His embrace is hard and cold.

'Man, it's good to see you. I was hoping they'd bring you over here but I wasn't sure. I just arrived a few hours ago. This is Mulhaq al Mazraa, "the Annex to the Farm". It's much better than our old home at Scorpion Prison, but it ain't the Marriott Hotel.'

'And Baher?' I ask. 'What about him? Where is he right now?'

'I'm hoping he'll be here soon. I saw him this morning before they moved me from Scorpion. They took him to the National Security building for another interrogation but apparently they want to put us all in one spot for some reason.'

Mulhaq is an austere, highly disciplined place designed to keep its inmates from having any contact with each other. Physically our cell is identical to all the others. It is a simple rectangle, about 3 metres wide by 3.5 long. Part of it is sectioned off, with a toilet, sink and shower so tightly packed that you can't have a shower without getting soap in the toilet bowl. But at least we have running water and reasonably sanitary conditions.

Our beds are arranged in an L-shape to fit around the bathroom cubicle. Fahmy bags a bed along the front wall, while I take the top level of a bunk bed tucked in behind it. There is just enough room for two people to pass if you turn side-on in the cell (and, I notice, enough room for push-ups and sit-ups), and a bit of space in one corner to stuff a bag of clothes. There is a heavy metal-mesh window that lets in fresh air from the outside, though it is so high up and so thickly barred it's impossible to see anything out of, except glimpses of blue sky or grey cloud.

We are allowed exercise time, but only for one hour a day in a cramped, dusty courtyard behind the cellblock, and the prison staggers the time so that only two or three inmates are in the courtyard at any one moment. All of the prisoners except us are in solitary confinement. Between 9 a.m. and 10 a.m., two of them are allowed into the exercise yard. They go back to their cells, and then another pair goes out from 10 to 11 a.m., and so on.

The three of us will only be allowed out together. In theory, we are to have no contact with anybody else. We are not allowed out for food – that will be brought to us – so we are to spend twenty-three hours a day in that tiny space. And as I've already discovered, we are not allowed any books or distractions of any sort. No radio, television, games, cards or dice. Not even pencil and paper. Not even a watch.

'It's a maximum-security prison,' Fahmy says. 'It's where they keep their terrorists.'

I raise my eyebrows.

'Our neighbours are all Muslim Brotherhood. We've got practically the whole cabinet from the last government here, apart from Mohamed Morsi himself. It's a pretty big line-up. Gives you a clue as to how they think of us now.'

It is a deeply disturbing notion. In the eyes of the authorities, we are exactly where we ought to be – among the people they believe we were conspiring with to wreak havoc across Egypt.

Is placing us in Mulhaq intended to show the world that we are linked with these individuals – that we are somehow part of a grand Islamist conspiracy? The question is unanswerable right now, but it weighs on me like the tonnes of concrete and steel that surround us.

•

Baher eventually arrives late in the evening. He has spent most of the day being questioned at the National Security building, but when he's finally shoved into the cell, he's wearing a wide grin.

'Hey, hey!' he shouts in greeting before throwing his arms around me in a big, smoky hug. Then, turning to Fahmy, he says, 'I did it. I got the letter out. A guy I met who we've interviewed before smuggled it out through his brother. It will get to your family.'

Fahmy clarifies for me: 'I wrote a letter, like you. It explains everything – about how we were caught up in the politics of the dispute between Qatar and Egypt; that we were only doing professional, unbiased reporting; about how we are Al Jazeera English and not Arabic, which was supporting the MB – all that. It sets out our whole defence case.

'We don't know how they will conduct the trial,' he continues. 'I don't even know if we will get a chance to defend ourselves. If we get the letter into the media now, everyone will know our defence arguments and they will know we did nothing wrong. It will be on the record, so the prosecution won't be able to twist it in court.'

I am worried by this. We have been formally charged and our trial is due to begin in the next few weeks. Under Australian law, and indeed in most Western legal systems, once a person has been formally charged the matter is sub judice, and that person is forbidden from making any public statements about the case. To do so is seen as an attempt to pervert the course of justice by influencing public opinion and putting pressure on the judges. Even if this isn't technically illegal in Egypt, it could easily be used against us.

I understand Fahmy's thinking, of course, but I released my statements long before we were formally charged. To my mind, Fahmy's letter will be in the papers dangerously close to the start of the trial.

In my letters, I also spoke about the general principles of press freedom that I believe are being violated in our case. I deliberately avoided going into the details of our defence, except to broadly deny the allegations and point out that there is no evidence against us.

It seems much safer to let experienced trial lawyers handle the specifics of our defence, playing the cards as they see fit in this game of legal and political poker, than to reveal our hands to the prosecution before we've even entered the courtroom.

But above all, I am troubled by Fahmy's approach of accusing Al Jazeera Arabic of somehow contributing to our arrest by having a pro-Muslim Brotherhood bias. In effect, he is confirming the government's conspiracy theory that we are employees of a company that is in league with the MB, but then denying that we are a part of it. That seems suicidal.

It also concedes the high ground that we have staked out for ourselves. Our professional colleagues have already started supporting us with a 'zipped lips' campaign, posting selfies with their mouths taped shut. Diplomats and politicians have begun to treat our arrest as an assault on media freedom. With each day we spend in prison we seem to be building support. To imply that there is some other agenda going on, or to suggest that we have been involved in anything other than work of the highest editorial standard, or that the network has somehow contributed to our situation, could well undo all that vital backing and see our support dissolve like a sandcastle in a rising tide.

Finally, it starts a public-relations battle we're in no position to win. The first rule of an effective PR campaign is to dominate the media messaging and respond swiftly to any new development. Although we have a huge number of media supporters and our own families to help keep up public support, it's incredibly difficult for the three of us to be heard directly from inside a cell. While the government is able to call a news conference or issue a statement at a moment's notice, we can barely respond in a matter of weeks. In short, we don't control the narrative – they do.

For now, though, I hold my tongue. I don't know the details of the letter, and anyway, if it is as Fahmy has described it, I hope a few of his family members might also be worried about the consequences of publishing so close to the trial, and talk him out of it. I'd much rather let others have that argument than start a row between the three of us inside this tiny pressure cooker where we have to live with one another for twenty-three hours a day.

•

The first night is difficult. Up in the top bunk, on the thin mattress laid across the metal frame, my world wobbles every time Baher shifts. He also snores, and that'll take some getting used to. But Fahmy is the worst. He is a natural insomniac at the best of times but now, with the stress of imprisonment, he is up most of the night, pacing around the cell or staring out the tiny window in the door. He tries to be quiet, but I am constantly aware of his restless presence.

The next morning I wake red-eyed and short-tempered, ready for an argument after churning the previous day's conversation over and over even in my dreams. But Fahmy has finally passed out, and through the early hours I let him sleep and my irritability cool.

Once the exercise yard is cleared, our cell door is opened and a guard escorts us into the walled compound behind the cellblock. The time outside is some reprieve, but not much. The compound is a dust bowl about the size of half a football pitch, with a ragged fringe of bone-dry grass. In fact, at either end of the rectangle is a set of goal posts, rusted at the base and skewed like a schoolboy's failed geometry homework. But there is no ball, and no play here. Overlooking us on top of each corner of the wall is a small sandbag-and-barbed-wire guard post with a tin roof full of holes. A rampart runs along the top so the guards ambling with their Kalashnikovs can keep watch over us.

Fahmy looks grim as he paces around the dusty quadrangle. Clearly his shoulder is still hurting – the bed is hardly hospital-grade, and he has no drugs to ease the nagging, persistent ache. He walks with a lolling wide-legged stride that has all the menace of a gunslinger.

By contrast, Baher is naturally optimistic. He smiles often, and has an easy charm that he deploys very effectively when enticing otherwise reluctant subjects to talk on camera. Here, he turns it on the guards, offering them expensive American cigarettes and chatting to them about their kids.

'It's not their fault we are here,' he explains once they've left. 'They're just doing their job and trying to raise their families. Ahmed here comes from a district not far from where my family has a property.'

He walks for a bit, making conversation with Fahmy in Arabic. I don't understand any of it and in a way I'm relieved. I'm not in the mood to chat – there is more than enough time in the cell for that. Here, I want to use the opportunity to sweat.

I pace out the distance around the edge of the compound. As near as I can tell, it feels to be about 30 metres down either side, and 20 across the short ends: a nice, round 100 metres per lap.

And so I run, with a gum-chewing guard disdainfully watching from above. We are not allowed shorts at Mulhaq, and so we must jog in our long prison uniforms. It doesn't take long before I feel the pants grow heavy and sticky. Nor does it take long for me to tire. I'm surprised by how little I'm able to do, even after all the exercise I pushed myself through at Lumen. After almost thirty laps, my lungs are heaving and my legs are starting to wobble. I can feel my face starting to flush, but I can't possibly stop now. I promised myself forty laps, so I push on. Five more is all I can manage, and I slow to a walk.

I'm angry with myself. I know I can do more, and yet I have given in. I can't afford to do that if I am going to get through this ordeal. We don't know how long it will take, but it has already gone on far longer than any of us anticipated, and we will need all the discipline and determination we have to make it through intact. So I resolve not only to set targets that stretch myself, but always to meet and exceed them. I have to prove to myself that whatever I think my limits might be, I can always go beyond them.

Besides, I'm going to have to work hard every time we come out if I'm going to make it through all the other hours of inactivity and get to the end of each day tired enough to sleep. I also know that when I don't sleep properly my mood darkens, I don't think clearly, and I'm prone to arguments. None of those things will help us here.

Cruelly, the hour flies by in an instant. It seems almost as though some sadistic demon has his finger on the clock and is spinning it faster every time we go out for exercises or I get a visit from the Australian Embassy, and loading it up with lead whenever we are inside the cell.

The first days feel as though we are neck-deep in mud. Everything happens with agonising slowness. Here in Mulhaq, as in Lumen, the sun filters through the meshed window for a few hours each morning, drifting across the opposite wall to help mark time. But even those weak rays of light seem to drag their heels.

We talk, of course. There isn't much else to do. But as much as we try to move our conversations to memories and stories and ideas, we somehow always return to the case against us, like a desert wind that might drift tantalisingly around a little before swinging back inexorably to the same tiresome compass point.

•

One day, about a week into our time at Mulhaq, Baher suggests a radio show. They began something similar at Scorpion, and he thinks it will work here.

'Not exactly a radio show, obviously,' he explains, 'but it will work the same way. We broadcast around the cellblock – Fahmy here can reach most of Cairo if he yells a little bit.'

The idea is that each day after lockdown we host structured conversations with our neighbours, shouted through the bars in the door hatches – so we might begin with a news bulletin, asking anybody who has any visits to share the news they have got from the outside, and interview the other guys in the cells about the 2011 revolution and their time in government.

'We can ask them everything you ever wanted to know about the MB but were afraid to ask. They can't really hit you if they're not happy with the questions,' Baher jokes. 'But I'm deadly serious. We can have discussions and debates. Whatever we want. After all, we're a bunch of journalists, aren't we? That's what we do.'

'The guards will be listening in, of course,' I say. 'But to hell with them. They can revoke a few privileges if they don't like it, I suppose. I reckon it's worth doing.'

Fahmy's face is alight. He loves the idea too.

'We're in journalist heaven here. We've got access to almost every senior MB official we've ever tried to interview over the years. We can ask them about what went wrong when they were in government, and what happened to them after they were kicked out. We can get the inside story of every drama we ever covered and wanted to talk to them about. It's perfect,' he says.

So that night, after the last of the guards has turned the locks on the outer doors, Baher climbs on the end of Fahmy's metal bed-rail and stretches to reach the window high in the door. Drawing a deep breath, he cups his hand around his mouth like a megaphone and in a strong, clear voice that echoes up and down the cavernous prison block, he incants the opening phrase of the Qur'an: 'Bismillah al Rahman al Rahim.' ('In the name of God, the Most Gracious, the Most Merciful.')

Then, with Fahmy giving me a running translation, he says, 'Welcome to Radio Mulhaq, gentlemen. We are, after all, reporters so we have decided to begin our own daily radio program. It will be a forum for news, debate and opinion. We will host the show from our cell, but this is not just about the three of us in our little box – this is for everyone. It is a chance for us to exchange views, to talk. Because our neighbourhood is a bit restrictive, we haven't had a chance to get to know everyone in here, so we would like to begin by inviting you to introduce yourself, and explain a little about how you came to be in this institution of ours.'

And so we do a rollcall of the cellblock, as each man fills in a bit of his background and tells us about his charges.

Mohammed Badie (pronounced 'BA-dee-yeh') is first up. He is in the cell just to our left, and as the 'Supreme Guide' of the Muslim Brotherhood, he is the most powerful figure in the organisation after the deposed president Mohamed Morsi. He is, in effect, the Brotherhood's spiritual leader, and while he doesn't exert direct power, he is hugely influential. If you go by the rap sheet, he is also a very bad man. He is accused of inciting violence that on numerous occasions led to multiple deaths, and of murdering a policeman himself – charges that seem utterly at odds with the soft-spoken, pious old man I glimpsed a little earlier.

This isn't his first experience of prison. In 1965, he was arrested in a nationwide round-up of activists and sentenced to fifteen years. He served nine before President Anwar Sadat released him as part of a general amnesty.

'I think it is going to be a while before I get to spend time with my wife and children,' he concludes, with an ironic sigh.

No one in the block has quite the same set of blood-soaked allegations as Badie, but all are facing similar kinds of court cases, whether for murder, incitement, terrorism or corruption. In the cell directly opposite us is Mohamed Saad El-Katatni, the former parliamentary speaker, charged with, among other things, conspiring to storm prisons in the 2011 uprising.[26] In the cell immediately to our right is Abou Elela Mady, the leader of the Al-Wasat Party, which split from the Brotherhood in the 1990s and whose deputy is languishing in prison back in Limen. Two men share a cell on the other side of the block – one is the former minister of labour, Khaled Azhari, and the other is his colleague Bassem Ouda, who used to be the minister of supply. They're accused of helping members of the Brotherhood escape after they were deposed. Mahmoud Al-Khudairi, the frail old judge I got to know in Limen and who can barely walk unaided, was moved here ahead of us, on charges of torture. Upstairs, with his long, thin beard, vast frame and booming voice, is the colourful Salafist lawyer and politician Sheikh Hazem Salah Abu Ismail. He is accused of incitement to violence. The ousted president Mohamed Morsi's political adviser Mohey Hamed is also in a cell above us, for helping his old boss evade capture after the coup, while a little further to the right is the former prime minister Hesham Qandil. He is serving a one-year sentence for failing to carry out a court order to overturn an executive decision.[27]

Then, we three introduce ourselves. All the other inmates have heard about us, of course, but there seems to be collective disbelief at the charges laid against us. I can almost feel their heads shake as we explain the allegations and the work we were doing. In particular, when I explain my own background, I can hear quiet tut-tutting up and down the corridor.

'We are so very sorry for you,' says Dr Badie. 'This is not the Egypt we wanted to create. It is wrong for journalists to be treated in this way, and I am sorry my country has done this to you.'

As the conversations continue, it becomes clear that everyone is listening intently. If someone at the far end of the block misses something, another prisoner in the middle acts as a relay, and so the information flows back and forth along the corridor. It is a little awkward and disjointed, but I can feel a collective sense of relief at the sharing of news and information. After extended periods of solitary confinement, *any* human contact comes as blessed respite.

•

The Muslim Brotherhood is a difficult organisation to understand. There is no membership register. You can't send in an application form, find a sponsor and get a membership card. It isn't even clear at what point someone moves from being a 'supporter' to being a 'member'. Like a cloud, from a distance it seems easy to define but the closer you get to it the more the edges blur and the harder it is to get a grip on it.

Its history is clear enough. The Brotherhood was founded in 1928 by a schoolteacher and imam, Hassan al-Banna, building on anger at the injustices of the British authorities who then controlled Egypt, and outrage at the way modernisation was undermining the popular commitment to Islam. It was, first and foremost, a charitable social organisation, with each branch running a mosque, a school and a sports club. Its original aim was to 'Islamise society through the promotion of Islamic law, values, and morals'.[28] Its founding motto was 'Islam is the answer'. In time, the Brotherhood became ubiquitous across the slums, operating as a de facto welfare state and providing an economic safety net for millions of poor Egyptians. With that came an aggressive program of political activism.

Banna himself was no pacifist. His paramilitary 'Special Interests' section carried out bombings and assassinations against the British Imperial administration. But it was Banna's successor, Sayyid Qutb, who emerged as the most influential thinker among radical Islamists; in 1964 he wrote his manifesto, *Milestones*, which many Sunni Islamist groups, including Al Qaeda and Hamas, have used to rationalise their more militant tendencies. The government executed Qutb two years later, turning him into a martyr for Islamists across the region.

In the 1970s Anwar Sadat pressured the MB into renouncing Qutb's philosophy, but a Brotherhood splinter group, al-Jihad, assassinated Sadat over what they saw as his token commitment to sharia law, and his 1979 peace treaty with Israel. Since then, the old guard, who prefer relatively peaceful political transformation from within, have struggled with the more radical militants who believe that only violent insurrection can bring about the Islamic society they want.

Ironically, it is that old guard who occupy the cells around us. The charges they're facing make them look like dangerous people, and I suppose it is possible that they have ordered murders to advance what they have decided is a higher cause, but I still can't reconcile the passionate politicians I find around us with the figures described by the allegations. If we are in prison on an utterly fabricated case, it is possible that they are too.

•

A gentle buzzing accompanying soft voices and gentle chuckles drifts up from the inner courtyard. Baher presses his face to the bars on the door and, with a grin, beckons me over. One of the MB prisoners has opened up a barbershop.

In the middle of the yard, in a puddle of dappled sunlight filtering down through the grille high above us, the dignified former minister of labour, Khaled Azhari, is waving a set of electric hair clippers over Abou Elela Mady, the founder of Al-Wasat (The Centre), the moderate MB breakaway. Elela Mady is swathed in a cotton sheet and is holding a plastic mirror while Azhari combs and trims his sideburns.

Is there something about the buzz of clippers that loosens men's tongues? The pair smile and chat amiably while a guard watches from the shadows a few metres away.

Baher calls the guard: 'Hey, Ibrahim. What about us? We've got to look decent for the court in a few days. You don't want the world to think you treat us like a bunch of shaggy animals, do you?'

There's a brief discussion with another more senior guard, who disappears into the shadows, presumably to talk to his bosses. Eventually word comes back.

'Okay. Get ready for a haircut. Who is first?'

Minutes later, the hot shears vibrate gently against my neck as thin locks fall gently down on my shoulders and prickle my face. It feels wonderful. If I close my eyes, I can transport myself back to my favourite Nairobi barber with his classic red-and-white pole.

Khaled is a warm soul. He isn't especially old – if I account for the prison's ageing influence, I place him in his early forties. His own hair is thick and dark, and though his beard is flecked with white and the lines across his forehead run deep, he brings a gentle broken-English chatter and easy humour that fill the courtyard. The experience is comforting and humanising, and I can feel my dignity return with each sweep of his shears across my scalp.

•

'Islam is all about peace,' insists Dr Badie one night on the radio show. 'The Brotherhood will never advocate for violence. We have never ordered any violent attack or called for insurrection, and none of our members have ever been involved in acts of violence.'

During Radio Mulhaq, I have asked how the Supreme Guide and his colleagues at the top of the organisation have tackled the young hotheads who wanted to fight back against the state with bombs and Kalashnikovs.

'There is no division among us,' Badie says. 'We all believe in peaceful change.'

It is hard to believe. In fact, we know from our own reporting that it simply isn't the case – we know that some of the more radical members have helped extremist groups to attack government forces in the Sinai Peninsula and detonate the occasional bomb in Cairo. And on the streets, we have met young MB activists who spoke of their frustration with a pacifist policy that in their eyes is another way of saying, 'We give in'.

I am keen to push Badie on the point, but we all know our evening program is being monitored and he is hardly likely to acknowledge links to violence or even suggest there is any dissent. (The next morning, as we pass Bassem Ouda's cell in the courtyard on our way out to the exercise yard, he whispers at me through the bars: 'Thank you for your questions – it is good that we talk about these things. Those debates are happening, and we don't know how to manage them.')

The Brotherhood won Egypt's first elections in 2012 because it was easily the largest and best organised political force in the country, its charitable work having built up a grassroots network in the densely populated slums that go back generations. It knew how to organise and mobilise people better than any other group. But running a network of charities is not the same as running a country, and many secular middle-class voters – those who started the revolution – didn't really feel that 'Islam is the answer'. Most *had* voted for the MB but they did it holding their noses, rather than back the alternative – a representative of the old regime – and throw away all that they'd sacrificed during the revolution.

It took only a few months for the public mood to turn sour, so we push the former politicians around us to tell us why their government failed so spectacularly.

The organisation made a few colossal beginner's mistakes. First, it overpromised. Morsi laughably declared that he would fix Cairo's notorious traffic within his first 100 days – a classic example of an inexperienced administration overconfident of its own authority and its ability to solve problems.

Second, the Brotherhood had existed in its own political bubble for a very long time, and misunderstood what democracy really means. Too often in emerging democracies, the victors assume that winning an election means the right to govern as they please. They think 'majority rule' means there is no need to worry any longer about the minority, that because they have a 'popular mandate' they can ignore the views of everyone else. They fail to appreciate that if democracy is to work, it needs continued negotiation, public debate, and often compromise on policies for the sake of holding on to public opinion and national unity.

It is also much easier to survive as a government if you have control over your security and intelligence agencies and the loyalty of their staff. From the outset, the Brotherhood faced outright hostility from the very civil service it had been elected to direct. In one fell swoop, it moved from being the number-one target of the intelligence agencies to being their master – a screeching, tyre-burning U-turn that the world's most professional security services would have struggled to cope with, let alone ones that were as overtly politicised as the Egyptian military and police.

And third, there was the media, divided between the conservative mainstream and online dissidents. Once the MB took government, the traditional press rarely gave it any quarter, and fuelled the growing howls of protest at some of the more openly Islamist policies the government tried to introduce.

•

Finally, after several weeks in Mulhaq, the date of our first court hearing approaches. We struggle to contain our excitement, our fears and our hopes. Surely the judge is going to have to toss the case out of court at the first hearing for lack of evidence. And if he doesn't, there's a very good chance that he'll give us bail at least. Even though somebody thinks we are dangerous enough to lock up among those they regard as hardened terrorists, we can hardly be considered a threat to society. We haven't been accused of crimes of violence; we were carrying no weapons; and none of us has any record of violent behaviour. I'll be prepared to surrender my passport and make daily visits to a police station if it pleases your honour.

The pressure of the impending hearing also brings out the strongest traits in each of us, as if it is stretching and distorting our personalities into caricatures of our normal selves.

Baher, ever the optimist, gets increasingly jokey, trying to lighten the mood by talking up our chances of a quick exit, or bail at least. He starts fantasising about seeing his kids and his wife again, who he has just learned fell pregnant in the days before we were arrested, about roughhousing with his young son on their lounge-room floor and taking them on a holiday to the beach. I worry that all the upbeat talk is leaving him unprepared for the admittedly remote prospect that we will have to stay where we are for a few more weeks. Far safer, I argue, to contemplate a more serious outcome than to get excited about something that hasn't happened yet and over which we have very little control.

Fahmy, on the other hand, gets nervous and argumentative. He hates being powerless, and is determined to get his letter published before the trial begins. But his family is deeply worried about the effect it might have on public opinion and on the judges themselves. As I'd hoped, his fiancée, Marwa, has argued against publication and held on to the letter against Fahmy's demands. His lawyer, too, is opposed to the idea. The only one who thinks it is a good plan is Fahmy himself.

'Nobody knows the Egyptian media like I do,' he fumes, pounding the air with his good fist. 'Nobody knows Egyptian politics like I do. And nobody knows our case like I do, so nobody else knows better how to handle the case than I do. They have to do what I say. I am paying my lawyers to carry out my instructions, so they have to do what I say. And Marwa is my fiancée. If she wants to be my wife then she has to do what I say.'

At night, Fahmy paces the cell. He stares out the bars in the door. He writes notes to his lawyers, to his family, to Al Jazeera, to be smuggled out during the next family visit. And we can feel the heat in the cell rising.

And me? I withdraw and go quiet. I argue the case with Fahmy, of course, but unless he or Baher raises it, I'd rather not churn it over and over in an endless cycle of argument and analysis with no new conclusions or insights. We've talked it out, and unless we've got something original to say it is better to shut up and try to relax. Or talk about the weather.

Eventually, the day comes. None of us sleeps much that night, and we wake early, expecting to picked up by the prisoner transport van any time from 8 a.m. We have freshly laundered white clothes and we fuss over the uniform, trying to make it look as smart as possible. We know it is likely that there will be a few cameras in court, and we want to look positive, strong and well groomed. We are determined to walk into court with our dignity intact. And we might need to be ready for a few media interviews afterwards.

We don't have a mirror – the prison authorities think that's too dangerous – so instead we work with our barely recognisable reflections in the shiny flat surface of a light switch. Fahmy sets his jaw and fusses over a lick of hair that won't stay down; Baher keeps pressing down the creases in his shirt as though his hands are an iron.

Eight o'clock comes and goes.

Then nine o'clock . . .

Then ten.

Fahmy keeps pacing. Baher is lying on his bed, staring at the bunk above him. I sit on mine and try to meditate.

Finally, there is a clatter of footsteps, the jangling of keys, bellowing voices.

'Yalla [Hurry up],' says the guard. 'Get moving. The truck is here. You boys are going to court.'

8

THE RENEGADE NETWORK

By any standards it was a world-beating scoop, the kind of thing that would have made almost any self-respecting foreign correspondent insanely jealous.

As the West prepared to retaliate for 9/11 by invading Afghanistan, the one interview everyone wanted was with the man accused of orchestrating the attacks: Osama bin Laden. Tayseer Allouni got it.

Allouni was a rapidly rising star with Al Jazeera. He had been appointed to set up the network's Kabul bureau in 2000, a time when all other foreign news agencies had either abandoned the city as too dangerous or been forced out by the Taliban. At the time, Al Jazeera was barely five years old and broadcasting only in Arabic, but it had already upset its competitors with aggressive, independent journalism that was vastly different from the heavily censored pro-government output of most its Arabic competitors.

Allouni watched the 9/11 attacks unfold from his office in Kabul and understood immediately that he was at the centre of the coming war. As American bombs landed on Afghanistan in retaliation, he took his cameras into the streets and filmed some of the consequences: horribly burned children, flattened homes and destitute villages. His reporting was seized on by critics of the US campaign, who declared it to be evidence of American hypocrisy: bombing and killing innocent civilians in the name of a just 'war on terror'.

Then, five weeks in, he received a call.

'It was Osama bin Laden,' Allouni later told the ABC. 'He sent some messengers to Al Jazeera office and they carry me with blindfold. They carry me to Osama bin Laden, and I made the interview with Osama bin Laden.'

•

Al Jazeera had already put the Al Qaeda leader on air. In the weeks immediately following 9/11, the station broadcast an old bin Laden interview and gave time to several commentators who said US foreign policy was at least partly responsible for provoking the attacks on the Twin Towers and the Pentagon. A furious Secretary of State Colin Powell met the Emir of Qatar, Sheikh Hamad bin Khalifa Al Thani, and demanded he use his influence to get Al Jazeera to tone down its rhetoric. (One senior American official told CNN 'the emir was "defensive" about the issue and countered that while his government was aware of US sensitivities on the issue, it did not feel al-Jazeera was any more inflammatory than any other Arab media outlet'.[29])

The meeting didn't seem to have any impact. Four days later, Al Jazeera broadcast another statement from bin Laden praising the attacks, and then another in November.

For many in the Bush administration, and indeed across the United States and its allies, giving an outlet to these bin Laden statements seemed to confirm what they had always suspected: that far from being the genuinely independent news service it claimed to be, Al Jazeera was a mouthpiece for Islamic extremism – a kind of Terrorist News Network.

'This isn't playing with fire – this is using a flamethrower in terms of the potential impact on the governments in the Islamic world,' James Morris of Britain's Institute of Arab and Islamic Studies at the University of Exeter told the *Christian Science Monitor*. 'This is Osama bin Laden's loudspeaker.'[30]

If there is one media house that embodies the challenge to

journalism posed by the War on Terror, it is Al Jazeera. With its bureaus bombed (twice), its journalists killed and imprisoned on terrorism charges, and government sanctions (from both Middle Eastern and Western administrations) on its broadcasting, no other network has found itself to be such a target – both metaphorically and literally – of those forces engaged in the conflict.

More than any other news organisation, Al Jazeera has forced the West to confront difficult questions about how far it is prepared to go to defend the idea of a free press, about whether it is willing to accept a company that has the capacity and the appetite to present its opponents' view of the world, and about whether Al Jazeera is just an observer or a participant in the War on Terror.

It turns out that the answers are as complex and conflicted as the questions.

•

Al Jazeera was established in 1996, soon after the BBC closed its Arabic-language news service in a dispute with the Saudi royal family and its satellite carrier, Orbit, over several controversial broadcasts. Orbit finally cancelled the deal when the BBC broadcast a documentary on human rights in Saudi Arabia that included footage of a beheading. (The BBC executive who set up the channel, Ian Richardson, later wrote: 'During the short life of BBC Arabic Television, there were several angry "liaison meetings" with Orbit and the guarantees of editorial independence proved to be a sour joke, only barely obscured by a thin smokescreen about the BBC's alleged failure to observe "cultural sensitivities" – Saudi code for anything not to the royal family's liking.'[31])

The Emir of Qatar agreed to lend US$137 million to support the fledgling network to fill the gap the BBC left. Where other local broadcasters would assiduously avoid putting to air anything that might embarrass their home governments (Qatar had its own official TV station as well), Al Jazeera was pitched as an independent news source and an unapologetically provocative platform for discussing issues relating to the Arab world. A lot of the BBC's Arabic staff migrated to the new channel.

The network has often been accused of being anti-Israel, yet it was the first Arab broadcaster to put Israeli officials on air (often speaking Hebrew). In his 2005 book, *Al-Jazeera: The Inside Story of the Arab News Channel that Is Challenging the West*, British journalist Hugh Miles said interviews with Israeli army officers and military spokesmen were 'truly shocking for the Arab public', especially because 'many Arabs had never seen an Israeli speak before'.

Lively, provocative talk shows, particularly a popular, confrontational program called *The Opposite Direction* (modelled on CNN's *Crossfire* program), were a constant source of controversy. In the space of a few months in 2000, for example, Qatar's neighbours protested for a variety of reasons. Libya abruptly withdrew its ambassador after Al Jazeera broadcast an interview with a Libyan opposition figure. Then, when the network reported the enormous expenses of Saddam Hussein's lavish birthday party, the Iraqi government lodged a complaint with Qatari officials. Tunisia's ambassador complained about a program that accused his government of human-rights violations. And a week after that, the Iranian daily *Jomhouri-e Eslami*, a conservative newspaper aligned with Ayatollah Khamenei, accused the station of 'attributing false news to the esteemed leader of the revolution' after it reported that Khamenei favoured the annulment of Iran's February parliamentary elections. Kuwaiti officials regularly complained that Al Jazeera's news coverage was too sympathetic to Iraq. Saudi officials insisted that its programs were anti-Islamic.

One commentator wrote, 'Every Arab regime has found something in Al-Jazeera's programs to complain about – which is precisely why it is by far the most popular satellite news channel in the Middle East.'[32]

So when the United States added its voice to the list of official critics, particularly over airing the bin Laden tapes, it was more of the same for Al Jazeera's management.

'Osama bin Laden, like it or not, is a party to this present crisis,' news editor Ahmed Sheikh told the BBC. 'If we said that we were not going to allow him the air time, then we would have lost our integrity and objectivity and our coverage of the story would have become unbalanced.'[33]

•

On 13 November 2001, viewers tuned in to BBC World and saw correspondent William Reeve dive beneath his dimly lit desk in Kabul during a live broadcast as that American missile hit the Al Jazeera bureau next door.

Initially, military officials said it was a mistake – a 'targeting error' – but it would take several months and persistent inquiries from Al Jazeera and other journalists before the Pentagon finally admitted that it had taken out a building it believed was harbouring Al Qaeda operatives.

•

Less than two years later, as US forces advanced on Baghdad in 'Operation Iraqi Freedom', Al Jazeera kept on working from the capital, broadcasting images that continued to challenge the US government's claims that it was making 'surgical strikes' on military targets to avoid civilian casualties. As one Al Jazeera reporter grimly described it, the network 'broadcast the horror of the bombing campaign, the blown-out brains, the blood-spattered pavements, the screaming infants and the corpses'.[34]

Again, Washington complained. Defense Secretary Donald Rumsfeld described Al Jazeera's reporting as 'propaganda', 'inexcusably biased' and 'vicious'.

Mindful of what had happened in Kabul, Al Jazeera headquarters had not only sent the Baghdad bureau's coordinates to the Pentagon, it had placed huge banners with 'PRESS' emblazoned across them around the sides and top of the building. But on 8 April 2003, another

US airstrike hit the office, killing reporter Tareq Ayyoub and wounding cameraman Zohair al-Iraqi. At a briefing at the operation's headquarters in Doha, the US brigadier general, Vincent Brooks, said, 'This coalition does not target journalists. We don't know every place journalists are operating on the battlefield. It's a dangerous place, indeed.'

(On the same day, an American tank fired a round at the Palestine Hotel, where most other foreign media groups were staying, killing two other reporters and wounding three more. After an investigation, the New York-based Committee to Protect Journalists accepted that incident as a genuine accident.[35])

There is no doubt that Al Jazeera Arabic had (and continues to have) a pro-Arab bias to its reporting. Rather than adopting the US's preferred language of 'liberated Iraq', it tended to portray the country as 'invaded'. And instead of showing American soldiers handing out sweets to Iraqi children, it showed wounded children with bandages over their eyes and blood on their faces. But it also gave due coverage to the US-led coalition and its political leaders, with interviews with Britain's prime minister, Tony Blair, and the US secretary of state, Colin Powell.

There was truth in both the US media's and Al Jazeera's reporting – there really were lots of civilian casualties, including children, and American soldiers really did dole out candy – but in the light of the ongoing resistance to US occupation and the continuing war in Iraq, it now seems as though Al Jazeera's coverage might have been a more accurate portrayal of the way Iraqis saw Operation Iraqi Freedom, than the triumphant images of adoring crowds that dominated American reporting.

So was Al Jazeera's reporting biased?

All reporting has bias: true objectivity simply does not exist. Even the act of deciding what stories to cover and what to ignore reflects a certain bias. Is it better to turn your cameras to the cheering throngs welcoming US tanks into Baghdad, or to look at the devastating cost borne by civilians during the campaign? Both are legitimate stories, but with limited time and resources it isn't always possible to cover everything, so hard choices have to be made.

Even American reporters admitted biases. On being accused of being pro-war and pro-administration, CNN's Aaron Brown responded, 'I think there is some truth in it.' Fox's Neil Cavuto was blunter: 'You say I wear my biases on my sleeve? Better that than pretend you have none but show them clearly in your work.'

That doesn't mean reporters should simply give up and forget about objectivity, but the fact remains that bias will always find its way into their work.

Cavuto's comments echoed Al Jazeera's Ramallah correspondent, who told a *60 Minutes* program about the Arab–Israeli conflict: 'To be objective in this area is not easy because we live here. We are part of the people here. And this situation belongs to us also, and we have our opinions.'

This is the heart of the matter: Allouni and his network provided a view of the war that their Western counterparts simply could not see. Allouni was able to explain the impact the bombing was having on Iraqi psychology not just because he happened to be living in Baghdad at the time, but because as a fellow Arab and Muslim, he had obvious sympathies for those who saw themselves as being 'invaded' rather than 'liberated', and so he was able to get access to those he connected with far more successfully than his Western counterparts.

•

Sami Al Hajj was a Sudanese journalist working for Al Jazeera, filming the Taliban's operation in and around its headquarters in Kandahar. He had been covering southern Afghanistan since the war began in October 2001, moving back and forth across the border so often that he got to know the Pakistani border guards by name.

On the night of 15 December 2001, after the Taliban had been driven out of Kandahar, Al Hajj tried to cross once more, hoping to film the city in the wake of the Islamists' departure. This time, though, the guards pulled him aside and told him he was under arrest.

Al Hajj was moved first to Bagram Air Base, the US military's main operational centre north of Kabul, where he was questioned about whether he knew where Osama bin Laden was.

'Of course, they were mistaken,' he said. 'I had never met nor interviewed bin Laden. But their questioning revealed that even if this was a case of mistaken identity, they were in no doubt as to the fact that I was a journalist.'[36]

Then, six months later, he was transferred to Guantanamo Bay, accused of being an 'enemy combatant'.

Al Hajj was never formally charged with any crime. In March 2005, the Combatant Status Review Tribunal, set up to decide if Guantanamo detainees were being legitimately held, ruled that he was indeed an enemy combatant, on the grounds that he had allegedly run a website that supported terrorism, had trafficked in arms, entered Afghanistan illegally in October 2001 while US airstrikes were underway, and interviewed Osama bin Laden. He and Al Jazeera denied all the allegations, and at no point did the American authorities give any evidence to back up their claims.[37] It was also never clear why interviewing someone – even Osama bin Laden – should be considered a hostile act.

In protest, Al Hajj went on a hunger strike. To keep him alive, the guards forced him to eat. Force-feeding was, he said, a form of torture in itself: 'They would tie us up by our hands and our legs and then force a tube up our nose. Most of the time, the fluid would enter our lungs. We'd be coughing and choking as our lungs filled with liquid. Often, they'd overfeed us so that we vomited. But even as we threw up, they'd keep on going. The vomit would dry on our faces and bodies. We weren't allowed to clean it away so the smell became unbearable. And they'd use the same tube for multiple prisoners without cleaning it.'

Eventually, after six years at Guantanamo Bay, he was finally released without explanation or apology.

Al Hajj's story is another deeply disturbing example of the way the American military made assumptions about a journalist. In his case, as in ours, the authorities assumed that because he worked for an organisation that they took to be hostile, he must therefore be a part of a terrorist group. His imprisonment became both an assault on the principle of a free media and an attack on a network that challenged the American government's orthodoxy.

Just after the destruction of the Twin Towers, President Bush told a joint session of Congress that terrorists 'hate our freedoms, our freedom of religion, our freedom of speech, our freedom to vote and assemble and disagree with each other . . . We are in a fight for our principles, and our first responsibility is to live by them.'

'Freedom' became President Bush's mantra in speech after speech, and yet in this conflict over ideologies, the US seemed willing to abandon its core principles. It attacked a network that exercised freedom of the press by giving voice to those who disagreed with it. It set aside its cherished commitments to the rule of law by locking up suspects, including a journalist, without evidence or trial for years on end. And in the process, it handed a kind of pyrrhic victory to Al Qaeda, chipping away at those very freedoms that Bush acknowledged the militant Islamists wanted to end.

•

Sami Al Hajj was only the first Al Jazeera journalist to be locked up over allegations of links to terrorism.

After covering the invasion of Afghanistan and then Iraq, Tayseer Allouni returned to Spain in the summer of 2003 for a badly needed holiday, and to recover from surgery for a heart condition. As he was taking a shower at his flat in Granada, Spanish police broke in and arrested him. He was charged with being a member of or having links to Al Qaeda.

Both Al Jazeera and Allouni dismissed the first charge as utterly ridiculous but freely acknowledged the second. He was, after all, a good reporter who used his contacts with radical Islamists to work effectively in Afghanistan and Iraq, and it was those contacts who had helped him get to Osama bin Laden. In fact, any reporter who operates with any integrity in war zones will have numbers for members of all sides in his or her contact book.

But as the investigation continued, the charges became more specific. Allouni was accused of having links to Mohamed Atta – the ringleader of the group that hijacked the aircraft in the 9/11 attacks – and of being a courier of cash and messages for Al Qaeda agents living in Chechnya, Turkey and Afghanistan.

Again, Allouni denied any connections to Atta but acknowledged carrying money for his own friends, who, he said, were simply trying to get help to their families living in conflict zones.

A colleague of Allouni's told the *Los Angeles Times* that his arrest was: 'going to make us [Al Jazeera] very popular in the Arab world. It shows Spain and the liberal democracies are just as hypocritical about freedom of speech, and of journalists, as the countries in the Third World are. Maybe it will hurt us in the States, but in Europe, no.'[38]

As with our case, Allouni's arrest triggered a global campaign to have him freed. Eventually, with his heart deteriorating, the then 48-year-old was released on bail, on condition that he hand in his passport. He continued to work, reporting on events in Spain, and in March the following year found himself covering terrorist attacks on Madrid's rail network that killed 192 people and injured about 2000 others. This created a bizarre paradox: a man accused of being an Al Qaeda operative found himself talking to government officials who were accusing Al Qaeda of being behind the attack.

Allouni was eventually sent to trial in 2005, and although he was cleared of being a member of a terrorist group, he was convicted of collaborating with Al Qaeda by carrying messages and money to Afghanistan. He was sentenced to seven years, six of those under house arrest for medical reasons.

Was Allouni colluding with terrorists? He has always argued that he was only doing his job as a journalist with good contacts inside a group considered to be the enemy in the War on Terror. He said the charges were the result of a judiciary keen to ingratiate itself with the United States that tossed out basic principles of due process and the presumption of innocence. (The European Court of Human Rights agreed: in 2012, the judges ruled that the Spanish judiciary had denied Allouni a fair and independent trial, and ordered that he be released and paid compensation.)

Allouni says he didn't know his contacts were Al Qaeda members, and that by carrying cash he was only following cultural traditions: 'If you refuse, you are looked upon badly. What is more, I was interested in these people because of the information that I needed.'

Al Jazeera was not the only organisation angered by the sentence. 'It sets a dangerous precedent, particularly for anyone who seeks to interview bin Laden in the future,' said Jean-François Julliard from Reporters Without Borders. 'Journalists have always investigated terrorist groups. It's part of our job.'[39]

But if there is no evidence that Allouni consciously and deliberately helped a terrorist group, there is still the question of whether he crossed an editorial line and became sympathetic to a group of militant extremists. As a reporter sharing culture, language, religion and life with the people he was reporting on, indisputably it would have been hard to remain utterly detached. And if Allouni is guilty of setting aside his journalistic integrity to become something more like an activist for one particular side in the war, then the same charge must surely be levelled at all but a handful of Western reporters who covered the conflicts in Afghanistan and Iraq.

There was no doubt that Allouni went after stories that challenged US claims of military success, and broadcast the views of people opposed to the US-led coalition attacking both Afghanistan and Iraq. That should be no crime in a world that claims to hold dear the idea of a press free to publish views and opinions that are uncomfortable for the establishment. But there is no evidence that he went beyond reporting what it was like for those living underneath the bombs and giving a microphone to Al Qaeda, into siding with the Taliban or the extremists. And even if he did, he arguably provided a balance to our understanding of the conflict that Western networks were simply unable to provide.

•

On 15 November 2006, Al Jazeera English went live. It was to be no mere translation of the Arabic service but its own network, editorially independent and staffed by some of the best broadcasters available.

Al Jazeera poached people from across its rival English-speaking networks. AJ Arabic had received its fair share of criticism for biased reporting, but it had also disrupted coverage of the Middle East and forced its competitors to rethink their approach to journalism. The English service's management promised a similar shake-up.

The new network pledged significant resources (including high salaries), as well as a commitment to covering news 'wherever it happens'. It promised to place editorial judgement above the more prosaic forces that influence editors, giving reporters the freedom to cover whatever they felt was important rather than having to chase stories that would draw large audiences or fitted a particular political line. By being based in the Middle East, it was geographically and philosophically well placed to honour its commitment to 'reversing the flow of information from the North to the South'. Instead of offering up a US or Anglocentric view of the world, it would spend time and resources looking into an obscure but bloody rebellion in the province of South Kordofan in Sudan, for example, or the politics of Hugo Chavez in Venezuela.

It was an appealing mix for lots of journalists, and some of the world's most respected news organisations, including the BBC, CNN, NBC and Reuters lost experienced reporters, producers and camera crews who were keen to take part in the new experiment. (Those were some of the reasons I joined Al Jazeera as its East Africa correspondent in 2011.) Riz Khan defected from CNN, along with the BBC's ageing heavyweight interviewer David Frost. Dave Marash from the American ABC's *Nightline* program was another: Al Jazeera English was 'too good, too significant, to not have a market in the US, given the complete abdication of American networks and cable channels from actually covering international news,' he said.

Such rhetoric didn't wash with American conservatives, who viewed the high-profile Western recruits like Marash as Islamofascist quislings. When the network began talking to Frost, John Gibson from Fox News sneered, 'That's a little like one of the royal family consorting with the [London, 7 July] bombers, isn't it?'

And Marash, who had worked with Bill O'Reilly in local news in New York City, appeared on *The O'Reilly Factor* only to have the host introduce his interview by telling his audience, 'As you may know, the television network Al Jazeera has a close-knit relationship with Al Qaeda and other Islamic terror outfits.'

With such vitriol aimed at Al Jazeera from some of America's most popular commentators, only a handful of cable carriers agreed to include the network in their line-up, afraid of losing advertisers and viewers in protest. It was available in New York and Washington, DC but few outside the big east-coast cities were able to watch. Gradually, though, Al Jazeera English won converts and began rivalling the BBC in its international news and analysis.

Then it struck what it called its 'Gulf War moment' (a reference to the story that turbocharged CNN's reputation).

In late 2010, as the Arab Spring swept across the Middle East, the American networks were caught flat-footed without people or resources on the ground, and struggled to make sense of the cascade. But Al Jazeera was perfectly placed. It had deep knowledge of the region and its history, a well-established network of correspondents, and an unrivalled list of contacts who were able to unpack the unfolding events.

The US secretary of state, Hillary Clinton, startled American viewers when she told the Senate Committee on Foreign Relations that a TV in her offices was permanently tuned to the network. Al Jazeera offers 'real news', she said, rather than commercials and 'talking heads'. She went on to suggest that the US was failing to win the information war in the Middle East.

It was an extraordinary turnaround in the West for Al Jazeera English. Suddenly, it had the respect of world leaders, was on screens in offices across the United Nations and in boardrooms around the globe, and was picking up both awards and audiences.

And yet in the Middle East, the Arabic service was once again the target of pressure from diplomats, the public and, ultimately, the security services.

If the Arab Spring was a watershed moment for Al Jazeera English, it was also a moment that challenged the Arabic service's view of itself and its place in the region's politics and society. With its philosophy of supporting the underdog and challenging established regimes, it gave significant amounts of airtime to the most prominent underground political force in the region: the Muslim Brotherhood.

The Brotherhood had been born in Egypt, but it had either formed affiliates or inspired like-minded groups in just about every country across the Middle East and North Africa. Some of those offshoots had taken power, such as Hamas in the Gaza Strip and the National Islamic Front in Sudan, while in places like Jordan, Iraq and Syria, it had formed influential underground movements.

When Mohamed Morsi won the elections in Egypt, the Qatari government pledged billions of dollars in investment to help the new regime and thereby undermine Qatar's rival and the region's other great Sunni power, Saudi Arabia.

While there is no direct evidence that Qatar ordered Al Jazeera Arabic editors to support the Brotherhood – and its editors always vociferously insisted that the network remained editorially independent – suspicious audiences across the region detected a clear alignment with Qatar's foreign policy and a bias in favour of the MB. Al Jazeera Arabic always referred to Morsi's ouster as a 'coup' (a term that even the American government was hesitant to use) and routinely gave Brotherhood activists a place in front of the camera. Even secular activists like Alaa Abd El-Fattah, who was with me in Torah Limen and who benefited from its coverage, complained of bias.

According to one analyst, Yigal Carmon from the Middle East Media Research Institute in Washington, DC, the network 'regularly' exaggerated the strength of pro-Brotherhood protests by zooming in on small crowds to make them appear larger. 'They attacked the military in every way possible and defended the Muslim Brotherhood in every possible way,' he said.[40]

•

Al Jazeera was set up to be provocative. It was designed from the outset to challenge the way news had traditionally been handled across the Middle East, to upset the established regimes, and to push debates into the open that had previously been left to hushed conversations in dark corners of coffee shops.

With that kind of mandate, it was always going to anger politicians and provoke their security services. But Al Jazeera was not a subversive agency working secretly to overthrow governments. It was a media company, aggressively seeking out alternative views and challenging established narratives.

Did it cross an editorial line, as reporters like Tayseer Allouni were accused of doing, to become so close to the Muslim Brotherhood that it became an apologist for the movement? Quite possibly, but it is easy to forget that in the heady environment around the Arab Spring, the Brotherhood was the single most influential and the best-organised political force in the region, and giving it generous airtime, particularly as the voice of the region's poor, had its own editorial logic, just as covering the consequences of American bombs in Kabul, or broadcasting statements from Al Qaeda, did. And in any event, what was true of Al Qaeda was true of the Brotherhood: both were parties to their respective conflicts, and journalists had a professional responsibility to cover both.

The problem facing news organisations operating across the Middle East was the same one we had struggled with before we were arrested in Egypt. By branding the MB as a terrorist group, the Egyptian government made anybody who identified with it a 'terrorist'. By giving airtime to anybody who argued the Brotherhood's case, journalists suddenly found themselves guilty of 'promoting terrorist ideology'. It was a radical redefinition of the political 'centre' that made it impossible to produce fair, balanced reporting without crossing that line.

What both Al Jazeera's Arabic and English services did was expose the government's assumption that those who dared to publish the views of 'the enemy', or question the regime's security policies and political strategies, were no longer just doing good journalism. They were being treasonous.

For its part, the US government and its allies never formally charged Al Jazeera with sponsoring or promoting terrorism. But by making the allegations informally, bombing its bureaus and arresting its reporters, the US and its allies were sending the same message as the Egyptian government: if you do your job and report from across the battle lines, you will be treated as 'enemy'.

9

THE TRIAL BEGINS

20 FEBRUARY 2014

The prison transport van is a truck with a cavernous steel box on the back. Light filters in through a couple of tiny, heavily barred windows, illuminating the dust in bright shafts. A seat runs around the edges with room for at least twenty, but on this ride it is almost empty. There are just the three of us – me, Baher and Fahmy – cuffed together in our prison whites.

We sit in silence as we move along the roads towards our first court appearance. The truck rattles like a tin can filled with marbles, and each of us sits silently contemplating the trial in front of us.

We are all concerned, of course – it's hard not to be when you are in an oversized paddy wagon on your way to court on charges of terrorism – but none of us seriously believes the prosecution's case will survive the first few hearings, and we all believe we'll get out on bail. We're not charged with violence, we don't have past convictions, and it is hard to see how we can be considered a threat to public safety and security. We also suspect the trial will be closely watched and that human-rights groups, diplomats and, of course, our colleagues will want to make sure that due process is followed. Surely the authorities will want to be seen to be acting with integrity in such a high-profile case.

Eventually the truck groans to a halt. There's more rattling of keys and locks and the door swings open, but rather than being ordered out of the cage, we are joined by three young men barely out of their teens, who climb in with boyish grins. Immediately Fahmy's and Baher's faces light up as they all exchange greetings and embraces. The three are university students who were arrested a few days after us and were a few cells along from Fahmy and Baher in Scorpion Prison.

Although none of us had ever met any of the students before their arrest or even knew of their existence, they have been included in our case, on the same incomprehensible set of charges. The only apparent connection with us is the fact that they had cameras in their car when police stopped them.

By now, I suppose we shouldn't be surprised, but why on earth should three random strangers somehow appear alongside us as co-conspirators?

Sohaib Sa'ad, Shady Ibrahim and Khalid Mohammed are intelligent, idealistic young men who are opposed to the old regime. While they are instinctively supportive of the Muslim Brotherhood, they all insist they have never been members of the organisation or worked for it. They were arrested in the early hours of New Year's Day as they were driving home after spending the night chatting at a popular lookout above Cairo.

A few minutes later, we stop again and two more young men climb in. They introduce themselves as Anas Beltagy and Ahmed Ibrahim. Anas is the son of one of the Muslim Brotherhood's feistiest political figures, who is also in prison on treason charges. Anas and Ahmed were watching TV in the Beltagy family home when the police raided it. It appears they will be charged with us too.

Our van eventually arrives at the court. The prisoners' entrance is a dusty staircase up to a caged door at the back of the building, out of sight of the public and any media who might be trying to get a glimpse of us. The authorities are treating us as though we are hardened killers: two ranks of riot police with batons form a corridor from the truck to the steps and then all the way up to a holding cell on the second floor. Still cuffed together, we are hustled up the stairs and into the cell.

It's another bare concrete room with a few high windows, the only furniture a concrete knee-high shelf that runs around the edges. Anti-government graffiti covers the walls, written with smuggled-in marker pens. Someone has drawn a cheeky cartoon of Defence Minister Sisi as a donkey, and there are crude drawings of the four-fingered salute that has become the symbol of the anti-government coalition, and of crossed swords – the Islamic symbol of resistance. The names of prisoners who've been through the cells before us also cover the walls. Among them I find 'Ahmed Maher' and 'Mohammed Adel' – the two April 6 leaders who were my neighbours in Limen. It is oddly and unexpectedly comforting. We are the latest in a long, noble line of campaigners and human-rights activists, and whatever the prosecutor might say, I feel no shame in being here.

Baher and I are still cuffed together, so while the others chat, he and I pace around the cell. Walking becomes a rhythmic, meditative exercise and we find a kind of groove that moves my mind away from the imminent hearing to the physical act of taking each step.

With no watches we have no idea how much time passes, but after what feels like at least an hour, we are finally called. The door swings open and we march out, through another corridor of riot police.

'Hold your head up,' booms Fahmy. 'Let 'em know we're strong.'

•

The special terrorism courtroom is a vast indoor amphitheatre. The public gallery is steeply banked so that everyone has a clear view of the judges' bench at the bottom. We are kept in a steel cage down one side of the court that has clearly been added as a modification to the existing courtroom. The cage separates us entirely from the public seating, but there is yet another barrier – a rank of bored police who fight off sleep as they sit through the day's proceedings – to keep friends and family back from the defendants.

It is all highly theatrical – more like a stage for a Shakespearian drama than a place to mete out justice.

As we walk in at the top of the court, I am staggered by the number of people filling the public area. My brother Andrew is there – he arrived a few days ahead of the hearing and came for a brief, emotional visit to the prison, where we discussed the case and the prospects for release – but I can barely see him amid the gaggle of reporters, photographers, diplomats, lawyers and human-rights observers. As we walk down the side of the cage to take our seats, the journalists surge forward and point their cameras in our direction, shouting questions across the space.

It's heartening to see the crowd gathered here. Although I don't know many of the local press corps, there are a few familiar faces, including an old BBC colleague and rival. Orla Guerin is a tough, fiercely competitive journalist I have always admired and respected though never much liked, yet all of a sudden, I feel a surge of warmth and gratitude at the sight of her and her cameraman.

Baher and Fahmy point out others they have worked alongside over the years. There is Patrick Kingsley from *The Guardian*, John Lyons from *The Australian*, Ruth Pollard from the *Sydney Morning Herald*, reporters from the Associated Press and Reuters, and local journalists and photographers. Normally a pack like this would be extremely intimidating for anybody on the sharp end of their cameras, but we know they are with us. We can feel it.

As soon as we're in the cage, they shout questions at us across the courtroom.

'How are you being treated?'

'What have you got to say about the charges?'

'What message do you have for your families?'

We answer as best we can, but my voice barely carries across the gulf. (In profiles I would be routinely described as 'soft-spoken'.) Instead, Fahmy and Baher bellow our answers.

'We have done nothing wrong,' Baher shouts. 'The charges are completely baseless, but we trust that the judge will see that and either throw the case out or give us bail. If the justice system has any integrity at all, it must release us in the end.'

Fahmy picks up the thread: 'These charges are purely political. We have faith in the justice system, but we must be released as soon as possible. We are being held in a tiny cell for twenty-three hours a day. We have not been physically abused, but I need medical attention.'

He waves his right arm, still wrapped in a black sling, like a broken wing.

The journalists scribble down every word, but then the bailiff calls the court to order as the judges enter, and everyone returns to their seats.

•

As the room falls silent, the judicial panel march in and take their seats. There are three on the bench: the chief judge sits in the middle, flanked by two advisers. All three sport thick moustaches. The one to the right is a small, balding man who looks more like a manager in the tax office than a judge, and the one to the left has narrow eyes and no chin. (My mother always warned me: 'Never trust anybody without a chin.') But it is the chief himself who draws all the attention.

Judge Nagy Shehata is a big man. His sagging jowls give him the appearance of a basset hound who's been stuck in the house for too long, and we find him almost impossible to read. His watery eyes give very little away when you can see them, and are almost always hidden behind dark sunglasses.

'He looks like a bullfrog with a hangover,' whispers Fahmy.

First there is a rollcall of everyone on the charge sheet. The list of defendants is staggering. There are twenty in all, including the three of us, the five students, five other Al Jazeera journalists and producers, and a host of names that none of us can place, including 'Susan Melanie' and 'Rena Netjes'. There are only eight of us in the cage, so it seems the rest are on trial *in absentia.*

There's no time to work out where all those names have come from. The first order of business is to sort out our lawyers.

An extraordinary gaggle of barristers is fighting to get to the lectern. It looks as though there are about thirty shouting and elbowing one another aside to be recognised as our representatives. It's a confusing, confronting mess, but apparently a routine part of the judicial process. Lawyers with nothing better to do show up at hearings hoping that a desperate prisoner will hire them. I expect that someone in there has been hired by Al Jazeera, but I have no idea who it might be.

Fahmy has already decided to go it alone and his family has apparently organised their own advocate. When he is asked to name his legal representative, he points out a small, confident-looking man, sharply dressed in an expensive Italian suit. It's Khaled Abu Bakr, a famous lawyer who has his own late-evening television talk show. It is in line with Fahmy's strategy to isolate himself from Al Jazeera by not using anybody paid from Doha.

Then the judge calls on me to nominate my legal representative. No lawyer has been to visit us, and we've had no messages about who might represent us or how the process will work. One well-known human-rights activist shouts out that I should name her. She would probably do a great job, but I don't know whether she's been formally hired and I don't want to unwittingly undermine the strategy that I'm sure has been worked out.

Confused, I look over to my brother, who is standing up and clearly trying to mouth something. I have no idea what it is. He makes a series of equally incomprehensible gestures, and I hold my hands apart and shake my head.

I. Don't. Understand.

He furrows his brow, sits briefly and scribbles something on his notepad in big letters. He holds it over his head and I see that it reads 'AJ LAWYER'.

Before I can respond, the judge bellows into his microphone. He is speaking in Arabic and I still don't have an interpreter, so I haven't got a clue what's going on, but the court is in turmoil and something is clearly wrong. Before Baher can explain, court security guards rush to Andrew and drag him out of his seat to make him stand before the judge.

'He's in contempt of court,' whispers Baher, 'and the judge is really pissed off. He isn't allowed to communicate with you. The judge is telling him that he can be thrown in the cells for that. He could be in real trouble if they want to make an example of him.'

I can feel my stomach in my throat. The last thing we need is another Greste in an Egyptian prison cell.

The lecture is long and stern. There's a lot of finger-wagging and head-shaking, and the room is silent as everyone waits to hear the judge's ruling. My teeth are clenched as I try to read signs that suggest which way it's going to go.

But the judge seems in a benevolent mood. He lets my brother off with a warning, and as Andrew returns to his seat he flashes me a cheeky grin.

The court session drags on with a drawn-out argument over who should be representing the rest of us; over whether I should have an official translator; over countless procedural issues I have no understanding of. It ends as it began – in turmoil, with none of us apart from Fahmy knowing who our lawyers are and no progress at all in our case. The judge declares a two-week adjournment and bangs his gavel.

•

Two more weeks. An eternity.

None of us spoke openly about walking out of prison today, but inside we all hoped it would happen. We all felt there was a better-than-even chance that we'd be eating hot food and sleeping in soft beds tonight.

Instead, when the prison guards finally shove us inside, the cell feels brutally harsh and unforgiving. Another two weeks in here will be interminable, insufferable.

As we talk through the day's hearing, Baher suddenly raises his eyebrows as he remembers who 'Susan Melanie' is.

'It's Sue Turton,' he says. Sue is another Al Jazeera correspondent who has been a regular in Cairo. 'Melanie is her middle name.'

Then Fahmy furrows his brow and shakes his head. He remembers that Rena Netjes is a Dutch journalist who came past the Marriott Hotel some weeks earlier to get his advice about the Sinai Peninsula, where she planned to travel. It seems the investigators have simply pulled their names from the hotel records and added them to the charge sheet, regardless of their association with us.

The craziness is enough to send you mad. And so, I narrow my focus. Instead of looking to that impossibly distant fourteen-day horizon, I work on getting through just as much as I can manage. Even one week feels a long way off. Making it past the next twenty-four hours is hardly a challenge, though, and anyway, there are far too many of those between now and the next hearing. Instead, two day-chunks seem both challenging and survivable. There are only three and a half of them in a week. Once we are through one week, well, there will only be one more to go to the next court appearance. Then surely we must be on the way out.

Once again, I try to take pleasure in small things.

The food at Mulhaq is much the same as elsewhere – standard prison-issue fūl and flatbread supplemented with fresh tomatoes and boxes of feta cheese – but we are allowed to order the occasional meal from the prison caterer, paid for from an account that our families top up. Those meals are important for two reasons: first, they provide us with morale-boosting nutrition, and second, they come wrapped in aluminium foil.

Our cell is painted a bilious, glossy lime green, presumably to expose any attempt to scratch it off and dig our way out. The walls are featureless slabs apart from a few holes that the guards tell us were drilled to hold flat-screen TVs for the sons of Hosni Mubarak, who were guests here before us. The space is flat, dull and depressing, like a hospital corridor, so Baher and I decide to do something about it.

We carefully smooth out the foil and, with a bit of experimenting, discover that if you smear it with wet soap it sticks quite nicely to the paint. And because one side of the foil is matt and the other is shiny, by alternating the sides we can make mosaics.

Then we make another discovery. The labels on the plastic water bottles peel off and have a handy bit of glue on the back that helps stick them to the walls. When they're arranged into giant letters, the labels lose their promotional quality and take on the appearance of abstract art.

It takes ages to collect enough water-bottle labels, but eventually I spell out, in giant capital letters, 'FREEDOM NOW'and add a big arrow pointing to the door. I then start collecting and pasting matchbox-sized pieces of foil onto the wall to create a shimmering silver halo around the sacred words.

When we are done, I feel incredibly proud of it. The mural sits plastered on the concrete where we can all see it from our beds, and at night it shines in the weak, grey light that filters through from the courtyard outside the cell. The words demand what we know to be our most fundamental right, and seeing them there gives all of us great comfort.

On another wall, Baher uses water-bottle labels to write in Arabic 'ALLAH U AKBAR' – 'GOD IS GREAT'. The West has come to think of this phrase as the Islamic battle cry, but for Baher it is reasserting his faith in God's ultimate wisdom. As the days pass into weeks, he rediscovers and takes refuge in his faith.

Before our arrest, Baher was, like so many other young, middle-class urban Egyptians, notionally Islamic but hardly radical or devoted. He professed a belief in Allah and would pray when he found the time, but would also happily join us for a quiet whisky after work.

Now, though, Islam becomes a central source of support for him, and his faith seems to run deeper and stronger with each passing day. To a confirmed sceptic like me, who struggles to see 'God' in anything, it is as touching as it is alarming.

For Baher, as with many mainstream Muslims, the Qur'an is superior to the Bible because the archangel Gabriel dictated it to the prophet Mohammed. It is quite literally the word of God. For Baher and the Brotherhood leaders around us, that makes the Qur'an incontestable, and every detail in it the literal truth.

Although the already-vast gap between our ideas of God – Baher a devoted Muslim, and I a fiercely sceptical agnostic – has widened further, our conversations on the subject are still respectful and considered.

Fahmy is much more conflicted about his religion. He declares himself a Muslim, believing in the truth of the Qur'an and its fundamental tenets, but he is also deeply sceptical. More than that, he is fiercely, angrily critical, particularly of what he regards as the blind, unthinking devotion of our neighbours and, by implication, of Baher as well. With Fahmy involved, our discussions are less conversations than they are an exchange of assertions, with Fahmy delivering lectures about the stupidity and hypocrisy of the more conservative believers. That would be fine were it not for the confines of our cell, where faith is not just a question of personal belief but central to an inmate's psychological survival. Fahmy's loudly delivered, unbending views grate sharply on everyone in earshot.

•

And so we try to find other diversions.

Sometimes the water bottles come with blue tops, sometimes with red tops, and occasionally we get a rare white one. We save five red and five blue tops, and once we have a white one, we have all we need to play what we call 'prison petanque'. It is our version of the French game of boules, with the white top serving as a jack tossed along the floor down the long edge of the cell. We compete to get our own bottle tops as close as we can to the jack and knock our opponents' out of the way in the process. The game soaks up hours of otherwise empty time, and infuriatingly, Baher quickly develops a fine knack for tapping my best-placed pieces aside just when it looks as though I'm about to nail him.

Once we have ten red and ten blue tops, I realise we can make board games like draughts and backgammon and I shift our focus, hoping to find some other sphere in which I can beat Baher. Backgammon is an institution in Egypt, as it is across the Middle East, and Baher is keen to figure out how to make a board. That's easy enough – we have a cardboard box and can scratch out the classic sharp triangles on the bottom. The big challenge is dice. I spend a few hours trying to figure out how to make a die out of paper or foil, or even a piece of carrot. Then it occurs to me: a die is nothing more than a random number generator. At their last visit, Baher's family brought a packet of pumpkin seeds, so we pick out twelve of the biggest, divide them into two sets, and scratch the numbers from one to six into them before we drop them into a cup. All we need to do is shake the cup, dip our fingers in and choose two seeds at random, and voila – we have our dice.

I'm delighted until I realise once again that Baher is a lot more experienced and skilled than he has let on. With a glint in his eye, he hammers me relentlessly game after game, only occasionally creasing his brow in sympathy at my pain.

Fahmy, meanwhile, doesn't seem interested. He is happy to watch us play our games and give advice, but prefers to sit on the sidelines. It bothers me that he won't join in – for me, the games and the murals are a way of focusing on something other than the prison. The games take us out of our box, so for a while, at least, they allow the walls to fall away. So too with the murals: the walls stop imposing constraints and instead become galleries for our own creativity.

But Fahmy prefers to lie on his bed and let us get on with it. His insomnia means he often sleeps through the day, but when he's not sleeping, he is constantly scheming and planning, trying to figure out ways of challenging the authorities, gaining public and political support, and turning the balance of power in our favour.

Baher salvages a stick from the garden when we have our run. 'Why don't we make something like a wind chime?' he asks.

So we set about unpicking the hated rough cotton uniforms and tearing and shaping sheets of foil into small triangles and balls that we will suspend from a beam running across the ceiling. When we are done, although it is no work of great craftsmanship, the gently swinging silver shapes fracture and splinter the light in a way that none of us anticipated. They send shards of yellow onto the walls that twist and dart about and for a while make the place feel a little bit lighter – fluid, almost – and somehow less permanent.

•

One day, Andrew makes it in for a visit. The visiting area is a concrete space with a tin roof just outside the main prison compound; guards watch from a few metres away. Visits are a strict forty-five minutes and it is staggering how quickly those minutes sweep past.

The trial is at the top of our agenda. Al Jazeera *had* hired a lawyer for us, but he didn't get past the guards outside the court until it was too late. He is Farag Fathy Farag, who runs a practice specialising in corporate law. I ask Andrew to get Farag to visit so he can prepare our defence, but my brother has memorised a list of questions about our work in Cairo in case he can't (paper and pens can't be brought into the prison). Once we work through those, we realise that almost half our time is up.

Prison visits can be traumatic for the visitor, who must navigate through security in an unfamiliar system and foreign language, and for whom any difficulties are amplified by the heat and dust. But the biggest distress is imagining the suffering of the prisoner, conjured out of countless movies and TV series depicting rat-infested hellholes with no water or food, abusive guards and even more abusive inmates.

So I spend some time talking Andrew through our prison conditions, hoping to ease the mental burden on my whole family. It's tough, I say, but it's not a *Midnight Express* nightmare. Then I slip him a note. I've been allowed to write one letter a month to my family, but the letters have to go through censors before they are let out and I am not allowed to say anything about life inside. That's not enough for me, so I've written a longer note on toilet paper, using a pen smuggled in by one of the other prisoners. (Toilet paper turns out to be quite effective. The guards are generally pretty thorough with their pat-down searches before we go out for visits, but they are a bit squeamish about getting too intimate, and a tightly rolled-up length of toilet paper slipped inside my underpants doesn't feel out of place – though it soon becomes clear that there are limits to how much I can write without looking suspiciously excited to see my family.)

There is a risk, of course: Andrew and I could both be severely punished for smuggling notes about life inside or messages for the media. But I also feel I have no choice but to keep up the communication, and so when I notice the guards talking to one another, I move rather awkwardly as if I'm scratching my groin, slip the note out and palm it to my brother. It must have looked comically clumsy to anybody watching closely, and I can feel my face flush with expectation as I wait for a heavy hand on my shoulder or a whack across my head from an angry guard. We try to make small talk, both of us painfully conscious of what we've just done and how obvious it must have been. Our conversation stutters. We try not to look around . . . I ask about the weather . . . and . . . it doesn't come. Nobody has noticed.

•

As the next hearing approaches, I have a panic attack. It comes in the deep night when I am lying flat on my back listening to Baher's gentle snoring. Fahmy is typically restless, tossing around in his squeaky bed, though he seems to be asleep. In the weak light, as I slowly focus my eyes on the ceiling, it suddenly occurs to me that I might not get out of this place for years. It seems an obvious thought, I suppose, but until now I have avoided confronting the prospect. We have worked hard to literally paper over the concrete and iron, and while I intellectually understand the seriousness of the cell, I have managed to circle around the idea of being inside for a Very Long Time. I went through something like this in Limen, but this attack is a different order of magnitude.

Now, suddenly and inexplicably, I feel it rise from my gut like nausea, only worse. This can't be purged in the toilet bowl. The feeling grips my chest like a cold iron band and I struggle to breathe. Calling it a 'feeling' doesn't seem enough – it's not an abstraction or an emotion any longer. My limbs fill with tingly panic as the walls start to close in. This is real in the way that being punched in the face is real. I know it can't be, but my body refuses to acknowledge the truth. My jaw feels as though it is screwed shut, and I am very, very scared.

If I can't control this, I know it will beat me. There is only one way for it to end, and madness is not something I am ready to contemplate. It feels like a physical struggle, beating down this internal monster, and I close my eyes to focus. I think about meditation. It seems impossible right now, but I force my mind to focus on the physical – the physiological feelings in my limbs, my skin, my bones, and my organs – and ignore the fact of the walls.

Meditation teachers instruct you to observe yourself from the outside as dispassionately as a scientist studying a subject in a lab. They ask you not to judge the sensations in your body, merely to note them in the finest detail possible, and to understand the connection between emotion and sensation. I try it now, this process of separating mind from body, to pull out of the vicious spiral. I can feel the black hole where the more energy I use to escape, the darker and denser it will become.

As I teeter on the edge of the abyss, I force myself to drag in air in ever-deeper breaths, and slowly the walls seem to recede. The room feels lighter, softer almost, and the panic fades.

•

We are back at court for the second hearing. I still don't have an official interpreter, and although Fahmy and Baher are skilled translators, I make a point of ignoring the judge when my name is called. How can I understand what's going on if I don't have anybody official to translate for me? Erika Tolano from the Australian Embassy underlines this in a submission to the court, and although the judge seems unamused, I think he gets the point.

The courtroom seems just as crowded as before, and once more there is an unseemly fight among the lawyers over who should be representing us. Most of them must be pretty low-rent street lawyers, because our case has already become so politically toxic that very few with a reputation to protect are willing even to consider taking us on.

Eventually, though, Farag manages to catch the judge's eye, and Baher and I confirm that he and his associate are indeed the lawyers we want to represent us. The court is cleared of excess legal expertise and we begin.

Farag half-heartedly argues that because the police overlooked a host of regulations and made some serious procedural errors, the case should be dropped altogether. None of this sticks, though, and the judge orders the prosecutor to begin presenting his evidence.

A group of court orderlies march in, carrying boxes with tags. It is our equipment, which the prosecutor says contains proof that we have been collaborating with terrorists. At last, the trial is about to get underway.

10

SYRIAN HELLHOLE: THE STORY OF JAMES FOLEY AND STEVEN SOTLOFF

We heard about James Foley and Steven Sotloff while we were in prison. The shocking news filtered through the usual channels – a mix of rumours passed along the prison grapevine from snatches overheard on local radios or through the guards – and was later confirmed by Australian Embassy staff on one of their visits.

Foley and Sotloff were two American journalists who had been kidnapped separately in Syria. Both were tough veteran reporters who'd been working on the front lines of some of the most dangerous conflicts in the Middle East. Both had earlier worked in Libya. In one incident, Foley had been kidnapped by forces loyal to the deposed leader Colonel Muammar Gaddafi and spent forty-four days in captivity. Sotloff had been one of a team of reporters who went to Benghazi in October 2012 to investigate the murders of the US ambassador and three other Americans the previous month.[41]

The two men had spent enough time on the front lines of the Middle East to understand the risks of operating in Syria's chaotic battlegrounds, and neither would have gone there without appreciating the very real danger of being picked up by one of the many groups operating at the time, or the consequences of getting caught by Islamic extremists.

There are plenty of war reporters who are in the business for the drama and excitement, but Foley wasn't one of them. He was in it because he believed deeply in the need to record the stories of those who were suffering, regardless of the risk. As he said in an interview after his first abduction, 'There is physical courage, but that's nothing compared to moral courage. If we don't have that moral courage, we don't have journalism.'

The stories of Foley and Sotloff are important for this book for two reasons: first, because of what they reveal about the way the forces on the other side of the equation – the extremist groups (and Islamic State in particular) – control both the media and the message; and second, because of what they tell us about the way the media itself responds to extremism. Neither tale is particularly edifying.

•

James Foley was the first to be caught. He was in Syria late in 2012 with another journalist, British front-line photographer John Cantlie. In a tragic irony, they had been working together on a story for *GlobalPost* about Cantlie's abduction and dramatic rescue earlier that year. On 22 November, as they left an internet cafe in northern Syria on their way to the Turkish border just a few kilometres away, a group that the FBI later described as an 'organised gang' abducted the pair. It still isn't clear who their captors were – *GlobalPost*'s editor, Philip Balboni, believed the Syrian intelligence services were responsible,[42] and others suspected Islamist rebels. Regardless, somehow the two men found their way into the hands of Islamic State – not an unusual occurrence in an environment where hostages have become a tradable commodity, a kind of currency to be exchanged for goods, favours or cold cash.

Steven Sotloff arrived in Syria some nine months later, on 4 August 2013, crossing the border with his fixer in the other direction, from Turkey. His other companions were a respected operator called Yosef Abobaker, with whom Sotloff had worked before, and Abobaker's cousins, hired as security guards. Abobakar later told CNN that about twenty minutes after they entered the country, fifteen masked gunmen jumped out of three cars and forced them into their vehicles.[43]

Abobaker and his cousins were released after about two weeks, but Sotloff disappeared into Islamic State territory.

Sotloff was a seasoned freelance reporter who worked for a range of respected publications, including *Time*, *Foreign Policy*, *World Affairs* and the *Christian Science Monitor* ('One of the most courageous, talented and insightful journalists that I have met', his editor at the Media Line, Felice Friedson, would later say[44]).

Sotloff's family kept the kidnapping secret for much of the following year, fearing that if it went public it would complicate negotiations to get him out.[45] Efforts to find and free both men took place largely out of public view, and on 12 August, Foley's parents received an email from his captors. The note was not so much an attempt to move negotiations forward as a statement of intent. It was addressed to 'the American government and their sheep-like citizens', and accused the US of refusing to pay ransoms and so passing up 'many chances' to negotiate the release of its nationals. It also said that the US had no motivation to deal with Muslims 'except through the language of force':

> You do not spare our weak, elderly, women or
> children so we will NOT spare yours!
> You and your citizens will
> pay the price of your bombings!
> The first of which will be the
> blood of the American citizen, James Foley!
> He will be executed as a DIRECT result
> of your transgressions towards us!

A week later, on 19 August, IS uploaded a video to YouTube titled 'A message to America'. It starts with President Obama announcing the first US airstrikes against Islamic State in Iraq, and then cuts to Foley kneeling in the desert next to a masked IS figure clad in black, and reading a long message expressing regret. After Foley stops, the executioner condemns the US airstrikes and warns that any aggression by

America 'will result in the bloodshed of your people' before drawing a knife across Foley's throat. The video doesn't show the actual beheading but it soon cuts to a blood-soaked, decapitated corpse lying in the dust. It ends with Foley's executioner declaring that unless the US stops airstrikes against Islamic State, Steven Sotloff will be next.

Anybody in the United States who hadn't already heard of Foley or Sotloff quickly knew about the two men. The image of the reporter with his shaved head kneeling in the desert in an orange jumpsuit and stoically facing the camera moments before his death became one of the most recognised videos in US history, second only to the footage of two planes hitting the Twin Towers in 2011. It marked a moment when the militants showed not only their ruthless brutality, but also their mastery of both social media and traditional news.

Michael Ware is an Australian journalist with more experience of Iraq and its Islamist militants than almost any other reporter. He has the dubious distinction of being one of the few men to survive a kidnapping by Islamic State, and understands the group's thinking remarkably well. Shortly after the video was released, Ware spoke to the Australian Broadcasting Corporation.

'These guys are so savvy when it comes to message,' he said. 'They always have been, in terms of accessing new media and new technology, in crafting the nature of their message. They don't do anything like that without thinking about its import, about the iconography of it, or about the statement behind it.'

The aim, he said, was to make the West look impotent:

> It very much reminds me of the situation that happened to three poor contractors in Iraq in 2004. Two Americans and a Brit, Kenneth Bigley. They were grabbed by [Al Qaeda leader Abu Musab al-] Zarqawi's people. They rolled them out in the videos and said, 'Look, if President Bush and Prime Minister Blair do not withdraw their forces, we will execute these men.' Everyone knew that Bush and Blair were not going to withdraw their forces, but

> one by one they started beheading these guys. With the Brit they left him till last. It seemed to have gone on a little bit longer as if to torment the British prime minister, because who doesn't want to save one of your own nationals? But you know he's just not going to. There's nothing [he] can do. It's a very effective way to stick in the dagger and twist it.
>
> Do you think President Obama is going to cease airstrikes over this? No. He can't. He can't stop. Not now that he's started. And they know that. But it's got you and I talking about it. In fact it's got most of the Western world talking about it.[46]

Three weeks later, IS released a second video showing another execution. This time Sotloff was the victim.

•

That Islamic State has no tolerance for a free media is self-evident. But as I am arguing in this book that governments are overstepping the mark in shutting down journalistic inquiry, I also need to pause on the unapologetically brutal way insurgents have worked to control both the message and the messenger. They have been extraordinarily sophisticated, giving the propaganda war as much emphasis as the physical guns-and-bullets battle.

Undoubtedly Foley and Sotloff were executed because they were Western hostages, but they were also executed because they were journalists. Islamic State was holding other hostages, but they chose to murder these two because, as Ware pointed out, IS understood the twin messages that the killings would send. The first was an assault on the ideal of free inquiry and a warning to every other reporter considering working in the area. The second was that publishing images of the bloody murder of someone they knew would have maximum impact on the victims' friends and colleagues.

These murders revealed how IS media operatives tailored their messages for the very media they were attacking.

This is no accident. IS has invested a vast amount of time and energy in its propaganda machine, even to the point of directing field operations for their impact on the media. An investigation by the *Washington Post* found that senior IS media operatives are treated as 'emirs' and have as much authority and status as front-line commanders, often being involved in decisions on strategy, and staging battles for the sake of the cameras. The *Post* described it as 'the most potent propaganda machine ever assembled by a terrorist group':[47]

> The group exerts extraordinarily tight control over the production of its videos and messages but relies on the chaos of the internet and social media to disseminate them. Its releases cluster around seemingly incompatible themes: sometimes depicting the caliphate as a peaceful and idyllic domain, other times as a society awash in apocalyptic violence.
>
> The dual messages are designed to influence a divided audience. The beheadings, immolations and other spectacles are employed both to menace Western adversaries and to appeal to disenfranchised Muslim males weighing a leap into the Islamist fray.
>
> A separate collection depicts the Islamic State as a liveable destination, a benevolent state committed to public works. Videos show the construction of public markets, smiling religious police on neighbourhood patrols and residents leisurely fishing on the banks of the Euphrates.

IS has clearly understood one fundamental truth that Western governments seem painfully slow to appreciate: that in our modern, highly interconnected world, the internet has become an extension of the battlefield. By using it, Islamic State is taking advantage of the openness of modern communications and turning it against the West. When governments talk of 'cyber warfare', they generally refer to malicious hackers trying to plant computer viruses to destroy things such as nuclear power plants, or to get inside military and intelligence computer systems. But to Islamic State, the cyber war means nothing more complex than using social media to both inspire its followers and terrorise its opponents.

The hideous snuff videos are the most obscene examples, but IS has kept up a barrage of messages on Twitter and Facebook as well. In an impressive study of IS's output over a one-month period from July to August 2015 for the Quilliam foundation, researcher Charlie Winter counted a total of 1146 'separate events' – discrete batches of propaganda – coming out of its media machine. They included photo essays, videos, audio statements, news bulletins, posters, theological essays and more.[48] That already-copious quantity of material is amplified by a virtual army of dedicated supporters around the world who duplicate and circulate the messages from countless bedrooms on every continent, making it almost impossible to control them.

Over half of the videos were related to civilian life in the caliphate. Winter points out that while the spectre of extreme violence was always a part of the output, the emphasis on an idealised image of ordinary life reflected the media unit's strategic priorities.

Winter comes to a number of worrying conclusions in his study. The first is that the sheer volume of propaganda flowing out of Islamic State far exceeds most previous estimates, and that existing efforts to challenge IS propaganda, whether by governments or independent groups, come nowhere close to matching IS's output in either quantity or quality. And so their narrative – or, perhaps more accurately, their mythology – has come to dominate social media in sophisticated ways.

One of the most intriguing examples of IS propaganda was a series of videos and online columns featuring John Cantlie, the British war correspondent who was with Foley when the pair were captured in 2012.

After vanishing for over a year, Cantlie reappeared in a video titled 'Lend me your ears' that IS released a month after Foley's beheading.

He was dressed in the familiar orange jumpsuit but spoke more like a talk-show host than a hostage. Rather than being filmed in the desert with an IS fighter holding a knife to his neck, Cantlie was seated indoors at a desk against a black background under professional-standard lighting, reading a prepared statement denouncing the West's policies in Iraq and Syria.[49]

'After two disastrous and hugely unpopular wars in Afghanistan and Iraq, why is it that our governments appear so keen to get involved in yet another unwinnable conflict?' he asked, before appealing to the British government to negotiate his release.

This turned out to be the first instalment in a series of seven videos featuring Cantlie as a news reporter in local civilian clothing. One released in July 2016 was typical. It appeared to show him walking around the destroyed ruins of a university in Mosul in northern Iraq and asking why the US would spend millions of dollars in weaponry to blow up a civilian institution intended only for education.

The videos were widely circulated online and reported across Western media because they were both familiar and shocking at the same time. They have all the look and feel of a well-produced news report from the BBC or CNN. They are well scripted, carefully shot and professionally edited. Cantlie looks tired and gaunt in the films, but there is no evidence that he has been forced into the role. It is easy to imagine that a group of IS gunmen might be loitering just off-screen to make sure he follows the script and makes no attempt to run, but there was no clear evidence of coercion. The disconnect between seeing someone who looks and sounds familiar – like one of *us* – talking up life in a place we have been told is violent and abusive makes the films disturbingly compelling, especially when we know that only weeks earlier Cantlie's friend and colleague has had his head hacked off. It's the same kind of can't-watch-can't-turn-away effect that a horror movie has.

•

The cases of the missing journalists were widely discussed in prison.

During the interrogations in the earliest weeks of our arrest, we were taken to a holding cell in the basement of the National Security directorate that had the look and feel of a dungeon. At the time, Foley and Cantlie were only rumoured to be missing, and Sotloff's kidnapping had yet to be reported.

The cell was a large concrete box, its walls scarred with graffiti left by hundreds of bored prisoners trying to kill time. For some, it was a simple 'Abdulahi was here'. Others left Qura'nic verses and political slogans.

Sometimes there were dozens of men crowded in, all of us on serious charges related to national security and terrorist offences. Some looked to me to be frightened innocents who had been swept up in police operations hunting for extremists in the slums of Cairo. Others were not only open about their violent hostility to the government but seemed genuinely proud of it.

Many of them carried the marks of torture – some had fresh wounds such as festering acid or cigarette burns; others had older scars from beatings or electrocutions. We were often held there for hours on end in large groups waiting until our interrogators sent word that they were ready for us, and a prisoner's name would be called before they were yanked out of the cell, cuffed and marched up for questioning.

In the meantime, we talked, with someone who spoke English whispering translations to those close to him.

'They [the journalists] should never have gone to Syria,' sneered one self-confessed jihadi. 'I don't know what's happened but they had no business there. They just wanted to spread more lies about Islamic State.'

'They were journalists trying to do their jobs,' I protested. 'They were doing what they're supposed to do, what we're all supposed to do – to go and see for ourselves what is really going on so we can report what we see rather than just what we hear. How can they be punished for that?'

'Impossible. They are Westerners. Christians. They can't understand what Daesh [Islamic State] is trying to do. They hate a place that lives with Islamic ideals, and never understand why that is such a beautiful thing to us. The West is corrupted – so far from what God wants for us that nobody from there will ever understand. They will only say things that make right bombings and killings of innocents. So those journalists who went to Syria – they are just spies, propagandists. Maybe they will be released – for their parents, I hope so – but maybe no.'

'But that is no excuse for kidnap,' I said. 'And if it is such an Islamic utopia, then what's wrong with having others come and see? What are you so afraid of?'

'You never report the truth,' another said. 'You only report what you think your readers want to hear. You only say that we are all murderers and rapists. And yet you ignore the fact that there are so many Muslims from around the world who are going to live in Daesh territory. Why would women come if they are all going to become sex slaves as you report? It's just more propaganda. You think somehow they are brainwashed, but that is even worse racism. It means you think anybody who comes is stupid and can't think for themselves or make their own decisions. Nobody forces them to come. They travel because they believe. They want to live in a place that is free of corruption of the West, but you can't see that and you will never report it.'

I was about to protest when another, friendlier prisoner caught my eye and, with a frown, gestured that I should back off.

A guard slid open the hatch in the door and called a name. The next to be questioned shuffled forward, and the crowd dispersed.

•

When the news of Foley's and Sotloff's executions filtered through, there was widespread sympathy. Despite some of the inmates' bitterness towards the media, those inside the prison recognised the common bond we shared, and all acknowledged the anguish we felt knowing that two of our colleagues had been executed in such a horrific way.

But one prisoner was also exasperated. 'I am sorry that your friends were killed,' he said with genuine feeling, 'but tell me something. Why is it that America calls them terrorists just like Sisi does to you? Why does America get upset and outraged whenever something like that happens? All those jihadis are trying to do is make you feel what Muslims in Iraq or Syria or Afghanistan experience every single day. American drones fly over villages and fire hellfire missiles, and the media says so many terrorists were killed. But they say nothing about all the women and children also murdered. They say nothing about how those families are starving because they can't get food or medicines because of sanctions, or because they keep our countries in war.

'America says this is a War on Terror, but it isn't. That is just an excuse for a war on Islam, and the people who are suffering the most aren't the families in New York or Paris. It is the millions of poor families who are struggling to stay alive every day, and yet when someone has the courage to become a martyr in a suicide mission to make the Americans or the French feel a small fraction of what we go through all the time, you call us the terrorists?'

He was not angry; his tone was matter-of-fact, unemotional. But he was reflecting the logic I had heard time and again: 'Of course those journalists will be treated as spies. We are at war. Why should we expect them ever to tell our side of the story? Why should we trust journalists to report honestly when they are part of the system that is attacking us in the first place?'

Sitting inside a prison overflowing with men who were waiting for their own terrorist trials, it was a hard question to answer.

11

THE CASE FOR THE PROSECUTION

18 MARCH 2014

A hush falls across the courtroom. All I can hear is soft fluttering and chirruping from a small family of swifts that has built a nest in the eaves directly above the judges' bench. The birds twist and dive in the cavernous room, bringing a surreal sense of ordinariness to these mad proceedings.

I settle into a corner of the cage as close as I can to my new translator. The court has at last found a genial former diplomat with good English, and while he isn't allowed inside the cage itself, he is sitting, close enough to whisper a running translation without interrupting things.

An orderly brings the first piece of evidence to the chief judge, Nagy Shehata. It's a large white envelope sealed with wax. The judge runs his finger under the seal and pops the envelope open before upending the contents.

'White envelope containing sixty-three photographs found to belong to defendant number seventeen, Peter Greste,' he announces in a phlegmy voice that sounds as though he has just woken up.

I have no idea where these photos have come from. My best guess is that they are printouts of one of my memory cards, but apart from a few standard tourist pictures I snapped on one of my walks around the city, I can't imagine what else they might have found, or how any of it could be incriminating even to the most dedicated conspiracy theorist.

The next one is a box. The judge fumbles with the knot, and the orderly steps forward, offering a pen to help prise it apart. Tittering ripples across the courtroom as the judge continues to fiddle with the knot, and the creases in his brow deepen into black furrows of frustration. Angrily, Nagy finally reaches for a cigarette lighter and burns the nylon string open with a pop.

'Medium-sized box, containing cables and one video camera,' he declares.

He reaches for another box. 'Medium-sized box, containing studio lights and more cables.'

The next one, I recognise. It's the battered rucksack that has carried my notebooks, laptop, cables and cameras through some of the roughest corners of Africa. 'Small backpack containing computer equipment.'

He pulls out my laptop – a silver MacBook Pro – and lifts the lid. Almost instantly, music echoes across the court from the computer's tinny little speakers, and I have to choke down laughter. It is the same song that I was listening to when the National Security agents burst into my hotel room and slammed the computer closed. It has buffered the song, and now that it is fired up again it simply resumes playing. For all the allegations of colluding with a terrorist organisation, the investigators have never bothered to open my computer.

I can't hold back any longer and let out a loud guffaw. Judge Nagy slams the lid closed before rebuking me for interrupting the proceedings.

And so it continues, box after bag after box, as Nagy compiles a complete inventory of all our kit. There are laptops, cameras, lights, cables, bags, TV screens, tripods, books, hard drives, a satellite phone and videotapes. The court has succeeded in proving that we are journalists, with all the equipment that a television team needs to do its jobs.

Then Nagy up-ends another envelope, this one containing an assortment of thumb drives, a few cables and what looks like a phone.

'One BlackBerry mobile phone, belonging to Peter Greste,' he says.

'That's not mine!' I shout. 'I have an iPhone!'

As far as I know, Fahmy is the only member of the team who has a BlackBerry. I have no idea what is on Fahmy's phone, but I know there will be a lot of photos, emails and messages that, if the prosecution believes it is mine, could make it look as though I was in Egypt at a time when in fact I was abroad.

'Silence!' Nagy retorts, before returning the phone to the envelope. 'One BlackBerry mobile phone, belonging to Peter Greste.'

•

The first witness is the Homeland Security investigator Major Ahmed Ayoub Mohamed Hussein, who led the operation to monitor our movements and raid our rooms. His report is the foundation for the prosecution's case.

The judge orders the cameras to be turned to the back of the court to protect Hussein's identity, but there is no mistaking the slightly pot-bellied, chinless leather-jacketed figure who makes his way down the steps to stand before the bench with his back to the public gallery and his hands clasped in front.

Fahmy's lawyer, Khaled Abu Bakr, is first to cross-examine, aiming questions at the back of Hussein's head.

Hussein says he investigated us because he'd been told we had cooperated with the banned Al Jazeera Mubasher Misr satellite channel. This is, of course, nonsense – Al Jazeera English was always careful to maintain both managerial and editorial independence from Al Jazeera's Arabic-language 24-hour news service. We have expected them to try to link the two organisations, and if that's the best they can do, this will be a very short trial.

Hussein's further allegations rely on 'secret sources' he won't reveal, but that he claims prove that we were running what amounted to a propaganda office for the Muslim Brotherhood from the Marriott. He alleges that we hosted meetings with MB figures at the hotel and manufactured false stories designed to undermine national security and further the MB's aims.

Of course we interviewed Muslim Brotherhood figures, as we did leaders and spokespeople from across Egypt's political spectrum. But we also deliberately never brought controversial interview subjects to the hotel because it might expose them, and us, to just this kind of attention.

The major's testimony is full of contradictions. While he acknowledges I first arrived in Cairo in December, he also alleges I was active in the infamous Rabaa and al-Nahda protests here six months earlier.

Then, under cross-examination, he appears to suffer from amnesia, regularly claiming he can't recall the details of his evidence and saying, 'I do not recall that and I stick to my statements in the investigations'.

My earlier smugness evaporates, and I can feel the fury rise in my throat.

Rabaa al-Adawiya was one of the bloodiest and most contentious outbreaks of violence between supporters of the Muslim Brotherhood and the Egyptian government in recent history. Accounts of what happened vary so wildly that it is almost impossible to know exactly what took place on 14 August 2013, but it was indisputably horrific.

After the military forced Mohamed Morsi from power on 3 July, MB supporters began to occupy two squares in Cairo, one outside the Rabaa al-Adawiya mosque near the Nasr City district, and a second, al-Nahda Square, in Giza on the southern edge of the capital.

What began as a protest quickly became a sit-in, with demonstrators vowing to stay put until Morsi was restored to the presidency. As the days stretched into weeks, Rabaa Square in particular grew to become a fully-fledged community, with shops, barbers, medical centres and even its own television station.

The camps became flashpoints for outbreaks of violence between pro- and anti-Morsi demonstrators, and although there were numerous attempts to negotiate a settlement, after six weeks the government issued an ultimatum: leave the squares or be forced out.

Nobody is quite sure how the shooting began, but on 14 August there was a bloodbath – what Human Rights Watch would call 'one of the world's largest killings of demonstrators in a single day in recent history'.[50]

The troops who surrounded Rabaa al-Adawiya Square claim that Muslim Brotherhood gunmen were hiding in the crowd and opened fire first, before the troops could move in with tear gas and water cannons; the protesters insist it was an unprovoked massacre of largely unarmed civilians. Whatever the truth, when the smoke cleared, the square was awash with dead and wounded.

The Egyptian Ministry of Health said 595 protesters were killed along with forty-three government troops. Human Rights Watch said, 'Security forces, following a plan that envisioned several thousand deaths, killed a minimum of 817 people and more likely at least 1000.'[51]

But the Muslim Brotherhood says those reports massively understate the death toll: it says about 2500 people were gunned down. And nobody has been held to account. It has become such a point of contention that 'Rabaa' is now shorthand – literally – for all that the MB is angry about. Its supporters have taken to waving a four-fingered salute, a play on the Arabic word for the number four, *arba'a*. They use it as a gesture of both protest at the government and solidarity with the victims, and the government has taken to arresting anybody waving it.

The Muslim Brotherhood supporters paid a high price, but so too did the media. Among those who died were four journalists, including Australian cameraman Mick Deane, who was working for Sky News. Deane was wearing a flak jacket and helmet and carrying a camera, which clearly identified him as a media worker, but witnesses said it appeared that a sniper still picked him out and shot him in the head. At least six other journalists were wounded that day, while *The Guardian*'s Patrick Kingsley, Abigail Hauslohner of the *Washington Post*, Alastair Beach from *The Independent*, the *Wall Street Journal*'s Matt Bradley, and McClatchy's Nancy Youssef were all threatened by Egyptian security forces or civilians. Soon after, the authorities raided the offices of Al Jazeera Arabic and forced it to close. One of its reporters, Abdullah al-Shami, was arrested, and as we stand in the dock, he is still in prison awaiting his own trial.

While the Egyptian government denied specifically going after foreign reporters, it released a statement complaining of 'feeling severe bitterness towards some Western media coverage that is biased to the Muslim Brotherhood and ignores shedding light on violent and terror acts that are perpetrated by this group in the form of intimidation operations and terrorising citizens'.[52]

The statement went on to criticise foreign media for failing to describe Morsi's ouster by the military as anything other than an expression of popular will, and for failing to highlight alleged links between the Muslim Brotherhood and Al Qaeda.

By trying to place me in Rabaa, Major Hussein is trying to make me part of what the authorities have cast as a pro-MB conspiracy. Except that at the time, I was watching the story unfold on a television screen in Juba, the capital of South Sudan.

When Judge Nagy finally bangs his gavel to deny us bail and declare the case adjourned for three more weeks, once again I slump in disbelief.

•

On the drive in the caged van back to our cell, we sit in silence as both excitement and anger churn within me.

What upsets me is the whole casual, sloppy nature of the investigation, which has holes so big that you could drive a herd of camels through them. Nothing is precise. It is so full of unsubstantiated assumptions and has so little detail and so many bizarre conclusions that the judges ought to toss the whole thing out to save any further embarrassment. And yet we remain in prison. Our fate is in the hands of an intellectually lazy, unprofessional fool of an investigator and the judges who beam down at him like doting grandparents.

Back in our cell, this time I'm the one who is unusually wound up. Baher and Fahmy stretch out on their beds in resignation, but I stride up and down the tiny space trying to settle my fury. I'm so angry that my thoughts can't move beyond the most basic of questions.

Four paces. Turn. Four paces. Turn. Four paces. Turn . . .

How could anybody take Hussein seriously?

Four paces. Turn. Four paces. Turn. Four paces. Turn . . .

How could anybody destroy the lives of others with such casual abandon?

Four paces. Turn. Four paces. Turn.

My eyes are focused only on the space where my next step will fall. Fahmy and Baher stare at the ceiling from their own beds until eventually I simmer down enough to climb up to my bunk, arrange a pillow, and sit cross-legged with my eyes shut.

I sleep, but only just. After what feels like a couple of hours of fitful half-sleep, I can hear Fahmy stir in his bunk. His bulk rises in the dim light that filters in from the hall outside and he begins shuffling up and down the track I left hours earlier, walking with heavy breaths. He works his right shoulder, his left hand resting on the muscle to ease the pain.

Eventually he returns to his bed, rolls onto his good shoulder and draws the sheet up to his chin.

Now it's Baher's turn. The bunk rattles beneath me as he climbs out and leans against the wall, with his face to the grille in the iron door. There's the snap of a lighter and I glimpse his gritted face in the brief flare of yellow flame. He draws deeply on his cigarette and watches the smoke curl through the bars.

It is a long night for all of us, and the next morning we are all short-tempered. As soon as the guards open the door for our hour of exercise

I bolt out, not wanting to talk, and stride around the dusty yard in a steady jog. The days are getting warmer now, and although it's not yet Sahara-desert hot, the sun has a sting in it that I haven't noticed before.

Just as I am finding my rhythm, Fahmy waves me down.

'I think we need to go after Fawzy,' he says.

Mohamed Fawzy is the cameraman the National Security agents picked up on the same night as us. Somehow he was released the next day and made it out of the country to Qatar.

'What are you saying? That Fawzy bribed his way out?' I ask.

'No, I think he did a deal. I think he's ratted on us. Why else would he have been released? The prosecutor obviously thinks he's got something over us, and if Fawzy bought off just the police, there's no way he would have made it through immigration and out of the country. He'd have been picked up at the airport.'

'But we don't know that,' I say, with more than a little exasperation creeping into my voice. 'We don't have enough to accuse him of anything, and even if it's true, I don't see how going after him is going to help our cause. All we're doing is defaming Fawzy on pretty flimsy circumstantial evidence.'

'But we've got to show how corrupt they are. It's a good way to undermine the integrity of the evidence,' he says.

'I still reckon that our best strategy is to stick to the moral high ground. Everybody, including the judges, can see that the case is bullshit. If they're going to convict us, it's because they've already decided to screw us. Dragging Fawzy into it all won't make a blind bit of difference.'

Fahmy gets angry.

'We've got to do it,' he growls. 'And I don't care what you think. I'm going on my own in this. I've got to look after myself. I'm not with you or anybody else, and I'm not going to throw away my future just to be nice.'

I argue with him, but he is set in his decision. It fills me with anxiety. The idea of publicly taking down one of our own colleagues seems to me more than unnecessary – it strikes me as dangerous.

Until now, our whole case has been seen as an attack on press freedom by an overbearing, paranoid government, and that is a fight we can win with widespread international support. If we start talking about traitors in our midst, the media attention could move to something entirely irrelevant to the bigger issues, making the story about our own disputes rather than about human rights.

Through the rest of the week, the pressure builds as we struggle to resolve the debate. Fahmy holds heated conversations with Baher in Arabic in the corner of our cell. It annoys me at first, but I am soon grateful for the fact that I can't get involved in the argument even if I want to.

Then, just as it feels as though the tension in the cell is becoming unbearable, there is sweet relief. I'm called to the office for an official visit. It's the Australian consular officer Erika Tolano, and when I walk into the room she stands, a huge grin splitting her face.

'We've had a breakthrough,' she says. 'The Interior Ministry has finally agreed to let you have some reading material. It only happened yesterday, so I'm sorry but we haven't had time to get you anything more than these.'

She gestures at a small pile of newspapers and magazines resting on a coffee table. There are several editions of the *New York Times, The Economist* and the *Guardian Weekly*. It is crack cocaine to a news junkie like me, and I can't help but do a little happy dance.

'It may take a bit of time because it all has to be cleared by the ministry, but we're trying to get you some books as well. Is there anything you'd like?' Erika asks.

Answers tumble out of me like a burst bag of oranges: regional politics, history, philosophy, any classic novels, some new novels as well, perhaps some adventure stories to keep us distracted. 'And I'd love some good science fiction. Any great Australian authors like Tim Winton would be fantastic too. Oh, and I'm always into a good biography, and what about some crime novels.'

Erika allows herself a grin.

'Let's stay away from romance and anything scary,' I say. 'Those are the last things we need here. But really, I don't care what you get. Bring the whole damned bookshop if they'll let it in.'

On the way back to the cell I can hardly contain my excitement, and when the guards open the door I dump my armful of papers on the floor with a loud thwack.

'It's Christmas, boys!' I declare. 'Or Eid, or whatever festival you like most for handing out presents.'

We pounce on the papers like a pack of starving hyenas and settle down to wallow in news. We read each paper cover to cover, chewing over the politics and international pages. We digest the financial pages, the house-and-garden sections and the cooking. We even linger over the ads. I roll about in the sudoku like a pig in mud, and though I hate crosswords I grit my teeth and sweat through the *New York Times* puzzle. For once in the room, all you can hear is the satisfying shuffle of papers and the occasional sigh or grunt or smirk at the latest unexpected development.

•

The next two hearings are a waste of time. In the first, on 24 March, the prosecution calls four more 'technical witnesses', who testify that we were holding 'unlicensed equipment' – computers, a BlackBerry mobile phone, a satellite telephone and Final Cut Pro editing software.

The sat-phone is a potential problem. We needed it for those times when the mobile network collapses, but it sits in a grey area: it is not technically against the law to hold one, but the working assumption in Middle East legal systems is that unless something is specifically allowed, it is illegal. At the most, though, it shouldn't attract anything more than a fine.

The rest of the kit is standard equipment that anybody can get off the shelf, and our lawyers try to show the court that the case against us is becoming more irrelevant and ridiculous with each subsequent witness.

Once again we ask for bail, and once again it is denied. The judge orders technicians to set up the court to view video evidence in the next hearing, and adjourns the case for another week.

When we walk back into court after the week's break, we are expecting big screens, video projectors and loudspeakers so we can see what the prosecution claims is the 'false news' in the charges. Instead, the room looks exactly as it has for every one of the previous sessions.

When the judges enter, a titter ripples across the courtroom. Judge Nagy Shehata is wearing dark glasses, and although it's hard to read his demeanour through them, I'm sure he is hungover. 'Where is the technical expert with the equipment?' he demands once they're seated. 'I told him to have everything ready so we can proceed with the trial.'

The prosecutor looks sheepish. 'I'm sorry, your honour. We don't know. We told him to be here, but he seems to have vanished.'

'Have him arrested,' he orders.

Then Fahmy stands, and with his fingers pressed through the bars of the cage he shouts across the room, demanding the right to address the court in person. With a sigh, Nagy tells the guards to open the cage and lead all of us out. In the absence of the technician, there isn't much else to do. We walk out and stand in front of the bench, our backs turned to the public gallery.

I can hear camera shutters snapping like a flock of hungry seagulls and can't resist turning to glance at the press pack as my face splits into a grin. (A friend would later tweet an image of me with my smirking head turned to the photographers, captioning it 'Greste shows how to photobomb a kangaroo court'.)

Each of us makes an appeal to the judge, explaining why the case against us is ridiculous and why we ought to be allowed out.

The students complain about the conditions of their cell in Scorpion Prison, and argue that they are just a bunch of passionate young men who happened to be caught in a police sweep.

Fahmy argues that he is a patriot who celebrated the fall of Hosni

Mubarak but supported the military when it ousted Mohamed Morsi and the Muslim Brotherhood. He says he enjoys dating women and drinking alcohol and is ideologically as far from an Islamist as it is possible to get.

Baher talks passionately about his pregnant wife and emphasises how much he wants to be reunited with his family.

Then it is my turn.

'My name is Peter Greste,' I say, pausing to give the court-appointed interpreter time to keep up. 'I arrived in Egypt two weeks prior to my arrest. As you can see I require a translator – I speak no Arabic. The idea that I have any association with the Muslim Brotherhood or work for an Arabic-language media organisation is preposterous. I believe the records held by the court and in my travel documents also show that I have not been to any place where I would develop a relationship with this group.

'Your honour, we have not been charged with any crimes of violence and nor were we found with weapons. We have no personal or criminal records of violence. I would like to emphasise that we pose no risk to the state of Egypt or to any individuals. Our only desire at this point is to continue to fight to clear our names outside prison. Our lawyers have made it clear that we are more than willing to accept any conditions your honour imposes as we see this trial to its conclusion.'

When we return to the cage, we can barely contain our excitement. It feels as though the judges are warming to us, willing to listen openly and with perhaps a tiny degree of empathy. I think I even saw Judge Nagy allow himself a brief smile through his dark glasses.

But when they resume their seats, Nagy orders us to remain in custody and sends us back to prison until the next hearing, ten days away.

•

The books in our cell have helped relieve some of the pressure. They give us a place to retreat to and help take our minds out of the box. The embassy officials bring in a few volumes every time they visit, but my brothers also spend a lot of their free time in one of Cairo's few English-language bookshops.

One book is a small, modest paperback that has an outsized impact on my approach to what we are going through.

Man's Search for Meaning is an extraordinary philosophical reflection on life by Viktor Frankl, one of the few Jews who survived the Nazi death camps during the Second World War. He made it through four of them, including the infamous Auschwitz.

If anybody was qualified to understand the way that hardship and suffering transform a person's view of the world, it was Frankl. He was an astute and intelligent observer of human behaviour who used his training as a psychiatrist and neurologist to study why some made it through the horror of the camps and others did not.

His key insight was the idea that to search for 'the meaning of life' is to ask the wrong question. It might well be true that a 'meaning' exists externally to us, whether it is in God or Allah, or Buddha, or Mother Earth, or tarot cards, but you can never be certain you have found it.

For Frankl, the better question was to ask how we can apply meaning to the questions life asks of *us*, especially when they involve suffering.

For some of Frankl's co-survivors, their family gave meaning to the horror they were experiencing. The idea that they simply *had* to get through the war alive so that they might search and care for their loved ones was all the meaning they needed. For others, survival was itself a form of resistance against a fundamentally evil regime. In each case the source of meaning was not abstract, but concrete and tangible. It didn't rest in a belief in heaven and hell, or in God's benevolence. It didn't require any great leap of faith into the unknowable assertions of theology.

Frankl found profound truth in a quote from Friedrich Nietzsche, who said, 'Those who have a "why" to live can bear with almost any "how".' He then wrote: 'In some way, suffering ceases to be suffering at the moment it finds a meaning.'

On reading that, I go back to the insight I had in Lumen, that our imprisonment was never personal. The gap between what we are accused of doing and what we actually did is so vast that it could never be about us as individuals. Instead, it has to be about something much bigger – about what we have come to represent. And to my mind, the only thing I can think of is an attempt by the government to suppress freedom of the press and, more broadly, freedom of speech itself.

Suddenly, I find great comfort in our situation. The idea that we have come to stand for something much larger than ourselves means that we have to fight on behalf of that bigger thing. It isn't just Peter Greste, Mohamed Fahmy and Baher Mohamed who are in the cage – it is every journalist working in Egypt. More broadly, it is every journalist working within any regime that considers using these kinds of tactics to silence public debate and critical voices.

Defending that cause is not just a heavy responsibility – it is a hugely empowering one.

As I contemplate all this on my bunk in our cell, I read one more of Frankl's thoughts: 'Everything can be taken from a man but one thing: the last of the human freedoms – to choose one's attitude in any given set of circumstances, to choose one's own way.'

•

At last, the courtroom looks as though it is ready to show us some vision. Two big screens have been rigged up on either side of the judges' bench, and a couple of projectors sit on tables in front of them.

This is the moment we've been waiting for. I am relishing the thought of defending my journalism. I am looking forward to arguing each story through, line by line if necessary. Of course there is always a chance that we might have got one or two details wrong, though I can't even begin to guess what they might be, but even if we have, the prosecutor still has to prove that those errors were both intentional *and* damaging to national security. And that is a very high bar indeed.

Once more the judges take their seats and call the court to order.

The technician who should have been ready with his equipment at the last hearing sheepishly steps forward and inserts the first thumb drive into his computer. He moves the cursor around the screen and, as a hush falls across the court, presses play.

To describe what is shown, it is hard to beat the Australian Embassy's internal report to Canberra for diplomatic brevity as dry as the Sahara:

> The following evidence was screened which was taken from a flash drive in Mr Greste's backpack:
>
> - Kenyan government press conference regarding the 'Westgate' incident.
> - 10 seconds of unidentifiable footage from Kenya.
> - Two still photos of Mr Greste's parents.
> - Mr Greste's award-winning 'Somalia' documentary (of which several minutes were viewed).
>
> The judge noted that it was not possible to watch anything more, as the correct equipment for specific file types had not been provided today.

We are sent back to the cells until the next hearing in twelve days.

12

PRESS FREEDOM IN THE LAND OF THE FREE

The United States has never quite been able to arrange a perfect marriage of its noble founding principles to its daily practice. Every time an American leader wags a finger at a despot over human-rights abuses or undemocratic behaviour, cries of hypocrisy follow.

It happened when President Obama stood at the podium at the end of a summit of American and African leaders and called on Egypt to let us go. 'In the specific issue of the Al Jazeera journalists, we have been clear both publicly and privately [that] they should be released,' Obama told the news conference.

While the Egyptian media couldn't ignore his statement, they dismissed it as the ranting of an imperialist power determined to interfere in the judicial system of another country while at the same time claiming that its own judiciary was free of political influence.

As with so many other developments, this filtered in through the prison walls, relayed by a sympathetic guard who heard it on his transistor radio. It was a huge moment for us – the leader of the Free World publicly rebuking Egypt for our imprisonment. We embraced and high-fived, knowing that whatever Egypt's media commentators said, Obama's statement must have an impact on Sisi, who by then had been elected president and who repeatedly presented himself as a democrat exercising the will of his people.

As Obama told the news conference, it wasn't the first time the US government had spoken in our support. The president had instructed his staff in the National Security Council and the State Department that in any meetings with Egyptian officials, our case should be the first item on the agenda. Obama might not be able to get us out of prison, but he wanted to make sure it would always remain a point of friction that the Egyptians would have to deal with. Although none of us were American citizens, the president saw our case as a useful opportunity to keep up pressure on the Egyptian government over its human-rights record and its lack of due process.

His remarks carried weight because of the moral authority that the United States presidency had established over the two centuries since the country was founded on the classical liberal values of individual freedom, democracy and the rule of law. It has often failed to live up to those ideals, of course, and every president standing in a pulpit to lecture other leaders has been rightly accused of hypocrisy. It turns out that a perfect alignment of a state with those ideals is impossible in a messy, complex world.

But their *power* has often helped the US push corrupt and abusive regimes towards better behaviour, and has inspired resistance among people living under the heels of dictators, often more effectively than the American military could ever have achieved alone.

'The Berlin Wall didn't come down because people were responding to American howitzers,' a former senior State Department official, Joseph Nye, told the *New York Times*. 'It came down under hammers and bulldozers wielded by people whose minds had been affected by the ideas of the West.'[53]

We will never know what ultimately pushed the Egyptian authorities to finally release us from prison, but the pressure from Washington undoubtedly played a significant role.

•

This chapter, however, will present a different angle of Obama's presidency and its relationship with the press. At the risk of sounding ungrateful, I want to show that despite his appearance as a glowing beacon of liberal values, Obama's administration in fact helped to cloud the media's ability to see into the workings of government to a greater extent even than that of his predecessor, George W. Bush.

In fact, before President Trump assumed office, some of America's most experienced media figures came to the startling conclusion that Obama was the leader who had done more to restrict press freedom than any other in the nation's history. When I spoke to him in 2017, James C. Goodale told me, 'President Obama will surely pass President Richard Nixon as the worst president ever on issues of national security and press freedom.' (President Trump – re-elected in November 2024 – may well claim that title, but more on that later.)

Goodale had reason to know: he was the *New York Times*' legal counsel who helped defend the newspaper against Nixon's attacks over releasing the *Pentagon Papers* in 1971.

As we have already seen, the rot set in around 9/11. Not only did it create a binary 'with us or against us' culture that made it incredibly difficult for anyone, including journalists, to challenge the US government's approach to the War on Terror, but it also triggered a rapid build-up of intelligence agencies, special military forces, covert operations and private contractors that together created what the *Washington Post* would later describe as 'top secret America'. In a special investigation that surveyed the extent of the US's security network, the *Post* found a total of 3984 federal, state and local agencies working on domestic counterterrorism alone. Of those, 934 were created or became involved in counterterrorism after 9/11. Nobody is entirely sure how much it all costs or how many people the agencies employ, but the *Post* estimated that around 850 000 people – more than one and a half times the population of Washington, DC itself – have top-secret security clearances. In total, some four million people have some kind of security clearance.[54]

Apart from an expansive and confused network of agencies with overlapping mandates and duplication, this has created a culture of secrecy in government that is at odds with America's foundational principles of democratic openness and accountability, and where the press is able to play its role as public watchdog. The founding fathers thought it so important that the first amendment they made to the constitution was a clause forbidding the government to pass any law that limited freedom of the press in any way. (Thomas Jefferson, who had a famously fractious relationship with the press, said, 'Were it left to me to decide whether we should have a government without newspapers, or newspapers without a government, I should not hesitate a moment to prefer the latter.')

The obsession with security, secrecy and war was not the fault of the government alone though: in the wave of patriotism that followed 9/11, many journalists suspended their usual scepticism and accepted the jingoism of the Bush administration, backing many of its policies in the War on Terror without question.

At the time, it all seemed perfectly natural. How could you *not* take sides in the wake of 9/11? How could an American journalist see those behind the attacks as anything other than terrorists, mass murderers and criminals? To be other than unquestioningly supportive of the government would have looked downright treasonous.

In hindsight, though, it is clear that the media lost its moral and ethical compass, with catastrophic consequences.

The most obvious failure surrounds the intelligence that the Bush administration used to justify the invasion of Iraq in 2003. The American government's accusation that Saddam Hussein had weapons of mass destruction was so frequently repeated that the abbreviation WMD was almost universally understood. In a stinging piece for CNN marking the tenth anniversary of the invasion, Howard Kurtz wrote: 'Major news organisations aided and abetted the Bush administration's march to war on what turned out to be faulty premises. All too often, skepticism was checked at the door, and the shaky claims of top officials and unnamed sources were trumpeted as fact.'[55]

Kurtz found that from August 2002 until the war began on 19 March the following year, more than 140 front-page stories focused heavily on the US administration's rhetoric against Iraq: 'Cheney says Iraqi strike is justified', for example; 'War cabinet argues for Iraq attack'; 'Bush tells United Nations it must stand up to Hussein or US will'; 'Bush cites urgent Iraqi threat'; 'Bush tells troops: Prepare for war'. By contrast, pieces questioning the evidence or rationale for war were frequently buried, minimised or spiked altogether.

As the war began, however, a few courageous journalists started to question and challenge the government more rigorously. In May 2003, as the government continued to insist that the search for WMDs was going well, *Washington Post* reporter Barton Gellman, who was travelling with the invading troops, detailed how the US taskforce had been unable to find any evidence that the weapons existed.[56] The following year, Seymour Hersh challenged the idea that the war was being fought in line with America's respect for human rights. In a piece for the *New Yorker* magazine, he exposed the widespread abuse and torture of prisoners by US soldiers at Abu Ghraib prison in Iraq.[57] Then, in 2006, James Risen from the *New York Times* upset the government further by publishing a book in which he exposed a failed CIA operation to sabotage Iran's nuclear program.[58]

It all created a sense of animosity between the Bush administration and what it eventually came to regard as a hostile press. But crucially, the administration reacted to that hostility by stepping up its efforts to sell the war and its security policies rather than shutting down media access altogether. It largely kept the doors to government open. 'Access was a routine matter,' columnist David Ignatius told the Committee to Protect Journalists.[59]

But when Obama moved into the White House, that already complex relationship quickly started to unravel.

•

The Espionage Act had been passed during the First World War to deal with anybody caught spying for foreign enemies. It had been rarely used since the end of that war until Obama's inauguration almost one-hundred years later. His administration invoked the act more times than that of all his predecessors combined. It might have been understandable at this time of conflict, but the people being prosecuted weren't spies giving the locations of US troops to Islamic State fighters or revealing secret codes to Russians. They were alerting the press to government wrongdoing, corruption or mismanagement.

A Hebrew linguist leaked transcripts of FBI wiretaps of the Israeli embassy that revealed nothing particularly sensitive except the embarrassing fact that the FBI was snooping on one of the US's staunchest allies. A decorated air-force officer and former National Security Agency executive went to the *Baltimore Sun* to expose what he believed was gross mismanagement within the NSA, and a State Department analyst gave a Fox News reporter an internal assessment of North Korea's likely hostile reaction to sanctions.

In each of those cases, the government prosecuted the leaker. Genuinely classified information was revealed only in one case, but even then the prosecution was unable to explain how it damaged national security. In none of the cases did anybody send anything to the enemy or place either the country or individuals at risk. Despite this, the Obama administration went after people who were doing their duty as public servants by exposing serious problems in the departments they worked in. The government generally avoided prosecuting the journalists themselves – who are protected by the free press principles enshrined in the First Amendment – but it did go after their sources.

Frequently, the government tried to obtain information far beyond a single leak. In 2013, the Associated Press's president and chief executive, Gary Pruitt, wrote to the attorney general, Eric Holder, to complain about the Department of Justice's secret subpoena of fax and phone lines for twenty of its reporters in an attempt to find the source of yet another embarrassing leak. Pruitt wrote: 'These records potentially reveal communications with confidential sources across all of the newsgathering activities undertaken by the AP during a two-month period, provide a road map to AP's newsgathering operations, and disclose information about AP's activities and operations that the government has no conceivable right to know.'[60]

In another case, the FBI used metadata to build a picture of communications between a Fox News journalist and a State Department analyst on a story about North Korea. The story 'revealed' the hardly surprising judgement that Pyongyang might lash out at any attempt to punish it for further nuclear tests, as it had often done in the past. Yet the FBI once again reached for the Espionage Act to prosecute the leaker.

Was that information important to the public? Was it helpful for people to know about both North Korea's nuclear weapons program and the thinking of State Department analysts? Was it right to have an open discussion about the ways in which the North Koreans might respond to any sanctions?

The answer to those questions must surely be an overwhelming yes.

The whole point of an effective democracy is to hold these kinds of discussions in public, to give people of all stripes a chance to weigh in with a range of opinions and assessments, and come to a broad consensus based on expert opinion and rigorous questioning. It is what the English philosopher John Stuart Mill argued in his famous treatise *On Liberty*, published in 1859. In his essay, Mill points out that the only way to be sure we have made the right choice in any situation is to test it against all the alternatives, and with access to all the facts. That can't happen without genuine freedom of speech, and in a democracy it requires a media that is free to interrogate all the arguments and protagonists.

It isn't always efficient, and anybody who has scanned the tabloids or followed debates on Twitter will know that it isn't always particularly edifying, but hundreds of years of experience suggest that openness and accountability are what keep democracies stable and functional.

This is not to suggest that every document the government produces should be freely available on the internet or that every analysis should be out in the public domain, but the starting position must surely be that unless national security is demonstrably at risk the public has a right to know, and that journalists therefore have a responsibility to investigate and report, and to speak to government experts, even if (*especially* if) those experts' assessments contradict the politicians. It is one of the reasons the courts have upheld in countless legal cases the right of journalists to protect their sources.

Of course, we will never know how many whistles have *not* been blown because government employees feared being charged as a spy. You can't prove a negative, after all. But the US Society of Professional Journalists has surveyed reporters across the country over the years and discovered a much broader trend towards the closing-down of government sources, whether related to security issues or not.

In the CPJ report from 2013, the *Washington Post*'s national security reporter, Rajiv Chandrasekaran, said, 'One of the most pernicious effects is the chilling effect created across government on matters that are less sensitive but certainly in the public interest as a check on government and elected officials. It serves to shield and obscure the business of government from necessary accountability.'

And getting behind that shield is surely the point of the media.

The author of the CPJ report, former executive editor of the *Washington Post* Leonard Downie Jr, said Obama's war on leaks and other efforts to control information was 'the most aggressive I've seen since the Nixon administration, when I was one of the editors involved in the *Washington Post*'s investigation of Watergate'.

Obama did not rewrite the rules, but he broke with a long tradition of accepting whistleblowers in all but the most serious of national security cases. He radically narrowed the government's understanding of what counts as justifiable leaking. The *New York Times*' lawyer

James Goodale was particularly scathing, saying, 'Until President Obama came into office, no one thought talking or emailing was not protected by the First Amendment.'

•

When it comes to media freedom, Obama's legacy lingers. In an article for the *New York Times*, James Rosen (who won a seven-year battle to protect his sources that went all the way to the Supreme Court) wrote: 'Mr Obama's record of going after both journalists and their sources has set a dangerous precedent that [President] Trump can easily exploit.'[61]

While Obama at least paid lip service to the principles of open and accountable government and publicly acknowledged the importance of a free press, Trump has openly attacked the media and its role in public life in what some of America's most respected media freedom advocates have described as the most serious threat to the press in a generation.

It might look alarming to American journalist groups, but as a person who has worked in some of the world's most oppressive places, to me Trump's strategy also looks disconcertingly familiar. In broad terms, there are four parts to the strategy, and Trump has followed each of them as if it was lifted from a textbook written by despots in Latin America and Africa.

The first is to berate unfriendly media and turn the public against it. That began long before he was first elected in 2016, with Trump posting a seemingly endless avalanche of tweets throughout the presidential campaign. Here is a sample of just some of the adjectives and phrases that routinely found their way into his tweets about the media: 'disgusting', 'incompetent', 'irrelevant', 'worthless', 'nasty', 'pure scum', 'boring', 'dumb', 'total disaster', 'sick', 'garbage' and 'fake news'. He repeatedly described the *New York Times* as 'failing' and the *Washington Post* as 'totally dishonest'. CNN became the 'Clinton News Network'. At countless election rallies he publicly vilified reporters, often leading the crowd in booing the press corps covering the event. And while Trump himself always stopped short of incitement (though calling the media 'the lowest form of humanity' comes close), he also never condemned those attacking the gathered reporters more aggressively. One of his supporters felt emboldened enough to wear a T-shirt emblazoned with the words 'Rope. Tree. Reporter. Some assembly required.'[62]

To many in the media, Trump overstepped the mark when in June 2017, he tweeted a short video of himself in a staged stunt at a 'WrestleMania' event from several years previously. In the video, Trump is seen body-slamming and beating a man with the CNN logo digitally pasted over his face. In his tweet, Trump used a hashtag, '#FNN' – 'Failing News Network'.

It was a joke, of course, but to many in the media, it seemed to be yet another tasteless example of a president not just giving license to the media's critics to physically beat them up, but metaphorically doing it himself.

At one of the most important conservative events of the American calendar, the Conservative Political Action Conference held just outside Washington, DC, Trump told his audience, 'I want you all to know that we are fighting the fake news. It's fake, phony, fake. A few days ago I called the fake news the enemy of the people. And they are. They are the enemy of the people.'

Then he warned, 'We are going to do something about it.'[63]

It all had disturbing echoes of Augusto Pinochet, Chile's right-wing dictator, who dismissed aggressive reporters as 'communist lackeys' peddling 'lies intended to embolden the leftists and weaken the resolve of the state'.[64]

Pinochet went on to introduce Article 6(b) of the State Security Law, which imposed harsh sanctions on 'those who defame, slander, or libel the President of the Republic, Ministers of State, Senators or Deputies, members of the superior courts, Commanders-in-Chief of the Armed Forces, or the Director General of the National Police'.

Article 6(b) became one of Pinochet's most powerful tools in silencing anyone who criticised him or his government.

That's the second part of the strategy – to use libel and sedition laws to build judicial fences around the media's work. The law is always presented as a legitimate means to protect victims of the press over-reach, but the legal definitions tend to be deliberately vague, making it easy to prosecute.

At a rally early in his campaign, Trump declared that if he was elected, he would 'open up our libel laws so when they write purposely negative and horrible and false articles, we can sue them and win lots of money'. Later he tweeted, 'My lawyers want to sue the failing @nytimes so badly for irresponsible intent. I said no (for now), but they are watching. Really disgusting.'

The threats to sue were related to a *New York Times* story about two women who had accused Trump of making unwanted sexual advances.[65] The newspaper defended its reporting and told Trump's lawyer: 'We welcome the opportunity to have a court set him straight'. A court case would have involved further witnesses and the prospect of the president's sexual history being dragged into the open, and he did not follow through with legal action. But he has repeated warnings that he wants to stiffen libel laws to make it easier for people (presumably including himself) to take media organisations to court for their reporting. It is highly unlikely that he could make good on that threat, either. Libel is dealt with under state law, so the federal government can't set the rules. But Trump's warnings remain as a form of intimidation.

A third part of the strategy is to control media access.

When some of the country's most respected news organisations critically reported on his campaign or had the temerity to fact-check his public statements, Trump's campaign managers denied them press credentials. The list of those shut out included the *Washington Post*, BuzzFeed, Politico, the *Huffington Post*, the *Daily Beast*, Univision and the *Des Moines Register*.

Then, once Trump was in the White House, Press Secretary Sean Spicer cancelled a formal press conference and replaced it with an informal briefing known as a gaggle, before again excluding a collection of media organisations. This time, the group included CNN, the *New York Times*, Politico, the *Los Angeles Times*, BuzzFeed and the BBC.[66] Spicer let through right-wing news outlets such as the avowedly pro-Trump website Breitbart News, the *Washington Times* and the One America News Network.

BuzzFeed's frustrated editor-in-chief, Ben Smith, said, 'While we strongly object to the White House's apparent attempt to punish news outlets whose coverage it does not like, we won't let these latest antics distract us from continuing to cover this administration fairly and aggressively.'[67]

At the same time, Trump and his cabinet favoured news services that have a record of friendly coverage towards him. After his 2017 inauguration, he granted his first interview as president to the Fox News commentator Sean Hannity, while his secretary of state, Rex Tillerson, went on a high-profile trip to Asia with just one reporter in tow, Erin McPike, from little-known conservative website the *Independent Journal Review*. (In explaining his decision, Tillerson told McPike, 'Primarily it's driven – believe it or not, you won't believe it – we're trying to save money.'[68])

It's a strategy that Turkey's president, Recep Tayyip Erdogan, has long used to powerful effect. He has a disturbing record of imprisoning journalists and shutting down critical media companies for 'supporting terrorism', but he has also deployed much more subtle tools, embracing supportive news organisations with exclusive access and interviews, and propping them up with lucrative government advertising deals.

Doling out access like sweets to well-behaved children is hardly going to shut down critical coverage. Determined leakers and skilled investigative reporters will still get around a government's attempts to control them. But the message it sends is clear enough: 'Follow the official line, or pay a price.'

•

The fourth part of the strategy is apparently aimed at disconnecting the 'facts' from reality. The list of Trump's generalisations, falsehoods, misstatements and downright lies would fill their own book, but a few stand out. He has claimed several times that he won the biggest Electoral College victory since Ronald Reagan (Reagan got 306 Electoral College votes, but Obama got 365 votes in 2008 and 332 in 2012, and Bill Clinton got 370 in 1992 and 379 in 1996.)[69]

He alleged there was 'massive voter fraud' during the 2016 election, despite no evidence of any fraud, and despite winning it himself. And of course, ever since he lost the 2020 election, he repeatedly – falsely – claimed that, too, was rigged.

In a speech at MacDill Air Force Base in Florida, Trump said radical Islamic terrorists were 'determined to strike our homeland'. He went on to say that terrorism was spreading but that the media was refusing to cover it: 'All across Europe you've seen what happened in Paris and Nice. All over Europe it's happening. It's gotten to a point where it's not even being reported. And in many cases the very, very dishonest press doesn't want to report it.'

At the time, there had been no evidence of *any* terrorist incidents in Europe that the press had ignored, and the White House declined to respond to several requests from the press corps to give examples.

He famously said the crowd at his 2016 inauguration was 'the biggest ever', but aerial photographs taken from the same position at Obama's inauguration show that Obama's crowd was significantly larger. And after his then press secretary, Sean Spicer, went to the briefing room to repeat the lie, CNN asked Trump's senior adviser, Kellyanne Conway, why the administration insisted on repeating it. Conway tried to brush it off, famously describing Spicer's remarks as 'alternative facts'.

It all seemed familiar to people who had read George Orwell's classic novel *Nineteen Eighty-Four*, about a dystopian world in which the government massages facts and twists the truth like plasticine: 'If all others accepted the lie which the Party imposed – if all records told the same tale – then the lie passed into history and became truth. "Who controls the past," ran the Party slogan, "controls the future: who controls the present controls the past."'

'Someone should let Kellyanne Conway and Sean Spicer know that Orwell's 1984 is a warning, not a guide,' quipped one Twitter user.

The strategy effectively discredited credible news services in the eyes of Trump's supporters, making the truth a fungible thing, as if reality were merely a matter of opinion. It gave the Trump administration the remarkable capacity to dismiss evidence of anything they don't like as 'fake news', and an excuse for his supporters to shrug off fact-checking and critical reporting as just the ranting of anti-Trump 'liberals'.[70]

In Idi Amin's Uganda, it became known as 'the information gap' – the ever-widening gulf between all the great things the brutal dictator said were happening in his country, and the reality of most people's lives. (He once enigmatically said, 'If we knew the meaning to everything that is happening to us, then there would be no meaning.') The information gap created a strange world where Amin's supporters and his opponents lived in parallel realities. Even when he finally died in exile in 2012, more than thirty years after his regime collapsed, some Ugandans refused to accept that the murders and executions that were a routine part of his regime ever took place.

Amin was famously unsubtle in his control of the media, also resorting to executing editors he didn't like, but Russia's Vladimir Putin has taken the strategy to more refined levels. State-aligned news outlets are flooded with the Kremlin's messages, while abroad he uses RT, an international TV news service formerly known as Russia Today, to shatter the West's monopoly on 'truth'.

I once sat in on a discussion about propaganda in Russia hosted by UNESCO where an editor from RT stood up to argue that there was no evidence that Syria's president Assad had ever used chemical weapons on his own people, despite verified media reports, and that

'Western journalists should admit there are facts they don't report' – a phrase eerily similar to Conway's 'alternative facts'.

•

If those strategies had come from one of the world's more despotic regimes, they would have triggered anxious calls of concern from democratic governments and human-rights groups everywhere. But coming from President Trump, with all the implied commitment to the US's core principles that goes with his office, they were deeply troubling.

It got so bad that even before the 2016 election, the board of the New York-based Committee to Protect Journalists decided it had no choice but to issue a rare public statement.

The CPJ was established in 1981 by a group of foreign correspondents who realised that they couldn't ignore the plight of colleagues reporting in countries with no regard for freedom of speech and whose work routinely put them at risk. Historically, the CPJ's focus has been on those working in some of the world's most oppressive states (the CPJ was actively involved in the campaign to get us out of Egypt), but suddenly they found themselves in the midst of a battle they had previously been fighting abroad. They wrote:

> While some have suggested that [Trump's] statements are rhetorical, we take him at his word. His intent and his disregard for the constitutional free press principle are clear.
>
> Through his words and actions, Trump has consistently demonstrated a contempt for the role of the press beyond offering publicity to him and advancing his interests.
>
> For this reason CPJ is taking the unprecedented step of speaking out now. This is not about picking sides in an election. This is recognising that a Trump presidency represents a threat to press freedom unknown in modern history.[71]

At the CPJ's annual awards ceremony in 2017, CNN's veteran war correspondent Christiane Amanpour told the audience, 'I never in a million years thought I would be up here on stage appealing for the freedom and safety of American journalists at home.'

•

I have always choked at the idea of American exceptionalism. It implies a God-given superiority assumed to be a given simply because America is, well, American. But as long as US leaders have spoken of that notion, however flawed it may be, they have also assumed a responsibility to uphold the ideals that underpin it. If they respect individual rights at home, support freedom of the press and obey the rule of law, they can legitimately criticise dictators and their regimes who don't.

Since its founding, America's leaders have recognised that the country's real authority – as opposed to merely its power – rests upon its moral standing. And as one of the world's most powerful nations, that is not a trivial thing.

The threats to press freedom in the United States are concerning, of course, but the power of the presidency is vast and Trump's actions had all the impact of an earthquake, with shockwaves reverberating far beyond America's borders.

To understand the significance of that quake, it is worth posing a rhetorical question. What would have happened to us – the Al Jazeera Three – if we had been imprisoned when Donald Trump was in the White House? Would we have been released?

Iraq's Saddam Hussein was 'a really bad guy', Trump has said, but at least he 'killed terrorists'. Syrian leader Bashar al-Assad may be a murderous tyrant, but, according to Trump, 'he looks a lot better than some of our so-called friends'. And when Fox News presenter Bill O'Reilly suggested that Putin had been assassinating rivals, Trump responded, 'There are a lot of killers. We've got a lot of killers. What – do you think our country's so innocent?'

Suddenly, startlingly, Trump abandoned any ambition to uphold those long-held principles of due process and the presumption of innocence, even if the United States had sometimes failed to live up its own standards. In the process he placed himself on the same moral plane as some of the world's most ruthless tyrants, and hinted that he'd have no problem with other governments doing much the same thing.

Did his 2024 re-election change anything? At the time of writing, it is too early to say with any certainty, but the evidence throughout that campaign served only to underline his earlier approach. At one rally, Trump spotted a small gap in the bullet-proof glass that protected him, and through it he could see some of the assembled press pack. 'To get me, somebody would have to shoot through the fake news and I don't mind that so much,' he told the jeering crowd.

He doesn't have to like the media – no president ever has – but democracy works because an unleashed and sometimes rabid press is able to hold the powerful to account. It might not always be dignified or edifying, but it is still a necessary part of the process.

It is worth a thought experiment here. If we were in prison in Egypt during Trump's term, would he have done as Obama did and raised our case with President Sisi?

It seems highly unlikely. Through the first months of his presidency, he showed no sign of criticising any regime – much less Sisi's – for its human-rights record. And as world leaders were gathering just before a 2019 G7 Summit, he called out, 'Where's my favourite dictator?'

Later, he said, 'We understood each other very well. He's a very tough man, I will tell you that. But he's also a good man, and he's done a fantastic job in Egypt. Not easy.

'Egypt has made tremendous progress under a great leader's leadership. It's what it's all about. And your staff also, who I've gotten to know – fantastic people. So, I want to thank you and I want to congratulate you.'

Even if he had mentioned our case to President Sisi, would the Egyptians have paid the slightest heed? Again, the answer must surely be no. Why would they, when Trump went to such extraordinary lengths to vilify the media and the work it does?

This is extremely troubling not just because of the damage Trump has done to America's standing across the globe, but because of the harm that the loss of authority does to the principles that have underpinned the liberal world order since the end of the Second World War.

Global institutions have, however imperfectly, tried to use respect for human rights, the rule of law and freedom of speech as their organising principles, and until now, the United States has been a kind of moral guarantor. This is not because the US has been perfect in its application of those principles, but because it has been willing to accept the rough end of the bargain – it has opened itself up to often painful media scrutiny, for example, and so has the authority to hold others to that standard.

It isn't just liberals in the West who are worried about this. Soon after Trump's inauguration, a columnist wrote that the shift in tone from Washington had been so marked that it was becoming hard to tell the difference between Donald Trump and an African dictator. You could dismiss the remark as mildly racist, except that its author was the editorial writer for the *Zambian Observer*.

Without a hint of irony, the paper published a stinging editorial calling for global solidarity in defence of press freedom in the United States.[72] 'What Trump is doing to the American media will soon be replicated across the world by dictatorial, tyrannical, intolerant, corrupt and abusive regimes,' the paper wrote. 'These will see open hatred for the media as a normal thing by those in power.'

It went on to reject the idea that Trump's criticism of the American media was harmless: 'This is ammunition for tyrants like Edgar Lungu [Zambia's president who won disputed 2016 elections] and others on the continent of Africa. What moral authority or influence will the United States embassies on the continent exercise in defence of press freedom in our countries as they used to do before, given Trump's conduct?'

13

THE CASE FOR THE DEFENCE

22 APRIL 2014

Understanding power becomes impossible when you do not know who is pulling the levers, how the rods are connected, or how exactly that power might manifest itself. It is a formless, threatening thing with no edges and no clear sense of reason.

Specific, definable threats are easy to manage – years on the front lines have taught me that. If you know where the bullets are coming from, you understand where to hide. You know which direction to run. And when they are no longer flying around, you can relax. But with incomprehensibility comes a sense of danger that cannot be defined. Nobody is holding a knife to your throat, there is no abyss looming on the road ahead, no sound of gunfire you can flee from. It is just a constant, sweaty sense that things are dangerously out of control. Like a whiff of smoke that tells you something is on fire somewhere, it leaves your adrenal gland drained and your sleep disturbed.

'This is the Middle East,' Fahmy tells me whenever we argue about how to tackle the case in court. 'You can't apply your Western logic here. It doesn't work like that.'

'Then how does it work?'

'It works on politics,' he says, as if that explains everything. 'You can only win if you play the game.'

But that's exactly what *shouldn't* work in a court of law, or at least not any court that I've been to. How are we supposed to play politics from inside a cage, when even our lawyers don't seem to understand the rules?

Of course, Fahmy is right that I am an outsider with an outsider's view of Egypt. And Egypt seems to work on implied truths, loose connections and disputed histories. To me, the law here feels malleable – it can be squeezed and shaped to suit whatever purpose its masters see fit. That might give us room to use influence with the judges and their political bosses, but in a case where I still have no idea what exactly we are supposed to have done wrong, it feels more like having extra rope with which to hang ourselves.

•

It is 22 April – the day of the sixth court hearing – and even our lawyers have been unable to see the physical evidence against us.

Soon after the hearing begins, Fahmy's lawyer, the always-urbane Khaled Abu Bakr, steps to the defence lawyer's lectern.

'Your honour, in this case the prosecutor is our opponent. And yet he has complete control over the evidence. Only he has seen it all. Only he knows what might be used against my client. How can this be fair? They have unsealed the evidence without any of the defence counsel there to witness it. How do we know that what is presented here in court is actually what they seized from the defendants? When they produce evidence supposedly against my client, how can we say that it has not been tampered with? It must be declared invalid and of no relevance to the case.'

It is such a fundamental issue that I expect the prosecutor to look embarrassed. I watch for a flicker of shame to pass across his face.

There is nothing.

Instead, Judge Nagy frowns as he looks across to the portly prosecutor, and then his face collapses into a genial, grandfatherly smile. 'This court is sure that there were no manipulations of the exhibits,' he says. 'The complaint is unfounded and dismissed.'

With the complaint dealt with, the court technicians once again dip into the files at random and the muffled sound of an audio recording bounces around the cavernous hall. None of it makes any sense to me, and the translator complains to the judge. There is more muffled video. The translator can't decipher it, either.

How do you mount a defence against this? How do you argue that you are innocent when the 'proof' that the prosecutor shows the court either doesn't show anything that might be incriminating in the first place, or is utterly incomprehensible?

It goes on for hours. There are more random photos, some taken from the students' computers showing them at protests. There are souvenir shots that Fahmy and Baher have taken during their fieldwork in Libya and across Egypt. There are press releases from the government and the Muslim Brotherhood.

At no stage are we called before the judge to explain our work, and after a while the students give up watching. Instead, they sit in a tight circle in a corner of the cage and chat among themselves while the trial continues.

The session ends with our lawyers demanding copies of all the files that the prosecutor has against us, so we can at least have some idea of what we are fighting.

•

For reasons that are never clear, our lawyers are either unwilling or unable to visit us in prison. My brother Andrew suspects it is because they consider it below them to go through the indignity of the prison searches and procedures to get through the gates. The lawyers insist that it is because it would be of no use and a waste of their valuable time.

The forty minutes we get for each family visit vanishes in an instant. You barely have time to greet one another, find out how everyone is doing and get news from the campaign before the wind-up comes. It is always unbearably brief, and never enough time to exchange all the messages and information we need, let alone swap the gossip and news we want.

Baher has managed to get hold of a pen that one of the other prisoners smuggled in and slipped to him as they passed in the yard one day. Never before have I appreciated the beauty and power that a communications device as simple as a pen can have. I continue with my toilet-paper notes.

On this visit, I have written a to-do list for Andrew. There is the mundane but important:

* *Please check if anybody has paid the rent on my house in Nairobi.*
* *Ask Jess (my neighbour) if the house is okay or has a pipe burst.*
* *I haven't paid my tax bill. Please arrange for someone to settle it and I will repay as soon as I am out.*

There is the exciting but unimportant: 'Please pass on my thanks to the Foreign Correspondents' Association of East Africa for electing me their honorary president.'

And then there are the questions for the lawyers:

* *Is there any way of identifying the videos that the prosecutor has refused/failed to show in court? We understand that the brief of evidence includes a written description of everything they have. It would help to know what the prosecution thinks was being fabricated so we can refute it.*
* *Other meetings with lawyers indicate that Baher's statement to the prosecutor may be a problem. Can they identify specific issues that we might need to prepare for?*
* *Can we get my passport and/or videos of my work to show that I was not in Egypt at the time the prosecutor claims I was at Rabaa al-Adawiya?*
* *Please advise the lawyers that all three of us strongly*

believe it would be a mistake to show AJE coverage of Egypt as they propose, because by definition it will be critical of the government and, while there won't be anything incriminating in there, we believe it might expose us to new questions, opening up an unnecessary front.

* *Why didn't the lawyers ask for bail at the last hearing?*

•

When we are allowed out for our daily exercise, Fahmy wants to talk. I am annoyed at having to curtail my precious running time, but he is insistent.

'We have to expose Baher's statement,' he says, once Baher has trotted off around the exercise yard and we are alone. 'If we don't, we will go down with him.'

'What do you mean? Denounce Baher? Deny what he's said when we don't know what's in the statement?'

'Yes. We've got to bring it up in court, because it will screw us,' he hisses. 'My family told me that he's said we manipulated the news to make Egypt look bad on orders from Doha, and that you brought in bags of cash for the Muslim Brotherhood.'

I'm not sure this is smart. I think it's hugely risky to raise something in court when we don't know exactly what is in the statement. The first rule of being a successful lawyer is never to ask a question that you don't already know the answer to.

I tell Fahmy we'd be flying blind with our fingers crossed and that it would be better to wait and see if the prosecutor presents it in court as evidence. If he does, we can challenge it then. Otherwise, we'll be introducing something that could backfire badly.

Fahmy visibly squirms. I'm not sure if it's his injured shoulder or building irritation, but I can see the tension under his skin.

'Don't be naive,' he growls. 'The judges will read everything in the prosecutor's file. It doesn't matter if it winds up as court evidence or not. They'll still go through it and it will still influence the way they think. We've got no choice.'

Fahmy may be right – after all, it's not as though the rules of evidence have been strictly applied before now. But we will be throwing Baher under a bus, and I don't want to do that – not just for his sake, but for all of us. 'We have to stay unified, together,' I say. 'If we don't, then the prosecutor and the local press will pounce on it.'

Finally Fahmy's anger erupts. 'I don't care what you think!' he hisses at me. 'I'm the one with the most to lose here! I'm the one who is supposed to be the bureau chief, and that makes me the ringleader of this little conspiracy. You're the white guy in this. You've got the support of your government and all those people out there who are putting pressure on Sisi. I'm going to look after myself.'

He walks off, his wide shoulders bunched up beneath his shirt.

A moment later Baher is at my side, breathing hard, with sweat running from his temples. 'What was that about?' he asks.

'You,' I reply. I hate confrontation, but there is no point in delaying the inevitable. 'Fahmy thinks we ought to bring up your statement in court. He's worried that it might cause us serious problems. What did you tell the interrogators?'

Baher's brow furrows deeply. 'Not much,' he says vaguely. 'I just told them what we were doing.'

'Well, Fahmy and I have heard that something in there is incriminating. Are you sure there is nothing to worry about?'

A little too quickly, he spits out his response: 'I don't know. It is possible that they changed the statement, I suppose.'

'Look, if there is anything in there that we need to know about, then tell us now. It's better that we find out here than in the courtroom – or worse, after we've been convicted.'

'There's nothing,' Baher says, wiping his sleeve across his forehead. 'Don't worry about it.'

He turns on his heel and resumes his run.

•

Back inside the cell, nobody speaks. Each of us is alone with his thoughts, and the air is thick with tension. I wash off the grime from my own run and change into clean prison whites. By the time I am done, Fahmy is curled up on his bed facing the wall, and Baher is smoothing out some foil.

'Come and help, dude,' he says. 'Let's make this place a bit prettier.'

•

'One point two million pounds,' says Fahmy's lawyer.

'I'm sorry?' I ask my stony-faced translator. 'Did he say 1.2 *million*?'

'That's what he said.'

I turn to Fahmy, who's been working across currencies for years.

'Yep,' he confirms. 'It's somewhere between 160 and 170 thousand US.'

We are at the next hearing, and Khaled Abu Bakr has just complained that the prosecutor is charging excessive 'administrative fees' for copies of the evidence. The prosecution simply says that these are the sums prescribed by the law, and Nagy shrugs and says, 'Well then. Those are the fees required. Now, let's continue with the case, shall we?'

Of course, the court can't be accused of denying us the evidence, if only we will pay the administrative costs – but our lawyers seem to have shrugged this off and moved on.

As I stew on it, Fahmy moves to the front of the cage. With his fingers pressed through the bars, he shouts at the judge, demanding an opportunity to address the court directly. Once more the guards unlock the cage and bring Fahmy to stand before the bench.

This worries me. Fahmy has been threatening to address the court, and while I've got no problem with him putting his case, I am worried that we haven't been able to agree on what he ought to be saying. We have generally tried to discuss our strategy beforehand, but as the mood in the cell has darkened, we've struggled to find any common ground. I know Fahmy has plans, but I have no idea what they might be. I guess I'm about to find out.

Once outside the cage and standing in front of the judges, he draws a deep breath and theatrically rolls his shoulder. 'Your honour, I have been denied the medical treatment that I need for my shoulder. As you can see, I am unable to raise my arm any higher than this.' He swings his arm in a wide, shallow salute, wincing as he does so.

'As a result, I am suffering from what I believe may be a permanent disability. I respectfully ask that I be moved to a hospital where I can receive appropriate care.'

Then, Fahmy draws attention to several statements from prominent opponents of the Muslim Brotherhood that his lawyer has presented to the judges; these attest that Fahmy drinks, does not pray and hates the Brotherhood. Having these allies is a major coup for Fahmy, and if the judge buys it I suppose it will help us all. But he is starting to sound as if he is defending himself and not the three of us as a group.

He continues: 'With regard to my colleagues Baher Mohamed and Peter Greste, I have great respect for their work, but I didn't know either of them before I began at Al Jazeera. I first met Baher on my second day on the job, on 11 September 2013. I only met Peter Greste on 15 December. I don't know anything about their backgrounds.'

Again, it feels as though he is placing distance between us, implicitly accepting the prosecutor's conspiracy theory but denying he is involved. I can't begrudge his efforts to clear himself of the charges, but I also can't shake my growing feeling of unease with his strategy.

'Your honour, I would also like the court to know that I sent an email to Al Jazeera English saying that any of the materials we produced in the bureau should not be aired on Al Jazeera Mubasher Masr [AJ's Egyptian affiliate]. We were aware that the station had been banned and we did not want our material to be a part of it.'

It is another statement that we have not agreed to. Once again, Fahmy is arguing against an allegation that hasn't been specifically made against us. He is guessing at the prosecution's case, confirming the government's conspiracy theories and trying to argue that we are not involved. No matter how many times I try to see his point, I can't bring myself to buy into that strategy. But he has said it, and it is now a part of the court record. No amount of recriminations or arguments is going to change that.

•

Andrew comes for another visit to Mulhaq, with news from the lawyers.

'We've finally worked out how the prosecutor managed to come up with the fee of 1.2 million pounds for the evidence,' he says, shaking his head. 'It turns out that they charge two pounds fifty for each single photo.'

I raise a questioning eyebrow. 'I'm a bit slow right now. Prison does that to you.'

'How many frames are there in a second of video?'

I guffaw out loud, catching the eye of the guard.

Like old-fashioned film, every second of video is made up of a series of still images – twenty-five of them – meaning that each second of video costs £62.50. Given the hours of video that the prosecutor seized, suddenly it is easy to see why the final figure is so breathtakingly high.

'I don't think Al Jazeera is going to pay that kind of money, on principle,' Andrew says.

'Well then,' I reply. 'We just have to make sure that our friends in the media make hay out of this one. We've got to make sure it embarrasses the hell out of them.'

•

Baher and I are playing backgammon on the floor of our cell.

It is a little risky – the guards have already confiscated one set, when they did an unannounced search a few weeks ago – but we need to stay active. I am beginning to regret it, though. Baher plays with a military officer's command of the board and an uncanny ability to get the numbers he needs from the dice.

On the original set, we naively scratched the distinctive triangles onto the bottom of the cardboard box we used as a socks-and-underwear drawer, and used red and blue plastic bottle tops that we painstakingly collected over the weeks. When the Interior Ministry goons found the box, they argued that backgammon was a form of gambling and therefore forbidden.

We got another box soon enough, but instead of the triangles we simply punched twelve holes down each side to mark the spots for each column of bottle tops. Each time the guards take something away, we learn to improvise.

•

As we walk back into court, Farag, the lawyer representing Baher and me, gives Fahmy a conspiratorial wink. 'This will be good,' he whispers. 'You watch today. I have a surprise for you.'

I have no idea what that means, but I am fed up with surprises.

We don't have to wait long. Almost as soon as the court session resumes, Farag approaches the lectern and shouts, 'Your honour, I am hereby submitting the resignation of myself and my colleagues as lawyers for the defendants Peter Greste and Baher Mohamed! We can no longer continue in our current capacity.'

Warming to his speech, he becomes louder and more theatrical, waving his hands in wide gestures and chopping them down on the lectern in an arc that begins high over his head. His voice rises in pitch and he spits out each syllable.

'I warned Al Jazeera Mubasher that their current lawsuit [against Egypt] would harm the case against my former clients. And yet they continued to go ahead with the case to sue our great nation. Al Jazeera doesn't care about the defendants. Their only concern is to give the world a bad image of Egypt – I have email evidence of this. I cannot defend my clients under these circumstances!'

I sit in slack-jawed silence. Farag has butchered our case, once again confirming the prosecutor's conspiracy theory without presenting anything to support his allegations. He hasn't said anything that might incriminate us, but he has effectively thrown us to the dogs and walked out.

At the end of his rant, he gathers his robe and his legal texts before turning to the cage and issuing one last, bitter smile.

'He's just fucked us,' says Baher through clenched teeth.

Fahmy agrees. 'He must have had his nuts squeezed good and hard by someone in the government. Who is going to represent you guys now?'

Before I can answer, a rotund, clean-shaven lawyer steps forward and says, 'Your honour, my name is Yousry El Sayed, and I am now acting on behalf of the defendants Mr Peter Greste and Mr Baher Mohamed.'

Yousry's words are hardly comforting. He is a wheezy, ruddy-faced lawyer who looks as though he has managed to find plenty of ways around Egypt's alcohol restrictions. He has been sitting through most of the hearings as a kind of back-up lawyer, but I have never met him and have no idea whether he is any good. But a first-year law-school dropout ought to be able to mount a convincing defence for us, and if he can't, nobody can. The thought gives me cold comfort.

'I am not here to defend any position related to Al Jazeera,' Yousry continues. 'I am here to defend just two people – one foreign and one Egyptian. I do not want the comments of my colleague to affect the case for my defendants.'

'Well then,' says the judge. 'We adjourn for closing arguments.'

•

'I don't think we've got any choice but to stick with Yousry at this point,' Andrew says as we huddle together in the visiting shed.

Farag's piece of showmanship has sent my family into a tailspin. They've been tied up in endless phone calls and Skype conversations trying to figure out the best way to handle his resignation. Do we go Fahmy's route and find our own legal counsel? Is it possible for a new lawyer to pick up the threads of the case and mount a credible closing argument at this late stage? Is it even possible to find a new lawyer?

The last question is the most vexing. Andrew agrees that someone powerful must have threatened Farag and forced him off the case, and that if the manner of his resignation was intended to send a message to other lawyers, it seems to have worked. Nobody with any credibility wants to touch us. It seems obvious that there is political interference, even if it isn't clear which political forces are doing the interfering. And in the new Egypt, nobody can afford to put their head above the parapet, especially with presidential elections due in just a few days' time. Field Marshal Sisi – the man who led the coup against the MB's Mohamed Morsi – is the leading candidate.

We have no choice but to cross our fingers and stick with Yousry.

•

Court hearing number nine.

Instead of closing arguments, the prosecutor announces that his 'technical experts' have at last been able to put together a collection of five CDs of video material and still images taken from our equipment.

We sit to watch the show – a random selection of pictures, half-audible recordings, irrelevant footage and stories.

My temper erupts. I start shouting out to the media in frustration.

•

Court hearing number ten.

Still no closing arguments.

Instead, the 'technical experts' who assessed our video are called to the stand. In their original reports, all three declared (in identical statements) that our work had been manipulated to make Egypt appear to be in a state of war, and to damage national security.

Khaled Abu Bakr's cross-examination quickly reveals the absurdity: all they are in fact asserting is that we edited the raw footage to make a finished story – the routine work of a television news team – and that by editing, we somehow distorted the truth and harmed the country.

When the lawyer asks one of the witnesses how he assesses a threat to national security, he replies, 'I am just a technical expert. I do not have the authority to make that judgement.'

'But you made that judgement in your report. You clearly said my client's work was a threat to national security.'

'I don't know. I do not have that expertise.'

'Why did you make your statement, then?'

'We were given the statements to sign.'

'Case adjourned until 5 June for closing arguments,' says the judge.

•

Court hearing number eleven.

The court is all but empty. My brother Mike is there with consular staff from the Australian and Latvian embassies, and Fahmy's brother Adel is also present, along with a handful of diplomatic and human-rights observers. But the press benches are strangely deserted.

'They can't get in!' shouts Adel from across the room. 'I don't know what's going on, but security won't let the journalists in.'

The lawyers and the prosecutor all seem to be dressed in their best suits. All the lawyers are armed with small stacks of notes, and I wonder what use any of it can be at this late stage, when all we have left is a summation of what has already been said. And yet, there is a restlessness and a sense of expectation – a sense of occasion that we haven't seen before.

Eventually the court is called to order, and once the judges are seated, from behind his dark glasses Nagy gestures to the prosecutor, Mohamed Barakat, to begin. Barakat is a round, pasty-faced, clean-shaven man. He leans forward to push himself to his feet, and as he shuffles his notes, I realise that apart from a few comments over legal procedure, he has hardly spoken throughout the trial.

He clears his throat and waits a moment for the murmuring to settle as I fix my gaze on him.

'In the name of God, the benevolent and the merciful,' he intones as he reads from his statement, 'the evidence unequivocally shows that these men were guilty of working with a terrorist organisation to undermine and destroy the great nation of Egypt.'

This opening line sets the tone for the rest of his performance – pious and pompous, with only the scantest connection to evidence.

'All the defendants are part of the same "cell" who worked under the direction of Canadian-Egyptian Mohamed Fahmy. Mr Greste and the other "foreigners" [those who are on trial *in absentia* – Britons Sue Turton and Dominic Kane, and Dutch freelance reporter Rena Netjes] assisted the rest of the defendants in damaging Egypt's reputation by providing them with "material" to which they had made alterations. This material was passed through Mohamed Fahmy.'

And then something odd: he claims that under orders from Doha we filmed a protest against Morsi in June, long before I was ever in Egypt, to make it look poorly attended. Not only is this absurd, it has never come up in any of the evidence presented in court.

'Fuck,' Fahmy whispers under his breath. I turn to look at him and realise that he is not looking at the prosecutor, but at Baher. Then the penny drops for me too – this must be one of the allegations contained in Baher's statement. According to that, we were instructed to underplay the scale of opposition to the Brotherhood and talk up the movement's support.

'Crap,' I reply.

The prosecutor is introducing Baher's statement as evidence now, and we have had no chance to challenge or rebut it. Fahmy might have been right.

Barakat goes on to say that our reporting about sexual assaults in Tahrir Square were designed to show Egypt negatively, and that Dominic Kane and I had brought in suitcases of cash to pay informants. These allegations must also be from Baher's statement.

I glance across at Baher, but his gaze is fixed on the prosecutor.

Barakat then argues that I was a kind of master propagandist who altered reports to show Egypt in a bad light. He blames Al Jazeera for the fall of governments in Iraq, Syria, Libya and Yemen, and accuses the network of colluding with the Muslim Brotherhood to ruin Egypt.

There is a commotion just outside the court, with lots of muffled voices. The door bursts open and the court floods with reporters, cameramen and photographers.

'They wouldn't let us in,' shouts one reporter furiously. 'Security.' They take their seats just in time to hear Barakat wrap up.

'Your honour, these are extremely serious charges. Mercy leads to the drowning of an entire society, which is why I respectfully request that the court impose the maximum penalty of up to twenty-five years in prison for all the defendants.'

Now it is Fahmy's lawyer's turn. Abu Bakr is astute and erudite, gradually picking apart the prosecution's case thread by thread. It isn't hard to do, but he is still an impressive player, dissecting the evidence like a coroner slicing open a decaying corpse and pulling it apart sinew by sinew to reveal the rotting mess within.

The performance takes him two hours, and when he finally slaps his file shut with a call for our unconditional release and a public apology for the suffering we have been through, the court bursts into spontaneous applause.

For once Fahmy looks pleased, but Baher's lips are pressed tightly together and his forehead is bunched up in thought. I am about to ask him about his statement to the investigators when his eyes widen. I follow his gaze.

Our lawyer, Yousry El Sayed, is weaving his way to the stand. His eyes look red and bloodshot, and he seems to be struggling with his breathing. 'There is no need for me to repeat all the points that my colleague has so ably explained to the court,' he wheezes. He adds a couple of technical details and sits down barely five minutes later.

Baher and I look at each other in stunned silence. Yousry's performance was cursory and superficial, as if he simply couldn't be bothered, and I can't help wondering if the portly lawyer is a little drunk.

His colleagues follow – lawyers for the students and Khalid Mohammed – and by the time we are done, six hours have passed. The end of the session feels like an anticlimax, an inconsequential full stop to an exhausting five-month epic.

Finally the prison van drops us back at Mulhaq, and we walk slowly to our cells, breathing in the sweet evening air and gazing at the unfamiliar pinpricks of light that dot the dark, milky sky. Suddenly I stop and laugh.

'What is it?' Baher asks.

'Do you realise that it has been more than six months since any of us has seen the stars?'

14

THE FEARFUL COUNTRY

When I returned to Australia in 2016 after twenty-five years on the road as a foreign correspondent, I found a country very different from the one I had left.

There was plenty that was familiar, of course – the cities had grown and developed but still had their old charm. Taringa, the neighbourhood where I grew up in Brisbane, had lost a lot of its old colonial-era homes, with their wide tin 'hats' covering demure, lazy verandas, but still had that sleepy subtropical feel with its sprawling mango trees and fiery-red poinsettias. Australians were just as obsessed with sport (no other country of the hundred or so that I've been to routinely devotes half of its news bulletins to sport), and somehow life still seemed to revolve around the beach.

A lot had improved, too. Suddenly we had become a nation of foodies. Even the pub that my friends and I used to flock to as uni students for post-lecture beers, the Royal Exchange, had moved the old pie floaters aside to make room for crispy-skin salmon with balsamic glaze. And somehow we seemed far richer – instead of the clattery old Valiants and Holden Commodores with leaky doors and sticky seats that used to cruise the streets, there were plenty of well-engineered Audis, BMWs and Hondas piloted by well-manicured folk in business attire.

At the same time, we seemed to have lost something essential in our national psyche: the much-celebrated larrikin streak.

We have always thought of ourselves as rebels at heart, as a nation of individuals who are sceptical of authority and would prefer to do our own thing rather than conform to regulations set by some higher figure. We used to see ourselves as adaptable, courageous and easy-going people, unafraid to express our opinions. But the Australia I returned to suddenly felt bound by stifling rules and regulations both small and large, by a pressure to conform that hadn't been there when I left in 1991. Suddenly, unexpectedly, we seemed fearful not just of authority, but of outsiders as well. We had lost our capacity to be ourselves and accept our neighbours in the same way, and as a result we felt more closed. It was as if we had accepted the cuisine of outsiders but not their opinions.

The effect was wider than that. The rhetoric of fear had infused political debates. 'National security' had become the go-to phrase for any politician wanting to impose another set of rules or restrictions, whether to do with immigration policy or the debate around the Racial Discrimination Act. The War on Terror had somehow insidiously seeped its way into our national DNA, displacing much of what we held dear about our nation and our place in the world.

•

If it were just about putting up with the inconvenience of extra airport security or constant surveillance by security cameras, it wouldn't be such a problem. But in the process of trying to make ourselves safer, we have allowed some of our most cherished freedoms to be whittled away, and in ways that do fundamental damage to our democracy. Among them are freedom of speech and freedom of the press.

This is more than just the gut instinct of someone nostalgic for an adolescent's carefree life that probably never really existed. In 2012, University of New South Wales law professor George Williams published a study of Australian national security legislation passed in the decade following 9/11. Before then, he could find only one statute, in the Northern Territory, that specifically dealt with 'terrorism'. After

9/11, he counted no less than fifty-four separate pieces of legislation that focused on terrorism and security.

In his study, Williams wrote:

> This legislation has been of unprecedented reach, including laws providing for: restrictions on freedom of speech through new sedition offences and broader censorship rules; detention and questioning for up to a week by the Australian Security Intelligence Organisation of Australian citizens not suspected of any crime; the banning of organisations by executive decision; control orders that can enable house arrest for up to a year; detention without charge or trial for up to 14 days; and warrantless searches of private property by police officers. As these examples demonstrate, powers and sanctions once thought to lie outside the rules of a liberal democracy except during wartime have now become part of the Australian legal system.

The trend has continued. At the time of writing, Williams told me his tally had risen to sixty-six, and the remarks he made in his 2012 study were even more pertinent.

While the overall direction is worrying, my particular concern as a journalist is the way that these laws have often directly or indirectly intruded on the media's role as a watchdog over government, and in the process chipped away at its ability to expose wrongdoing or abuses of the system and to hold those with power to account – in other words, to perform its core function in a democracy.

As I have argued throughout this book, this is part of a trend undermining democracies all over the world, and part of the same broad strategy that put us in prison in Egypt. I am not suggesting that Australia is necessarily on the slippery slope to becoming another Egypt or Turkey, but to a lesser or greater degree politicians everywhere are using the same arguments to nudge their countries in the same general direction, and damaging the foundations of democracy in much the same way.

Of course, the Australian government has consistently argued that the laws are not intended to limit freedom of the press. But they have often been drafted so loosely that they've had a smothering effect on the work reporters do. Disturbingly, the laws have been passed regardless of the party in power. Both the Liberal–National Coalition and the Labor Party have pushed through such laws or supported them in opposition.

One of the biggest problems is what has become known as the Data Retention Act of 2015. The government introduced this legislation to force telecommunications companies to hold the metadata of their customers for two years and to give a range of government agencies access to that information for investigations.

Metadata is essentially the electronic footprints we all leave on our computers and phones. It identifies who we call and text, and the people who call and text us. It can also identify who we email and message on our computers, and who contacts us through a multitude of social media and messaging apps. It can also include a record of the websites we visit, the places we've been with our mobile phones, and the routes we have driven in our cars, logged on traffic cameras.

While it doesn't include the *content* of any of those communications, data experts can still learn an extraordinary amount about us by building up a picture of who we communicate with, where we go, what we are interested in, what we buy, and so on. For an intelligence agency trying to track a would-be terrorist, it is an incredibly powerful tool.

The former general counsel for the US National Security Agency, Stewart Baker, has said, 'Metadata absolutely tells you everything about somebody's life. If you have enough metadata, you don't really need content.' At a debate in the USA in 2014, Baker's quote came up and General Michael Hayden, a former director of both the NSA and the CIA, said the comment was 'absolutely correct'. He went on to point out: 'We kill people based on metadata.'[73]

Think about that for a moment. CIA operatives are so confident about what metadata tells them that they use it to make decisions about who lives and who dies. It is an extraordinary, frightening admission.

But what does it mean for journalists? How does that tool intrude on a reporter's responsibility to keep track of those we entrust with power?

The answer to these questions turns out to be deeply troubling.

Veteran investigative reporter Ross Coulthart told the ABC that, if the authorities are trying to work out the story a reporter is investigating, 'If you know who I'm calling as a journalist and if you know who's calling me . . . who I'm emailing, who I'm getting emails from, you almost don't need the content of the information.'[74]

It is not as if the authorities need that legislation to look into our data. Police and other security agencies have always been able to search private property using the tried and tested warrant system. If they want access to someone's house, for example, they have to convince a judge that they have 'probable cause' to believe that criminal activity is occurring there, or that they expect to find evidence of a particular crime.

Crucially, the police can search only the place described in a warrant and only the property it mentions. They can't search a house if the warrant specifies only the backyard, and they can't hunt for weapons if the judge has authorised a search for, say, marijuana plants.

This system has been around for hundreds of years, and although it isn't perfect, it is still the most effective way we have of giving police the tools they need to carry out their jobs, while maintaining some kind of independent judicial oversight.

The data-retention legislation up-ends that system. It gives the police and intelligence agencies unfettered access to our metadata without the need for a warrant or the judicial oversight that entails.

Paul Farrell is one of the most intrepid reporters in Australia. He is smart, dedicated and instinctively sceptical of authority – the kind of reporter we ought to be celebrating. As a journalist with *The Guardian*, one of his first assignments was to look into the way Australian Customs Service (now Australian Border Force) ships had been intercepting boats carrying asylum seekers to our shores. In April 2014, he got hold of electronic maps that not only confirmed that the customs ship *Ocean Protector* had broken international law by sailing into Indonesian waters to turn back boats, but suggested that the customs officers on board *knew* that they had literally crossed the line, and that an internal panel that investigated the report lied by claiming the incursion was an accident.

Around the middle of that year, Farrell noticed a passing reference to an investigation into the incident at a Senate Estimates Committee hearing. Curious, he lodged a freedom of information request and then, when the Department of Immigration and Border Protection blocked some of the information, he appealed to the privacy commissioner, who ordered the release of the previously sealed files.

Farrell discovered that after his report, the immigration secretary had written to the Australian Federal Police asking them to find the source of the leak and prosecute that person under Section 70 of the Crimes Act. The AFP then went into Farrell's metadata to try to find out who was passing him the information.

'I had been very careful to protect my sources, so they weren't able to find anything,' Farrell said. 'But remember – this was at the same time that they were trying to push through the data retention scheme, claiming it was aimed only at dealing with terrorism.'[75]

At the time, the department claimed that *The Guardian*'s story had damaged national security by telegraphing its tactics to people smugglers.

'If you think about it,' Farrell said, 'the government is effectively saying it plans to continue with unlawful incursions into Indonesian waters, which is itself a very serious admission. It is hard to see their investigation as anything other than an attempt to deal with political embarrassment. The government was conflating politics with national security.'

•

It has happened before.

In 2005, *The Australian* published a customs report exposing the way that criminal activity had seriously compromised security at Sydney Airport. The report explained how motorcycle gang members with criminal convictions held airport security identification cards that got them into supposedly secure areas. The report's author, Allan Kessing, said it amounted to an open invitation for gun running and drug smuggling. But his report had been sitting on a shelf gathering dust for two years by the time *The Australian* got hold of it and released the findings.

Hugely embarrassed, the authorities tried to track down the leak. They used Section 70 of the Crimes Act to charge Kessing with being the source (something he has always denied) and used metadata records to argue that he had called the newspaper from a phone box close to his house. He was convicted and received a nine-month suspended sentence.

Once again, not only was there no damage as a result of the leaked report, but under intense public pressure, the government ordered an inquiry – which recommended a $220 million upgrade of airport security.

•

In the debate around the Data Retention Bill, the media demanded that the law require investigators to get a warrant before they could access journalists' metadata. This wasn't because those in the media are less likely to be a threat than the rest of the public. The news organisations were calling on the government to recognise the importance of the media's role as a public watchdog holding our elected officials – the ones who work for *us* – to account. Journalists can't do that unless they can talk to sources without fear of those sources being exposed.

In the end, the government relented and agreed to set up a special magistrate's court to hear warrant applications in secret whenever police want to search a journalist's metadata. Under the system, a government-appointed lawyer acts as a 'public interest advocate' to argue on the public's (and by implication the journalist's) behalf.

There are two rather awkward problems with this. First, the journalist will never know of a warrant application. Neither the investigator asking for the warrant nor the public-interest advocate is allowed to contact the reporter for more details about their work, which means that the advocate can only guess at the public interest they are supposed to be defending. It is hard to see how they can do that properly without fully understanding the story the journalist is pursuing.

Secondly, the sources themselves enjoy no such protection. Investigators are free to go into the metadata of anybody they suspect might be feeding a reporter the information the reporter is publishing. Even if it is a relatively thin fig leaf, journalists still have one extra legal layer between them and the authorities they are supposed to be monitoring – but their sources are exposed and vulnerable.

After the *Ocean Protector* story, Farrell reported on conditions in the offshore detention centres the government had set up to house would-be refugees and asylum seekers. The centres fell under another piece of legislation passed in the post-9/11 push for national security: the Australian Border Force Act.

The Act makes it a criminal offence (punishable by up to two years in prison) for any person working for the Department of Immigration and Border Protection to reveal *anything* that happens in the centres. Most legislation covering social workers and medical staff acknowledges that those workers' highest duty is to the wellbeing of the people they are attending to, and encourages them to report anything that undermines that. But because the Border Force Act is another piece of legislation marked as part of the national security system, it up-ends the usual priorities. Doctors and nurses, and the staff of organisations such as the Salvation Army, Red Cross, the United Nations and Amnesty International – anyone employed in one of the many functions the Immigration Department oversees – are forced to abandon their ethical and professional obligations to report physical or mental harm.

Nevertheless, some forty of those contractors and workers were so disturbed by the horrific conditions they found that they went to the press anyway, and in June 2016 they published an open letter defiantly challenging the minister to use his new powers of prosecution:

> Today the Border Force Act comes into force. It includes provision for a two-year jail sentence for 'entrusted persons' such as ourselves if we continue to speak out about the deplorable state of human rights in immigration detention without the express permission of the minister for immigration and border protection. This strengthens the wall of secrecy which prevents proper public scrutiny.
>
> We have advocated, and will continue to advocate, for the health of those for whom we have a duty of care, despite the threats of imprisonment, because standing by and watching sub-standard and harmful care, child abuse and gross violations of human rights is not ethically justifiable.[76]

It was a brave act of defiance, but did nothing to divert the government or the Opposition from the course they'd set. Two months later, in August, *The Guardian* released a cache of some 2000 incident reports leaked from the detention centres. The reports, which became known as the Nauru files, backed up the broad allegations contained in the open letter, with shocking details of assaults, sexual abuse, self-harm, child abuse and appalling living conditions.

One of the most disturbing cases was that of Hamid Khazaei, an asylum seeker who had been held on Manus Island and who died in September 2014 after a cut on his leg developed septicaemia. Using leaked documents, *The Australian* and the ABC current affairs TV program *Four Corners* ran the story as an example of the way the asylum seekers were suffering from institutionalised neglect. One of the most prominent figures in both reports was Dr Peter Young.

Dr Young was a psychiatrist responsible for overseeing the mental health of detainees in all the centres from 2011 until he resigned in the middle of 2014, saying he could no longer work in a system devised to make people suffer.

'You can't mitigate the harm, because the system is designed to create a negative mental state,' he said. 'It's designed to produce suffering. If you suffer, then it's punishment. If you suffer, you're more likely to agree to go back to where you came from. By reducing the suffering you're reducing the functioning of the system, and the system doesn't want you to do that.'[77]

The government appeared to dismiss the complaints with a rhetorical wave, but we now know that it was so upset by the leaks that the Department of Immigration once again tried to track down the people responsible for passing the information to the media.

We don't know if the AFP applied for a warrant to look into Farrell's metadata, and if they did, what the public-interest advocate might have said at the hearing, but it seems unlikely they even bothered. Why would they go to the trouble of a warrant hearing if they could freely look into the metadata of a relatively small group of people who could have been Farrell's sources?

When Dr Young learned about Farrell's experience with the Federal Police, he made his own application under the Privacy Act to see if he too had been investigated, and discovered that he had. The file revealed that the police had compiled hundreds of pages of case notes and documents, including his phone records, in a hunt for the source of the Nauru files. Young was never charged with any offence – he had resigned before Hamid Khazaei's death and didn't have access to those medical records, so it is unsurprising that the investigators couldn't find anything on him – but their intent was clear: to use metadata not to deal with any specific threat to national security, but to stop the source of acute political embarrassment.

•

Inevitably, it is hard to quantify the impact of the metadata legislation on the work that journalists do. After all, how do you measure the number of would-be whistleblowers who have decided *against* contacting a news organisation, or how many reporters have decided not to follow up a story, because of the risks involved? Coulthart said he has turned away whistleblowers after they have made initial contact using a traceable phone number because the risk that they might be caught and prosecuted is too great. But the wider impact is impossible to guess at.

•

In another example, journalists reporting on national security matters could unwittingly find themselves facing up to ten years in prison, under provisions in the Australian Security Intelligence Organisation Act 1979 (ASIO Act) that were introduced in 2014.

Section 35P was passed to stop unauthorised disclosure of any 'special intelligence operation' (SIO). On its face, this is a reasonable provision: nobody would argue in favour of publishing information about ASIO operations that might jeopardise the organisation's work or its people. An operation is designated as an SIO when there is significant risk to either people or property, so clearly ASIO has an interest in deep secrecy. But once an operation has been marked as an SIO, a dark, heavy blanket falls over it and any disclosure of information is prohibited for all time and punishable by five years in prison (and up to ten years for 'aggravated disclosure').

At the National Press Club, then attorney-general, George

Brandis, rejected the idea that SIOs could be used to cover anything up: 'They are unusual operations. They require unusually the fiat of the attorney-general . . . The idea that these could simply be rubber-stamped to cover up or gloss over anything that ASIO might choose to do is nonsense.'[78]

The problem is that, by definition, an SIO *designation* must itself be kept secret, so a journalist simply gathering information about the work of ASIO will never know if they are looking into something that is supposed to be hidden under an SIO cloak. There is no exception for reporters acting in good faith. Even a reporter simply talking to their editor about information they have is technically breaking the law. There is no 'public interest' defence, where a news organisation can argue that the public has a right to know about what the security services are up to, particularly when things go wrong or agents overstep boundaries. Nor is there any protection for insiders who believe they have no choice but to go to the media to expose wrongdoing.

There *is* a formal internal whistleblowing system through the inspector-general of intelligence and security (IGIS). In 2018, Justice Margaret Stone admitted that the system is shrouded in secrecy. Justice within the intelligence services is not only blind, it is blind to the public. The IGIS is not allowed to say anything about whistleblowers or the abuses they have exposed. Quite simply, we will never know if or when intelligence agents have broken the law.

Justice Stone argued that this was the price we had to pay for the kind of security we need in the face of modern threats such as terrorism and foreign espionage.

'There is no doubt that ASIO's new powers are chipping away at privacy in the digital age,' she said, 'but what the public doesn't know is how much oversight we provide. We have unrestricted access to all their files which we regularly exercise . . . I realise it isn't always very easy to hear when someone like me says "trust us", but we can't have both secrecy *and* open public oversight of the kind you are talking about.'[79]

Lawyers such as Bret Walker find Section 35P to be a deeply troubling extension of ASIO's powers. He believes that it creates an unnecessary cloak of secrecy that will inevitably be abused to hide embarrassing or illegal acts, and that it up-ends many of the conventional legal checks.

Walker is a former Independent National Security Legislation Monitor and one of the sharpest legal minds in the country. One of his functions as INSLM was to keep track of the consequences, both intended and unintended, of national security legislation.

'There are aspects of national security that would make the constitutional imperative to openness a suicide pact if there was full disclosure of all things all the time,' he told me. 'But it seems to me that there is something disgusting about supposing that you can properly enlist constraints of secrecy to prevent unlawful conduct from coming to light. That is a legal system that is cannibalising itself.'

The INSLM recommended a number of changes to Section 35P, and the government accepted them in principle, but according to Williams, they don't even come close to striking the right balance between ASIO's need for secrecy and the public's right to know when things go wrong.

•

In September 2015, Andrew Wilkie, the independent federal member for Denison in Tasmania, made a speech in parliament opposing a tranche of new national security laws, in which he said Australia was becoming a 'pre-police state'.

Wilkie understood better than most the tension between the culture of secrecy within the security services and the public's right to know in an open democracy. He began his professional life as a career soldier, rising to the rank of lieutenant colonel. In 1999, he was seconded to the Office of National Assessments (ONA) as an intelligence analyst. He left the following year to join the American defence company Raytheon, but in the heightened security environment after

9/11 returned to his old job at the ONA, where he worked on intelligence relating to Iraq's alleged weapons of mass destruction.

Wilkie's story would be unremarkable if he didn't have a conscience. The ONA has a broad mandate to provide assessments of international political, strategic and economic developments to the prime minister and the National Security Committee of Cabinet, but is also tightly integrated into the intelligence community, in particular coordinating and evaluating Australia's foreign intelligence. Nobody works there without top-secret classification.

As the United States and its allies continued to accuse Iraq of secretly developing and stockpiling WMDs in violation of UN sanctions, the security services scrambled to find the stockpiles. On 13 March 2003, Prime Minister John Howard went to the National Press Club in Canberra to explain why the country was about to join the US-led war, suggesting that Iraq was on the verge of supplying Al Qaeda with WMDs.

But Wilkie could not square the information he had been studying in his ONA office with what the government was telling the Australian public. He quit and went to the media.

'Iraq does not pose a security threat to any other country at this point in time,' he told ABC Radio soon after. 'Its military is very weak – it's a fraction of the size of the military at the time of the invasion of Kuwait. Its weapons of mass destruction program is very disjointed and contained by the regime that's been in place since the Gulf War. And there is no hard intelligence linking the Iraqi regime to Al Qaeda in any substantial or worrisome way.'[80]

(The interviewer, Catherine McGrath, went on to ask Wilkie how he thought things would play out if Australia did indeed join the coalition in a war against Iraq. With what now seems like remarkable foresight, Wilkie replied, 'A war at this time is just not worth the risk. I think there is too great a risk of a military or humanitarian disaster, and I think there's a real risk that a war now will further inflame popular anti-Western opinion in the Middle East and push Saddam

[Hussein] closer towards Al Qaeda, and push us all just that little bit closer to the so-called clash of civilisations that we've so far managed to stay well clear of.')

What Wilkie did was illegal on a number of levels. As an intelligence officer, he broke his professional code of secrecy, and as a civil servant, he violated Section 70 of the Crimes Act, which prohibits disclosure of any 'fact or document which came to his or her knowledge, or into his or her possession, by virtue of having been a Commonwealth officer'. (The Crimes Act is not specifically aimed at intelligence agents; it was originally drafted in 1914 to stop any government leaks as the country moved towards the First World War.)

The penalty for revealing information under the Crimes Act is two years in prison. Tellingly, the journalists who first interviewed Wilkie – starting with veteran Channel 9 political correspondent Laurie Oakes, who broke the story – were risking seven years in prison for publishing the information. In the end, nobody was prosecuted over the leak. Wilkie believes he had a degree of protection because his case had such a high profile.[81] He freely admits that he broke his own professional code of conduct, but he told me he felt he had no choice but to go public when, in his view, his primary responsibility was to the country rather than either his immediate bosses or his political leaders. He was a *public* servant, after all – and he considered his ultimate loyalty to be to the Australian people rather than the government.

'The trouble was that I could not address my concerns internally. There was no formal mechanism for it, and even if there was, I still would have been regarded as unreliable and lost my security clearance. I would have been sacked on the spot,' he said.

Justice Stone snorted a little when I raised Wilkie's case with her. 'Why didn't he come to our office? He could easily have done that. We would have investigated the matter and made a report, and the government would have had to answer it.'

When I went back to Wilkie with this, his retort was blunt.

'That's a bullshit response,' he said. 'She knows that IGIS is irrelevant in this matter because [her office's] remit is the activities of the intelligence agencies, while my complaint was with the conduct of the government. See what I'm still up against? Despite all that we now know about the invasion of Iraq, the [Australian Intelligence Community] still defaults to shooting the messenger.'[82]

•

To Wilkie, Walker and Williams, there is a vital need to protect the media's oversight role, and in particular its function as a whistle-of-last-resort for public servants who are genuinely acting in the interests of the public and feel that they have nowhere else to go.

Even though what he did was technically illegal, it is hard to argue that the country would have been better off without Wilkie's leak. It certainly didn't divert the government from joining the war in Iraq, but it did raise important questions about how the government handles classified intelligence briefings, and about the way it communicates with the public. In other words, there was a powerful argument that Wilkie's actions were defensible *in the public interest.* At the same time, they do not appear to have done any serious or lasting damage to the way the ONA or any other intelligence agency operates. The same applies to the actions of Allan Kessing and Dr Peter Young.

None of those whistleblowers actually went to prison, so doesn't that show that the system works? Walker says the answer is emphatically no. Relying on prosecutors or judges to use their own judgement about when to apply the law, he says, runs against one of the most fundamental principles of our judicial system: 'My view is that's contrary to the rule of law. We should not be dependent on prosecutorial or judicial discretion to temper the operation of a law that is more crude than is necessary.'

In other words, the law needs to make it explicitly clear that whistleblowers and journalists acting in the public interest to expose wrongdoing must be protected. Walker goes a step further, arguing that in creating a culture of secrecy in government, we've lost the most basic principles of public accountability.

This is not to suggest that the system has been deliberately skewed to protect guilty politicians and government figures, but we do appear to be creating a system with so much secrecy built into it that it allows scope for political abuse away from public scrutiny.

Walker believes that we ought to be thinking about the health of the nation in the same way we think about the safety of air passengers.

'Air safety has led the aviation industry to be way ahead of any other sector I know in encouraging people to dob on each other in the nicest possible way, and even to dob on themselves without thinking "I'm about to be sacked",' he said. 'They have a whole regime of protected disclosure about anything that undermines safety that is solidly policed, and even encouraged. It ought not be a spectacular way of dying that brings us to that realisation.'[83]

15

THE VERDICT

23 JUNE 2013

We have only one week to wait for a verdict. Seven days. One hundred and sixty-eight hours (give or take a few, depending on timings). And although there are a lot of possible outcomes, each of us feels a compelling urge to do a bit of planning.

'It'll take time for us to get our passports back,' Fahmy argues. He is lying on his bed, flat on his back with his good arm tucked up behind his head, as he stares at the paint flaking off the ceiling. 'We ought to use that time to maybe go and have a break in Sharm El Sheikh, or go diving in the Red Sea.'

'What about a party?' Baher is perched on his bunk bed with a gleam in his eye. 'We've got to have a party to thank everyone who helped us.'

'Of course there will be a party,' says Fahmy. 'It'll be huge. And we won't even have to worry about the hangover. We won't need to work again for a very long time. And then we will go on a holiday. Me and Marwa, Baher and Jihan, and you, Peter. After all of this shit, we owe it to ourselves.'

Fahmy rolls to look up at me out of the corner of his eye. 'What are you going to do once this is over, Peter? You could have your own show. CNN has offered me a job, but I'm not sure if I'll take it.'

I shift on my pillow and the bunk bed sways a little. 'I dunno. I'm not even sure we will get out of here after the hearing.'

'Okay – perhaps it'll take a day or so to organise the paperwork, but it won't take long.'

'That's not what I mean. What if they convict us? They've got to save face somehow after all this bollocks of a trial. It'll look really bad if they say it was all a big mistake and let us go with a handshake and an apology.'

Fahmy won't let me sour his mood. 'That might happen, I suppose, but even if they convict us of, say, operating without a licence, it would mean a fine and a few months in prison, max. We've already done six months, so we'd be out on time served.'

Oh my, it is tantalising. Freedom is so close I can almost taste it. There is a tickling in my limbs that won't let me sleep. My fingers and toes are fizzing with – what is it? Excitement? That noun is too mundane for this. There is an effervescence in my veins, almost as if my blood has turned to soda water and I can feel it bubbling through my skin making my fingers vibrate. I so badly want to join Baher and Fahmy in their fantasies. It is like watching them run off at Dreamworld and leap on ride after ride – the holiday coaster here, the family fun slide over there, the career carousel as soon as they can fit it in. But this dreaming, this fantasising, is taking us into places I'm scared we might never reach.

'Okay, guys. That's fantastic. Honestly, I'm right with you on the beach by the Red Sea. But for the sake of the argument, what is the absolute worst they could do to us? Our record on predicting things has been pretty lousy so far.'

'I suppose they could make a point and force us to sit it out for a few more months,' says Fahmy, wrinkling his nose.

'I bloody hope not,' sighs Baher. 'That means we'd have to sweat it out in this shitbox for the worst of summer *and* for Eid. And I don't want to miss Eid with the kids.'

He ticks the months off under his breath and quietly grits his teeth. 'It also gets us really close to the day my baby is due. There is no way I'm gonna miss that, even if I have to bust out of this stupid cube.'

•

Erika is smiling when I walk into the investigations officer's office. It is one of her biweekly visits, and I'm not sure why she is grinning so widely.

'Have you heard the news about Shami?'

'No. What's happened to him?'

'He is out. Free. They let him go last night. There was huge coverage all over the Egyptian press and of course on Al Jazeera. He is at home right now.'

The news is stunning.

Abdullah al-Shami was a reporter for Al Jazeera Arabic. Back in August 2013, four months before I arrived, he was arrested while covering the Rabaa massacre. He was never charged, but it was widely understood that he too had been held on suspicion of colluding with the Muslim Brotherhood. For more than ten months he had been in prison without charge; five of those on a hunger strike in protest at his conditions.

'They let him go on compassionate grounds,' Erika tells me, 'but we think it had more to do with the public pressure. It has been pretty relentless.'

'What do you think that means for us?' I ask, with more than a hint of hope creeping into my voice.

'As a diplomat, it is hard to say,' she replies, 'but personally I think it is a really good sign. It shows that they are vulnerable to pressure after all, and that the pressure can work. Your judge, Nagy, is a tough one, but I reckon this means things are definitely moving in the right direction.'

Then Erika looks sideways at the officer sitting at the nearby desk shuffling through his paperwork.

'We need to discuss travel plans,' she says under her breath. 'We will need to get you out of here as quickly as possible. Where do you want to go?'

'You mean out of Cairo?'

'I mean out of Egypt. We think we should get you out within twenty-four hours.'

'But what about my passport? They still have that.'

'Don't worry about it. It's been taken care of. We got your second passport from Nairobi. There is still a lot of anger here against Al Jazeera and we want to get you to an airport as quickly as possible.'

I pause to think, but for only a moment.

Nairobi. I want to go home to Nairobi. Since I left the rambling old timber Queenslander I grew up in in Brisbane more than three decades ago, Nairobi has been the only place I've lived longer than three years. For the first time since leaving Brisbane, I am somewhere I'm happy, with friends I care about, a job I love and a country that offers all the adventure I could hope for. And, most importantly of all, I have a contract that doesn't demand I move every two to three years – the BBC's preferred rotation. With Al Jazeera, you stay for as long as you (and they) are happy. And I still am.

I've had moments of dreaming about sailing in the Whitsunday Islands, of course, and I have yet to find a place that comes close to Australia's beaches, but my emotional attachment to Australia is now based on the undeniable bonds of family and nostalgia for a childhood that exists more in my own rose-tinted memory than in the reality of sweaty Brisbane classrooms or the pubs and service stations I used to work in. I am proud of my Australian heritage, and I will get there eventually, but in quiet moments in the cell, when I drift off to somewhere idyllic, it tends to be Sunday afternoon drinking tea or beer with my neighbours in the silken African light filtering through the trees to the back veranda of my house in Nairobi.

•

A letter to the family, on toilet paper:

> *In one of the Radio Mulhaq broadcasts, as we discussed what we were all going through, a thought occurred to me. All the things we think of as weakness, like loneliness or anger or bitterness or vengeance, are all things that make us human. And in their own way,*

they are emotions to be recognised and nursed. To see them as flaws or failings is to deny who we really are. They become weakness only when they dominate us, when they run out of control and drive our thinking.

There is no shame at all in acknowledging fear or anxiety. We are not automatons, after all. But true courage comes from facing down those emotions. Not from denying them, but recognising them as part of our human nature and placing them in context, as companions to the strength we've come to discover inside this box . . .

In our conversation, one of our prison mates talked about how our weaknesses – or at least the things we perceive as weaknesses – can in fact be points of strength, just as perversions of the things we regard as 'strength' can become self-destructive.

Courage is madness if it blinds us to suicidal risk. There is no point being brave if you lose your capacity for compassion in the process. Loneliness is a powerful motivator and a wellspring of love for those closest to us, as long as it doesn't become overwhelming or crippling.

I started today feeling tired and flat. I am finishing it feeling strong and determined. The buggers will not beat us down.

•

'Hey, Ibrahim,' Baher calls out through the cell door. 'Let's have those shears. We've got to spruce up a bit for the hearing.'

The guard eventually arrives with a cardboard box. 'Don't be long. I've got to have this back in half an hour,' he says.

Baher smiles as he opens the lid and pulls out the hair-cutting kit. 'If this journalism thing fails once we're out, maybe I'll open up my own barber shop,' he says. 'I kind of enjoy the challenge of making an ugly bastard like you look halfway respectable.'

'Let's go for a number two and number-three shears,' I instruct. 'Give me short back and sides. I want to look hard, like a marine.'

Baher laughs. 'Mate, you couldn't look hard if they built you out of concrete.'

Once I've stripped to my waist and a towel is draped around my neck, he sweeps the clippers across my scalp in clean, easy gestures. The hair tumbles onto my shoulders and across my chest, finally gathering in a dark-brown and grey puddle beneath me.

'Do you know what?' he says when he finally switches off the buzzing machine and surveys his handiwork. 'If I was a girl, I might even want to feel you up. Beautiful.'

•

Mike is due for one last visit before the verdict, and although we all remain as confident as ever, I realise that if things go horribly wrong we could easily disappear into the guts of the toughest prisons in Egypt, isolated from family and unable to smuggle out messages or make any public statements. So, by the nightlight filtering in from the courtyard, I write a letter I hope he will never have to use.

Dear Mike

I'll explain in more detail what I'd like you to do with this note when I see you later, but it's pretty straightforward. If the unthinkable happens, please release this statement on my behalf, through you, Mum and Dad, and AJE.

God, may all this be over soon!

Love,

Peter

I am extremely disappointed and frustrated by today's verdict. Throughout this trial, the prosecutor has consistently failed to produce a single piece of concrete evidence to support the outrageous allegations against us. At the same time, our lawyers have highlighted countless procedural errors and abuses of due process that should have had the case thrown out of court many times over.

That is why I intend to use every legal tool available to overturn our convictions, starting with an immediate appeal. But the verdict confirms that our trial was never simply about the charges against us. It has been an attempt to use the court to intimidate and silence critical voices in the media. That is why I know that our freedom, and more importantly, the freedom of Egypt's press will never come without noisy, sustained pressure from individuals, human rights groups and governments – anyone who understands the fundamental importance of a free press to Egypt's fledgling democracy.

We are all grateful for the extraordinary and unprecedented support that countless people have offered us throughout our ordeal. It has kept us strong and continues to do so. We must all remain committed to fighting this gross injustice for as long as necessary.

Peter Greste

•

Mike is annoyed with me. He isn't at all happy with my plan of going to Nairobi.

'You can't go there,' he says, shaking his head and irritated by my intransigence. 'If you do, you won't be able to hide and the local press won't leave you alone. We won't be able to hold the rest of the Aussie journos away, either, and the story will have gone before you get back to Australia. You can't hang out there and turn your back on everyone who supported you from back home. You just can't. Why don't you just take Mark's advice?'

Mark Colvin is one of Australia's most venerable broadcasters as well as one of its most seasoned foreign correspondents, and he has advised my family that I ought to go somewhere quiet and safe where I can decompress and gather my thoughts for a few days before facing the inevitable media 'onslaught'. (I use quote marks because I find it hard to imagine that the noun is appropriate when the press interest in our case is unlikely to last more than a day or two after we are released.)

'But Mike, you don't understand,' I tell him. 'That *is* my home. And if I don't go there first, I know it'll be months before I get back. There are documents and clothes and things that I want to collect. My driver's licence is Kenyan, so if I don't go back and get a copy, I'll be screwed until I can sort out a new one. And for God's sake, can't I have a chance to sleep in my own bed for a few nights?'

Almost as soon as the words come out of my mouth, I realise how silly they sound. Mike and Mark are right, of course. The best option will be somewhere quiet and neutral where I can lie low for a few days away from the media, get my thoughts and things together, and then go home – to Australia. If I go to Nairobi, it could be weeks before I get out of the place, and after all the help and support that Australians have given us, from shopkeepers to the prime minister, it would look disrespectful to head anywhere else.

'Okay,' I sigh, giving up. 'Where do we go? London?'

'Nah – unless you stick your head in a paper bag, you'll be spotted there pretty quickly. The story has been big in the UK, you know. How about Italy?'

'That might work, but I really want somewhere near the sea. Can you at least give me that?'

Mike sighs. 'Okay, but it has to be relatively close to an airport. We don't want to have to move you around too much.'

'What about Cyprus? It's in the middle of the Mediterranean, only an hour or so from Egypt; it's pretty quiet; and they've got cold beer and plenty of pork.'

'That's not a bad idea.'

•

'Have you heard the news?'

Fahmy is a little breathless as he comes back to the cell after a visit from his brother. 'A deal has been done. We're out of here.'

'What do you mean?' asks Baher.

'It's John Kerry. He has just had a news conference with [Egypt's foreign minister] Shoukry and they've announced they're lifting the arms embargo. They're going to deliver the Apaches! Apparently he mentioned human rights, the rule of law and press freedom in the conference. That means us. It can't be anything else.'

As the US secretary of state, Kerry is the highest-ranking American official to have visited Egypt since the coup. The Americans have been highly critical of the way Sisi seized power and of the new administration's human-rights record since then, so this visit is hugely symbolic. Simply by showing up, Kerry is giving the Egyptians the dignity of his presence and effectively acknowledging the government's legitimacy.

Almost from the beginning, the American administration has been explicitly vocal about our case, and Kerry and President Obama have publicly chastised Egypt for the way we have been treated. To underline his concern, Obama has left an arms embargo in place, effectively freezing the delivery of modern weapons systems, including a fleet of Apache helicopters that have been sitting in crates in the USA.

Kerry simply couldn't have come to stand side by side with his Egyptian counterpart, Sameh Shoukry, unless there has been some breakthrough. Anything less than an acquittal would be hugely embarrassing, so they *must* have sorted things out behind closed doors.

It is great news, and I can feel that fizz return to my skin, but I can also still detect a little tick of doubt gnawing away at the back of my skull.

'Has your brother had anything concrete? Have the Americans or the Canadians told him something that hasn't been made public?' I ask Fahmy.

'No. He hasn't had anything explicit, but can you imagine any other outcome? If we go down, Kerry will look unbelievably naive and stupid, and they won't let that happen. I also don't think even Sisi would have the balls to flip the bird at the Americans by letting us go to prison now. If he did they might even cancel the Apaches, and Sisi wants those more than he wants us.'

'Woohoo!' shouts Baher as he does a little jig, and we all slap hands with high-fives. 'We're gonna party, party, party . . .'

•

It is 23 June, and I am awake by 5 a.m. I know without looking that Fahmy is already up and has probably been awake for hours. Baher coughs.

As far as the universe is concerned, today is no different from any other. People outside are continuing their lives as they have always done. There is nothing unusual or special about it, and no reason to remark upon it. June 23 is pretty much the same as June 22 was and, in all probability, will be no different to June 24. The sun rises on schedule, the planets spin on their axes, birds chirp as usual, and workers still have to commute to their offices.

And yet here, inside Mulhaq al Mazraa, something is odd about the morning. The air has a thickness that feels out of place. There is both a density and a clarity that I struggle to describe because I've never experienced it before. It has a visceral viscosity. If I move my hand through the air fast enough I imagine I might find a bubble trail, and when I slap my tongue against the roof of my mouth there is a dull metallic taste.

After the euphoria around the news of Kerry's announcement, none of us has had much sleep. I'm not sure about the others, but as I rise, I find it impossible to hold my focus.

We take time to prepare for the hearing.

We have no iron, but we know there will be a few more cameras than usual in court and we want to look proud, dignified and strong. You can't do that in a wrinkled shirt. I put on the clean white polo shirt I have saved for the occasion, and wipe a damp hand across my chest to smooth out any creases.

True to form, Baher smokes and cracks jokes while Fahmy gets talkative, moving around with restless nervous energy. He can't resist the urge to plan for the party.

'We will have it at my house. Or on a boat on the Nile. It'll be huge. Everyone in the media will be there. We can invite all the people who supported us, as well as a bunch of celebs I know.'

His voice fades into white noise as I sit with my own thoughts.

I tend to go quiet, and right now the last thing I want is idle conversation. There is nothing left to say, nothing that we haven't ploughed through like a muddy field a dozen times already. We have talked about this moment for most of the past four months, and I am fed up with all the talk.

By 8 a.m. we have scrubbed ourselves down, dressed, made our beds, brushed our teeth, straightened our things, redone our beds, tried to read, paced the cell, talked about the party, argued about getting overoptimistic, stretched out, leafed through newspapers . . . and still the guards haven't come for us.

They could turn up any time between now and noon. Or later. Who knows? We have even heard of cases where the verdict hearings have been delayed at the last second because the judge is off sick (with a hangover, according to rumours), and our judge has never looked especially healthy.

('What if Nagy dies?' Baher asks with gallows humour. 'Then we'd have to have the bloody trial all over again.')

Finally, we hear the footsteps of the guards and the clatter of keys in the outer doors.

'Let's go, boys. There is a court waiting for you.'

Baher turns to Fahmy and me as the cell door swings open. 'Another day down, another day closer to freedom.'

•

When the door to the transport van swings open at the prisoners' entrance to the court, we are confronted by two ranks of fully-kitted-out riot police whom the locals call 'ninjas'. They line the short walk to the entrance of the building, the staircase, and the landing leading to the filthy holding cell – perhaps forty or fifty of them in all. Cuffed together in pairs, we march up to the cell, with the students defiantly shouting anti-coup slogans.

The guards refuse to take off our cuffs, so Baher and I pace around the cell, arms and legs moving together in step. He is much taller and longer-legged than I, but if we focus on one another we can make an easy, steady pace around the perimeter. If we lose concentration, drift out of the present and start thinking about the hearing just minutes away, we fall out of step and get into an awkward, gangling mess. It is a valuable lesson.

Eventually the hatch in the cell door slides open and a voice commands us to line up. Baher and I are in front, with Fahmy and Shady Ibrahim behind us and the rest of the students and Khalid Mohammed bringing up the rear.

As the door finally swings open, I turn to the queue behind me and say, 'Keep your heads up. Let the bastards know we're strong.'

We march through another corridor of armoured goons into the court, to the top of the steps leading down to the cage.

The room is extraordinary. It is packed with camera crews, photographers, reporters with notepads, family members, lawyers, observers, diplomats, and quite a few people I simply can't place. I try to count the TV cameras but give up after fifteen. They keep moving around, making it impossible to keep track of them all.

We march in a dignified line into the cage and take our places. Each of us presses against the iron mesh and scans the heaving crowd for familiar faces. I can see Patrick Kingsley from *The Guardian*, my old colleague Orla Guerin from the BBC, reporters from CNN and the ABC, John Lyons from *The Australian*. Sherine Tadros, a former Al Jazeera correspondent in Egypt who is now working for Sky News, is towards the front of the crowd (she blows me a kiss and my heart melts). There is the *New York Times*, the Associated Press, *The Times* of London, reporters from Al Arabiya, and countless others from local news organisations. Far too many to count.

I can see the Australian ambassador, Ralph King, and his counterparts from Latvia and Canada. Each has his or her collection of consular staff and advisers. Our lawyers are also there, of course, but there are many others I have never seen before.

The courtroom is heaving but still somehow feels light, and above the crowd I spot Mike. As I wave, I see Andrew's familiar grin hovering behind him. That wasn't expected – both my brothers are here! My heart bounces as Andrew waves his hand and punches the air in solidarity.

'See. You. Soon,' I mouth at them both with a smile as I give a thumbs-up.

Eventually the sergeant of the court calls the crowd to order, and the hubbub subsides as the cameras swing to the bench and the officials march in – first the trio of judges and then the prosecutors, who take their seats to the left of the court.

I settle into the corner of the cage as close as possible to the official translator, who is seated just outside it. He smiles at me, whispering, 'I wish you the best of luck, Mr Peter. I hope we can drink tea together soon.'

A hush settles as Judge Nagy intones the opening lines of the Qur'an: '*Bismillah hir-Rahman nir-Rahim.*' ('In the name of Allah, Most Gracious, Most Merciful.')

Then he picks up a page from his desk and begins reading the verdict, halting slightly as he stumbles over the sentences.

'The court finds that the defendants acted to depict the country in a state of rift and infighting, taking advantage of the noble media profession,' he says.

The translator's face turns grey. I hear his words, but their meaning takes time to sink in.

'This was, as they say, a marriage with the devil, twisting their profession from a "search for the truth" into a "fabrication of truth", simply to serve the cause of one of the outlawed terrorist groups, the Muslim Brotherhood.'

Judge Nagy then begins reading out a long list of names – all the defendants *in absentia*. The translator gives up trying to relay them all, instead squinting and leaning in to listen for the verdict.

'They are all guilty,' Nagy says at the end of the list. 'Ten years in prison.'

There is a collective intake of breath, as if the walls themselves have suddenly inflated in a gasp, and a shocked hubbub begins to ripple across the court. My brain simply won't process the meaning.

The translator creases up his face even further as he struggles to hear the judge above the rising din.

'Fahmy, Baher, you and three students – all guilty, seven years in prison. Only two students – Ahmed Ibrahim and Anas Beltagy – are not guilty.'

I look down at the translator in stunned disbelief.

'Yes – seven years,' he tells me. 'That's what the judge said. I am so sorry. And Baher gets three more years for having illegal ammunition.'

The judge bangs down his gavel and he and his panel rise to leave.

I can see the court erupting. People are shouting in rage, standing on the chairs and yelling, but my ears are ringing and I feel giddy with shock. I can't hear a thing beyond the words locked in a loop inside my head.

'Seven years. Seven years. Seven years. *Seven years . . .*'

The students begin chanting revolutionary songs and slogans, their combined voices filled with fury.

I press my lips together in a tight, thin line and hammer the cage with a single angry swing of both my palms. I can see Andrew's and Mike's faces above the crowd. Andrew is patting his heart in sympathy and I punch the air once more. I mean it to be a gesture of strength and defiance, but it is all I can do to keep my legs from collapsing.

•

One of our guards, Abdulahi, wipes a finger across his moist eyes as we tell him of the verdicts and sentences.

'That is very wrong,' he says in a conspiratorial whisper. 'I am so sorry. You should be going home, Mr Peter. Not stay here with us.'

He turns the key in the lock of our cell door and gestures us inside. 'Please forgive Egypt.'

As the door swings shut with a clang, Fahmy collapses on his bed face down, curls into a fetal position and closes his eyes.

At last my own legs give way, and I slide down the cell wall with tears streaming down my face. Baher's cheeks are wet too, as he finally lets go of the emotion.

'Ten fucking years. Fuck.'

'Baher, I'll have one of your cigarettes,' I say.

'But you don't smoke.'

'Today I do.'

16

CHARLIE HEBDO

Gérard Biard considers himself lucky. On 7 January 2015, he was in London speaking at a conference when two heavily armed men wearing balaclavas arrived at his office almost 350 kilometres away at 10 Rue Nicolas-Appert in Paris. There, the men confronted 32-year-old cartoonist Corinne 'Coco' Rey as she approached the building and forced her to punch her passcode into the security door that was protecting her colleagues at the satirical magazine *Charlie Hebdo*.

The story is shockingly familiar to anybody with access to the media early in 2015. The gunmen – brothers Chérif and Saïd Kouachi – were carrying an extraordinary arsenal: vz. 58 assault rifles, Škorpion submachine guns, a pump-action shotgun, a loaded rocket-launcher and pistols. Once inside, they sprayed the reception area with gunfire, killing maintenance worker Frédéric Boisseau as he sat at the desk.[84] They then ordered Rey to lead them upstairs to where the first editorial meeting of the year had just begun. Fifteen cartoonists, writers and editors had gathered in a jovial mood to plan the next few editions of the magazine. ('We thought it was a joke,' one of the survivors, Laurent Léger, later told reporters. 'Everyone was on top form and happy. Some of them had just come back from holiday. It was almost euphoric.'[85])

By the time the Kouachi brothers had finished their killing spree, a dozen people lay dead and three others were wounded. As they left the building they shouted, 'We have avenged the Prophet Mohammed!', and 'God is great!'[86]

At the time, the gunmen didn't make the reasons for their attack any more explicit than that, but as the drama continued to unfold with the police hunting for the pair across the city, a former deputy director of the CIA, Michael Morell, said their motive was 'absolutely clear: trying to shut down a media organisation that lampooned the Prophet Mohammed'.[87]

The magazine's director of publication, Stéphane 'Charb' Charbonnier, had already been under police protection after Al Qaeda issued death threats to avenge the magazine's caustic take on Islam and the Prophet Mohammed. The Kouachi brothers specifically asked for Charb before killing him and his bodyguard.

Gérard Biard was in no doubt, either. He had been the editor-in-chief since the magazine relaunched in 1992, and was already acutely aware of the threats it faced. He had steered his publication through some of its most provocative editions, which had resulted in a slew of death threats and lawsuits.

As France struggled to come to terms with the attack and to find an appropriate response, Biard knew exactly what he had to do.

•

In Egypt, we learned about the *Charlie Hebdo* killings within hours through the prison grapevine. I first realised something was up when I heard whooping, cheering and shouts of 'Allāhu akbar' from the exercise yard.

One of the prison officers saw the breaking news on a TV in his office, and it quickly spread through the ranks of the guards. They told the prisoners in the exercise yard what they knew, and as the prisoners returned to their cells, the news came back to us and the others in our block.

Like most of the West, I was staggered by the enormity of the crime – it was one of the deadliest attacks on French soil since the end of the Second World War – and found it incomprehensibly violent. I didn't know much about the magazine at the time, but others recalled that it had reprinted a series of cartoons lampooning the Prophet that were first published in Denmark and had triggered a wave of angry, violent protests across the Islamic world.

Charlie Hebdo is the only remaining paper in France with a long tradition of trenchant caricatures of the religious, the sacred and the powerful, and of openly mocking all forms of fanaticism. Some of its most provocative covers have been aimed squarely at the Catholic Church, attacking it for its positions on abortion, sexuality and women's rights. (One famous cartoon showed the Holy Trinity – the Father, the Son and the Holy Ghost – in a sexual threesome.) It has lampooned racism, the right, the left and political correctness. It has been flagrantly and unapologetically offensive to just about every 'ism' that ever existed. At times, it has seemed as though its sole purpose is to rile, jab and rankle.

Although I didn't see it as such at the time, I have since come to understand the attack as part of the wider assault on press freedom that we were caught up in. Once again, we were witnessing a full-frontal strike at a media institution simply because of the ideas it was publishing.

But those in Mulhaq Prison saw the Kouachi brothers' killing spree as an act of revenge for belittling Islam. Even among the guards, there was a sense of justice about the bloodshed. The magazine had, after all, once published a cover image of Mohammed with his head in his hands complaining, 'It is hard to be loved by arseholes.'

•

The question confronting France and the West more broadly was how best to answer an assault like that. Should the government declare 'war' on the attackers and effectively make France an extension of the American War on Terror? Should it target Muslims and immigrants who might share the Kouachi brothers' ideology? Should it try to stamp out the ideology that inspired the pair, and if so, how? Or should it treat the bloodshed simply as crime of mass murder and carry on as before?

The short-term reaction was unequivocally clear: millions of people around the world posted 'Je suis Charlie' on their social-media pages or shouted the slogan in demonstrations in support of the magazine and in condemnation of the attackers. Forty world leaders joined about 1.6 million Parisians – an astonishing two-thirds of the city's entire population – at a march four days later when they all cried it out in unison. Across France, officials estimated that 3.7 million people were on the streets that day, making it the most significant protest in the country's history.[88] One group carried a giant pencil with the words 'Not afraid' stencilled along its length. To anybody who believed in freedom of the press and the right to speak and to criticise, it was a deeply heartening, almost spiritual movement.

But as the shock and outrage dissipated, critics turned on *Charlie Hebdo*, echoing many of the complaints I was hearing inside the prison. 'They had it coming' was common.

'Okay, maybe murder was too much,' one fellow prisoner told me. 'But what did they expect after insulting Muslims like that? If you poke a lion with a stick, you should not be surprised if you get bitten.

'The magazine should mourn its dead and then they should close for good,' he continued. 'I hope they have learned their lesson.'

•

For the editor, Gérard Biard, his own response was never in question: 'We had to keep publishing, to honour the victims but also to keep fighting.'[89]

For security reasons, *Charlie Hebdo* doesn't like inviting people to its current address, so Biard and I met in the boardroom of his lawyer's office. Throughout our conversation, a short, wiry-looking man with a shaved head, a grim expression and a windbreaker loosely covering the pistol on his hip stands guard on the other side of the glass with one eye permanently trained on the front door.

Biard continues: 'I won't even allow self-censorship, because what we are fighting for is something we have been battling since 2006: the right to sketch, the right to blaspheme. The story of the Danish Mohammed cartoons that we reprinted that year is key.'

That series of twelve images was first published on 30 September 2005 by the Danish newspaper *Jyllands-Posten*. In Biard's eyes, the cartoons were relatively benign. One, for example, showed an exasperated mullah at the gates of heaven waving his hands at a queue of smouldering suicide bombers waiting to get in and telling them: 'Stop, stop. We have run out of virgins.' Certainly by the standards of *Charlie Hebdo*, which often dredges up social taboos, they were pretty inoffensive, though still undoubtedly sharply critical of Islam.

Even so, early the following year the cartoons had triggered a wave of angry protests that in several cases left people dead.

To Biard, the fact that the outrage took so long to surface – more than three months – is a clear sign that it was manufactured by religious leaders wanting to use it as a political tool to launch a debate and fire up Muslim anger, rather than any reflection of the way most Muslims felt. He sees it as a cynical attempt by conservative Islamic clerics and thinkers to manipulate public opinion, to turn it against the West and attack one of the most deeply held principles of Western democracy, the freedom of speech. The Danish cartoons were simply a means to deepen the divisions between Islam and the West. That is why Biard decided to join dozens of other news organisations around the world and reprint the images in solidarity with his Danish counterparts, who by that stage were receiving their own death threats.

As usual, though, the French magazine went further, following the Danish cartoons with a series of its own provocative images.

'We attack ideas, not the people,' Biard insists. 'With our sketches, we are told that we are abusing and criticising a whole group of people, but in fact we are sketching an ideology. We are drawing figures who represent that ideology, like mullahs. Neither *Charlie Hebdo* nor any of our journalists have ever said that all Muslims around the world should take responsibility for terrorist attacks. That is what racists do.

'When [the leader of France's National Front] Marine Le Pen and far-right figures in other countries demand that Muslims should condemn terrorist attacks, they are holding them implicitly responsible and so exposing themselves as racists. We do not do that. We point to ideas and individuals and criticise them, but never the group.'

In the wake of the attack on its offices, *Charlie Hebdo* continued to publish with all of its original irreverent, acerbic mischievousness. But in releasing more images critical of Islam, it drew fire from critics – including many journalists – who argued that the cartoons amounted to Islamophobic provocation.

In one opinion piece published in *USA Today*, Islamic scholar Anjem Choudary argued that even in the West, freedom of speech has limitations to prevent defamation and incitement: 'Muslims consider the honour of the Prophet Muhammad to be dearer to them than that of their parents or even themselves. To defend it is considered to be an obligation upon them. The strict punishment, if found guilty of this crime under sharia, is capital punishment implementable by an Islamic state. This is because the Messenger Muhammad said, "Whoever insults a Prophet kill him." However, because the honor of the Prophet is something which all Muslims want to defend, many will take the law into their own hands, as we often see.'[90]

In the *New Yorker*, writer Teju Cole was sharply critical of what he argued was a misplaced lionisation of the magazine and its Islamophobia: 'It is possible to defend the right to obscene and racist speech without promoting or sponsoring the content of that speech. It is possible to approve of sacrilege without endorsing racism. And it is possible to consider Islamophobia immoral without wishing it illegal.'

Biard scoffs at this idea and its implied pressure for self-censorship: 'The evil genius of creating this word "Islamophobia" is that you transform the right to criticise Islamism – a religion, and a political religion – into something bad.'

And yet, while the government hasn't explicitly limited freedom of the press (Biard jabs his thumb at the state-funded bodyguard behind him as an example of the French government's commitment to defending the media), he sees examples of self-censorship everywhere among his colleagues.

'What is really striking me now is that the aggression against us isn't coming from outside, as we expected, but from within the French press itself. Government pressure is not the reason many journalists have stopped writing criticisms of Islam . . . They are not writing because they do not dare to.'

The effect of self-censorship, even if it is born of a desire to avoid a backlash, is corrosive and damaging. Biard sees it as akin to a slightly more benign version of a Mafia protection racket where a standover merchant says, 'Pay me, or I will burn down your business.' In this case, the payment is in the form of quisling deference to thin-skinned people unable to take public criticism without a violent retort.

'What happens is that the cost always grows, and you will never escape the racket. It is never going to convince those who use the violence to stop, because if you show them that you are afraid, and that [their threats] have an impact on what you do, if you let them think their ways are working, it will only continue. Of course it is natural and normal to be afraid, but it is even more dangerous to let them know that these methods are effective.'

In May 2015, PEN America, a prominent literary organisation that supports writers and the free flow of ideas, gave *Charlie Hebdo* its prestigious Freedom of Expression Courage Award. In doing so, it faced a backlash from six authors who boycotted the ceremony (including Australian novelist Peter Carey, and Teju Cole) and more than two dozen others who signed a joint letter condemning the decision to honour the magazine:

> To the section of the French population that is already marginalised, embattled, and victimised, a population that

> is shaped by the legacy of France's various colonial enterprises, and that contains a large percentage of devout Muslims, *Charlie Hebdo*'s cartoons of the Prophet must be seen as being intended to cause further humiliation and suffering.
>
> Our concern is that, by bestowing the Toni and James C. Goodale Freedom of Expression Courage Award on *Charlie Hebdo*, PEN is not simply conveying support for freedom of expression, but also valorising selectively offensive material: material that intensifies the anti-Islamic, anti-Maghreb, anti-Arab sentiments already prevalent in the Western world.[91]

For Biard, the protest was both absurd and tragic: 'In Europe, we have this freedom of speech, this freedom of expression, but what happened to us [at *Charlie Hebdo*]? We were in the bizarre situation where somehow, because we were exercising our rights of freedom of the press – the freedom to criticise – we, the victims of mass murder, were somehow transformed into offenders. How did this happen?'

•

Gaspard Koenig is no fan of *Charlie Hebdo*.

'I hate it,' he tells me in the Paris headquarters of GenerationLibre, the think tank he has run since he founded it in 2013. 'I think *Charlie Hebdo* is vulgar, and often just plain wrong. It is very inaccurate, but of course I totally defend the right for it to exist, and I was with those people demonstrating on the streets, shouting "Je suis Charlie" too.'

Koenig is radical in his defence of free speech. Soon after the attack, on 11 January, the then French interior minister called a meeting of his counterparts from across the European Union. During their discussions, they focused on the internet and the way it has become a tool for recruiting and radicalising would-be terrorists, spreading hate speech and inciting violence. Among the meeting's initiatives was a move to get internet providers to help police hate speech and remove offending content.[92] In other words, the response to an attack on free speech . . . was an attempt to limit free speech.

'It's quite a paradox,' Koenig says. 'They ask social-media companies themselves to do the work of cleaning up their users. Of course, when somebody has extremist views, it makes you very uncomfortable. That's why mainstream French politicians want to ban Salafism, but I don't think that is the right response.' (Salafism is a radically conservative branch of Islam that demands 'personal jihad' – a personal struggle to be pious – but eschews politics.) 'I think the right response is *more* free speech, not less. I know it is uncomfortable, but [extremists] need to be able to say what they want to say so that we are able to refute them. Otherwise it is just a power struggle between two political groups.'

To support his argument, Koenig calls John Stuart Mill to the witness box.

Mill's *On Liberty*, published in 1859, includes a chapter called 'Of the liberty of thought and discussion', whose opening paragraph reads:

> The time, it is to be hoped, is gone by when any defence would be necessary of the 'liberty of the press' as one of the securities against corrupt or tyrannical government. No argument, we may suppose, can now be needed, against permitting a legislature or an executive, not identified in interest with the people, to prescribe opinions to them, and determine what doctrines or what arguments they shall be allowed to hear. This aspect of the question, besides, has been so often and so triumphantly enforced by preceding writers, that it needs not be specially insisted on in this place.[93]

It is worth restating the obvious here: that the practical and philosophical value of a free press was so well established more than 150 years ago that an author like Mill could brush it off as a given.

But a philosopher and intellectual of Mill's stature is also never going to make assumptions, and he spends the rest of the chapter laying out his deceptively simple yet powerful case for allowing no opinion to be suppressed, regardless of how wrong-headed or extreme it might seem at first glance.

In his view, since nobody is infallible or can claim to have complete knowledge, 'truth' can only be discovered and maintained if what we believe is constantly tested and challenged by alternative opinions. 'If an opinion is right, [we] are deprived of the opportunity of exchanging error for truth; if wrong, [we] lose, what is almost as great a benefit, the clearer perception and livelier impression of truth, produced by its collision with error,' he wrote.

Mill goes on to argue that any attempt to suppress alternative opinions is based on the assumption that the suppressor has some claim to infallibility – itself, supreme hubris.

The implication for the EU interior ministers meeting at the behest of their French counterpart is twofold: that only by exposing established orthodoxy to constant questioning and challenges can we make sure that the ideas that underpin Europe are true, strong and healthy; and also that the only way to defeat a bad idea – in this case a particularly violent ideology – is with a good idea. To apply Mill's argument, if we believe that militant Islamism is fundamentally and fatally flawed, the best way to snuff it out is by forcing it to confront better, healthier, truer ideologies. That would have the twin effect of both killing off the bad idea and confirming the value of the better one.

Clearly the alternative hasn't worked very well. The West has tried to shut down dangerous militant ideas since 9/11. As we have already seen in this book, online censorship, political pressure, imprisonment and drone strikes don't seem to have had a great deal of impact. In fact, those strategies seem to have made terrorism more widespread rather than less, and if killing an idea is tough, it is even more so in the age of social media and encrypted communications. Between secure chat rooms, data encryption and a minor explosion of secure social-media applications, policing every corner of the internet has become a hopeless endeavour.

'It is impossible to regulate freedom of speech on social media,' Koenig says. 'It is technically impossible.'

Of course, France's commitment to free speech has never been absolute. It has long been illegal to deny the Holocaust, spread 'hate speech' or incite terrorism. In fact, under article 421-2-5 of the French Criminal Code, 'provocation of acts of terrorism or public apology for such acts shall be punishable by five years' imprisonment and a fine of €75 000'.[94] (Curiously, the penalty increases to seven years in prison and €100 000 for anybody who makes their statements online – itself an implicit admission of the power of social media.)

In the space of just one week after the *Charlie Hebdo* attack, France's Justice Ministry said it opened thirty-seven cases against people allegedly 'condoning terrorism'. Among the cases, a man of twenty-two was jailed for a year for posting a video mocking one of the two policemen murdered in the attack; a drunk driver was given four years in prison after making threats against the police who arrested him; three men in their twenties were jailed in Toulouse for 'condoning terrorism'; and a man of twenty was jailed in Orléans for shouting 'Long live the Kalash[nikov]!' at police in a shopping centre.[95]

But the most notorious arrest involved comedian Dieudonné M'bala M'bala.

Widely known and loved among disaffected youth from the *banlieues* – poor, run-down suburbs with large immigrant populations – Dieudonné had become something of an anti-establishment hero and an example of what his supporters said was obscene hypocrisy in the wake of the *Charlie Hebdo* attack.

He had already been convicted of anti-Semitism and Holocaust denial and widely condemned for his signature *quenelle* – allegedly an inverted take on the Nazi salute – but it was his arrest for mocking the *Charlie Hebdo* solidarity march that drew attention.

On the night of the mass 'Je suis Charlie' marches, Dieudonné wrote in a Facebook post as the marchers were dissipating: 'Know that this evening, as far as I'm concerned, I'm feeling like Charlie Coulibaly.' (The post was soon deleted.)

The remark was a take on 'Je suis Charlie', but with a cynical twist. Amedy Coulibaly was a friend of the Kouachi brothers, and as the pair launched their attack on the magazine, he killed a policewoman near a Jewish school before going on to hold up a kosher supermarket the following day and murdering four Jewish hostages. In conflating Coulibaly with the 'Je suis Charlie' slogan, Dieudonné's comment sparked widespread outrage, including condemnation from the French prime minister, Manuel Valls.

'I'm being seen as an Amedy Coulibaly when I'm no different from Charlie Hebdo,' Dieudonné complained. The government disagreed. He was arrested and charged with incitement, and crucially, his shows were banned.

'Think about that for a moment,' says Koenig. 'He was silenced because of what he *might* say in his shows. That is unprecedented. You can say that someone has violated the law by making remarks *after* they have said it, but *ex-ante* [before the fact]? That is impossible.'

To get around the legal dilemma, the Conseil d'État (the supreme court for administrative justice – France's highest judicial authority) developed a new concept: the idea that preserving human dignity is a part of maintaining public order, and that by attacking and insulting Jews, Dieudonné's shows were therefore a threat to public order.

To Koenig, it is a form of censorship that is not only legally absurd but against Mill's fundamental principles behind freedom of speech. It turned Dieudonné into a hero, helped him draw hundreds of thousands of viewers to his YouTube videos, and at the same time isolated his supporters from hearing any rational debate about why his form of humour is so wrong-headed.

•

In France, the government lurched towards authoritarianism once again after the second mass attack in that horrific year. On Friday 13 November 2015, three groups of gunmen and suicide bombers launched a series of six distinct attacks across the northern Paris commune of Saint-Denis.

Once again, the blood-soaked details are familiar enough. Three suicide bombers signalled the start of the violence when they blew themselves up outside the Stade de France during a football match. Within minutes, mass shootings began at nearby cafes and restaurants, including another suicide bombing. Hardest hit was the Bataclan theatre, where hundreds of fans were enjoying a concert by the US band Eagles of Death Metal. There, the attackers took hostages in a stand-off with police. The gunmen were either shot or blew themselves up when police finally raided the theatre. In all, 130 people died on Black Friday, including eighty-nine at the Bataclan.

In a statement claiming responsibility for the attacks, Islamic State described Paris as 'the capital of prostitution and obscenity' and warned that it was the 'first of the storm'.[96]

'France is at war,' President François Hollande told a special joint session of the French parliament three days later. He ordered a state of emergency and vowed to step up military operations in Syria.[97]

In his address to the parliament, Hollande said, 'The law which governs the state of emergency of 3 April 1955 cannot really match the kind of technologies and threats we face today, but it includes two exceptional measures: house arrest and police searches. These two measures offer useful means to prevent terrorist acts. I want to ensure that they are fully implemented and strengthened.'

That reaction is hard to criticise, especially after the heat and emotion of such a brutal strike at the heart of French life. Politically, the government had no choice but to respond forcefully and make sure that French people felt safe and protected. At a minimum, that meant a heavy presence of security forces on the streets, and operations targeting anybody else who might pose a threat.

Hollande went on to tell the parliament that 'last night, more than 104 people were placed under house arrest and there were 168 police searches. And there will be more.'

The laws allow police to place anyone they think is a security risk under house arrest, dissolve groups who are deemed to be a threat to public order, carry out searches without warrants, and copy data and block websites that 'encourage' terrorism. Internet surveillance has become widespread. Curfews can be imposed, large gatherings or protests are forbidden, and movement is limited.

After extending the state of emergency for almost two years, the government finally called it off, but only after it had passed a new anti-terror law that made some of the emergency measures permanent. Those measures include easier searches of homes, and confining individuals to their home towns without judicial approval.

Yorric Kermarrec is an urbane lawyer for Madrigall, one of France's most prominent publishing houses, with a list of authors that includes novelist Michel Houellebecq. (Houellebecq is infamous for his book *Submission*, in which a moderate Islamic party exploits the divisions between mainstream parties to win an election and take control of the government.) In the wake of the *Charlie Hebdo* attack, Kermarrec's first concern was for some of his more controversial authors, who were already under police protection after receiving specific threats to their lives. He understood the need for a robust government response, but believes it went way beyond what was necessary.

'After the Bataclan attack, some people were placed under house arrest – that was important, of course. But there was the Paris climate change talks a few weeks later, and the police put environmentalists under house arrest too. In the War on Terror, "terrorism" is a very flexible, blurry concept. You can use it to convict people who are not linked to terrorism as most people would think of it. And yet this is what we see in the state of emergency.'[98]

In other words, the French government was already reinterpreting 'terrorism' to include anybody who posed a challenge to the state in far broader terms than originally intended. Islamic State fighters were obvious targets; less justifiable were IS sympathisers with nothing more than an objectionable opinion expressed on a Twitter account. But environmental campaigners?

Even the United Nations thought the government went too far. A group of special rapporteurs on the freedoms of opinion, expression, assembly and privacy visited France to examine the impact of the state of emergency. In a public statement, they concluded that the government was imposing 'excessive and disproportionate restrictions' on fundamental human rights.[99]

To guarantee the rule of law and prevent arbitrary procedures, the experts recommended that the authorities accept judicial controls over antiterrorism measures *before* they use them. The state-of-emergency law only allows judicial review retrospectively, long after the police might have overstepped the mark.

The UN experts also noted that a law giving the state powers to monitor international electronic communications, swiftly adopted after the attacks, expanded the power of the executive over the collection, analysis and storage of communications content or metadata without requiring any judicial oversight, either before or after the fact.

•

Koenig argues that the French government's overreach is dangerous for two vital reasons.

The first is that rolling back basic principles of human rights, rule of law, equality of all, and freedom of expression – the founding principles of Western democracy – is a form of capitulation to the extremists who were trying to undermine the French state.

'When we limit freedom of speech,' Koenig says, 'or when we push through laws [authorising] electronic surveillance on the internet, or when we say, "Well, it's fine if we imprison people without a trial because of the war on terror", and so on, we are giving up the very principles for which we were attacked. So when we do that *we* are being naive.'

The second is that when governments shelve their commitment to those ideals, even if it is for the sake of 'national security', they undermine the system that has made democracies among the most stable, prosperous and peaceful states in human history. When the United States suspended its principles after 9/11 and used extrajudicial killings, detentions and torture, it played directly into the hands of IS.

•

It is rare that Islamic State offers genuine thanks to an American president, but in February 2015, the organisation did exactly that. It published a cover story in its online magazine, *Dabiq*, titled 'The Extinction of the Grayzone' (sic).[100]

In the opening paragraph, the anonymous author wrote: 'Bush spoke the truth when he said, "Either you are with us or you are with the terrorists." Meaning, either you are with the crusade or you are with Islam.'

In this binary world, there can be no room for compromise, debate or interpretation. There is 'right' and 'wrong', and anybody who strays onto the 'wrong' side of the line is marked for brutal punishment. For IS, more peaceful, open versions of Islam are worse than disbelief altogether, because they challenge the hard edges of IS's own extremist interpretation.

The article makes it clear that one of IS's key strategies in its long game is to drive a wedge between Muslims and the West, forcing those who inhabit the grey zone (the 'hideout of the hypocrites', according to the article) to choose which side they are on.

'The grey zone is vital to our democracies,' says Koenig. 'We have to protect the grey zone even if it sometimes makes us uncomfortable.'

The call to eliminate the grey zone is especially troubling for journalism – after all, it is the space that reporters are supposed to inhabit. It is the region of difference that we have a professional obligation to explore, by seeking out and exposing opposing views. The idea is not to generate conflict, as IS would want, but to help understanding, push debate and test ideas. The whole point is to keep the conversations going so we *avoid* conflict. As Koenig says, it isn't always comfortable or easy, but it is necessary.

•

One evening in prison, after the guards had locked us in our cells for the night, we again started to talk about the *Charlie Hebdo* attack.

'You can't allow insults,' declared one of the more devout inmates.'What did they expect making cartoons? Of course we Muslims will get angry.'

'Don't you think it is good to be able to express your opinions freely and without worrying about whether you're going to be murdered for it?' I asked. By then I was getting exasperated.

'Of course it is. We all believe in freedom of speech, but there must be limits. You can't insult people and expect no anger.'

'Is your faith *really* so weak that some guy putting a drawing in a magazine can challenge it so much?' I said. 'They weren't criticising you personally. They were having a go at your beliefs, and if you have no response better than murder, if you have no good arguments yourself to deal with the criticisms and your best answer is to blow the place up, then you're the one that needs to look at your ideas.'

'My faith is strong,' he snorted. 'Nothing can move me from my faith.'

'Then learn to fight those kinds of attacks with better reasoning. That's how democracy and the media work.'

'Reasoning?' he spat. 'This is not politics. This is God's word – Allah's. You cannot argue with Him. Nobody can say what He *means*. Muslims must fight anybody who insults His faith.'

I could see this was an argument I would not win that day.

17

MAZRAA PRISON

24 JUNE 2014 – 31 JANUARY 2015

Once again, I have that feeling of dread. Once again we are to be moved, apparently because of our conviction, and, like an animal that has been prodded for so long that the cage seems like the only safe place left, I feel anxious about what they have in mind for us beyond these now-familiar walls.

The guards give us an hour to get our stuff together, and although we have very little in relative terms, it still takes surprisingly long to organise our possessions. Clothes, books, food – those are the easy things. But I have stashed a few notes and pens around the place (a letter to my ex tucked up inside a crack behind the cistern; a letter to my family pressed flat along the bed frame; a pen stuffed inside the hollow metal leg of one of the beds, held in place with a wad of toilet paper) and we are worried that either the guards will find them when they go through the cell after we have left, or that those responsible for wherever we are headed will be more thorough with their searches. The only safe option is to flush them down the toilet. It hurts.

Dread? Anxiety? Those are the wrong words for what we are feeling. Too weak. Let's put the proper word in here: it is fear. I am afraid of what they have in mind for us, of what our new companions will be like, and of what my family must be going through. But I also realise that fear has been with us for so long that it has become the white noise to everything else that's been going on. As we bounce along the rutted road in the back of the prison transport van, sitting on top of sacks stuffed with our clothes and books, I can feel it bubbling up like bile and suddenly I feel sick.

But 'fear' is a very blunt word. In English, we don't have the vocabulary to parse the various, multitudinous forms of fear. It is like trying to describe the light spectrum with a single word, 'colour'.

There is that intellectualised fear you have when you know in your head that something is threatening. It is a clear-headed, logical chain of thoughts that says, 'That noise is a gunshot. Guns mean bullets, and bullets can hurt. I should be afraid.' This kind of fear is more thought than felt. It only becomes that paralysing, gut-wrenching fear that explodes your adrenal glands in a firecracker blast after you have seen and experienced the muscle-tearing and bone-shattering damage that an AK-47 bullet can do when it hits a body at 715 metres per second. Then and only then does a loud bang from a backfiring car or slamming door instinctively drive you to the ground for cover.

Then there is that background fear that eats away at your brain like a cancer, twisting and gnarling it the way a strand of barbed wire tightly knotted around a tree bends and tortures it. It is always there, for the most part fading into the background while you focus on the challenges of getting through daily life. It is an insidious angst-filled sense of foreboding that creeps into every pore – a constant, nagging feeling that things are not right, that a threat is close but cannot be pointed at, much less fought off. It often feels stupid – without a specific thing to be afraid of, it is not something that can be rationalised – but it cannot be easily dismissed. And when the busyness of ordinary life fades away, quietly that shadow returns.

I have come to think of it like a dog. Not a friendly slobbering labrador or a tail-wagging kelpie, but a wolf lurking in the fringes of a forest. It can be held at bay or ignored, and at times, with enough sheer will, it can even be dominated, but when it is hungry enough and the forest is quiet, it emerges red-eyed and snarling.

Now, with nothing to do but sit in the van, I can hear the growling rise once more.

•

It doesn't take long before the van halts with a lurch and we are ordered out – the three students, Baher, Fahmy and me.

We are ushered in through the usual security procedures – a walk through a metal detector, a relatively benign strip search down to our underwear, and our things searched both physically and with an X-ray machine – and then ordered to stop in an unexpectedly lush courtyard garden surrounded by high walls, with an Arabic sign announcing 'Mazraa' and a path leading off to the right towards what must presumably be the prison blocks.

Translated literally, Mazraa means 'The Farm', and we have heard about this place. Prisoners speak of it in hushed, reverent tones, as if it is a Hilton hotel. It is hardly that, but neither is it the severe, blank austerity of Mulhaq, which is as blunt as the name sounds.

We are ordered to march in line behind one of the guards, who leads us past the vegetable gardens that give the prison its name. There are rows of tomatoes, spinach, cucumbers and kale. Our little column passes a large construction site to our right, apparently for a new cellblock on what clearly used to be basketball courts. On the left is a large, sandy space with collapsing goal posts at either end, and a long low block that the guard tells us is the prison hospital. Another small, squat building apparently holds a crude gym.

Slowly, the growling in the back of my head starts to fade.

Finally, we are led through another two sets of iron doors to a long, narrow corridor that runs between a pair of single-storey buildings. Each building is studded with three smaller, widely spaced doors and a series of tiny barred windows spread out along its length. The top of the corridor is covered over with iron mesh loose enough to let in a long shaft of filtered sunlight, and at the far end another barred door apparently leads to a small tiled courtyard and the prison mosque.

The corridor is filled with ambling inmates dressed in the regulation blue of convicted prisoners, and they watch us silently but curiously as we are led into the first door on the left.

Our new cell feels vast. Instead of the cramped concrete boxes of the past, this is a dormitory-style block about 20 metres long, with bunk beds down either side. Rather than being formally arranged in strict ranks, a few of the bunks have been moved to create more private spaces, some marked off with cloth-covered wardrobes. There are two fridges by the door, and at the opposite end is a wet area with toilets and showers. But best of all (and I almost praise God), to one side of the wet area is a crude kitchen, with three battered and stained convection ovens, each the size of a microwave, fighting for space on a bench alongside a small two-burner hob.

It feels like Christmas.

•

Our cellmates could best be described as a collection of gentleman rogues (or perhaps rogue gentlemen).

The closest we have to a cell leader (and one always seems to emerge) is Hossam, though for reasons I can't quite figure out, he prefers to be known as 'Bob'. He is a handsome, well-built man in his thirties with dark olive skin, a classic thick black Egyptian moustache, and fierce dark eyes. He squints and talks with a nervous energy that won't be bottled. His English is rudimentary at best, so our conversation is a combination of half-sentences, hand gestures and guesses at the gaps. He is also a man of fiercely held opinions and something of a patriot, with an Egyptian flag and a portrait of President Sisi above his bed. When I ask him about his children, his chest wells with pride and a suppressed mistiness passes over his eyes. Bob wound up in prison five years ago after he got mixed up in a scam involving forged US dollars; he is due out in a few months.

Mr Hussein is older – in his fifties, I'd guess – and has a mischievousness that I can't quite trust. He used to run one of the country's knackered old electricity plants, and got done for embezzling state funds meant to pay for repairing the generator.

The other three are portly white-haired old men who look more like the distinguished lawyers that we should have had than the white-collar criminals that they are.

Bob has been putting his time in prison to good use by refining his razor-sharp backgammon skills. Unlike at Mulhaq, here the authorities have allowed the cell to have an old, battered board inlayed with mother-of-pearl and cherry and walnut woods. It must have been quite spectacular once, but now it is scratched and chipped, and its refinement has lost a bit of its edge due to the dark patina of a thousand greasy hands.

Baher is good at backgammon, but Bob seems almost unbeatable. He plays with his hands resting in his lap and flicks the dice high into the air. The second they settle on the board, he slaps his stones down apparently without thinking. The movement is so quick and fluid that Baher feels compelled to keep up, dancing to Bob's percussionist beat. The rattle of the dice is followed by two sharp slaps as they smack the stones down. *Rattle, thwack, thwack. Rattle, thwack, thwack.* Bob is like some kind of backgammon zen-master – talking and joking all the time, apparently without paying the slightest bit of attention to the pieces, but always seeing the board in its entirety. There is no hesitation, no counting of pieces. He knows his moves before he rolls. And he always seems to win.

•

We might have backgammon, TV and a kitchen, but this is no holiday camp. Once again, we are confined to our cell for at least ten days, maybe more. Major Sami is the prison investigations officer and appears to be the man who wields the most power here. He is under orders to keep us separate from the rest of the prisoners.

'It's for your own safety,' he tells us without elaborating when Baher and I meet him to complain about the restrictions.

Sami is an unusually small man for such a big position. He is balding, clean-shaven and intelligent, with a disarmingly easy manner and a command of English that I suspect is much better than he lets on. He is also a surprisingly soft-spoken figure, who encourages us to approach him with any issues we have.

By now I am wary of any official within the system – I have learned that trust is a dangerous thing here – but we also need to cultivate friends in prison if we are going to either get out any time soon, or (God forbid) get through the next few years intact. Most urgently, Sami has the power to extend or curtail prison visits, and when Erika Tolano tells me my parents have decided to come to Egypt, I know we will need as much time together as we can get.

Baher and I are in his office, sitting down over a thick, oily Turkish coffee, and Sami seems in no rush to end the meeting.

'Why did you come here to make trouble in Egypt?' he asks, shaking his head with a sad smile. 'You are a man who knows the world, so surely you must have understood that you would get caught, and that this would be the consequence.'

'Major, we did nothing wrong.'

He raises a cynical eyebrow, and I continue: 'I know every prisoner in here probably tells you that, but in our case it is true. You don't need to take my word for it, though. We are accused of producing false news and of broadcasting Muslim Brotherhood propaganda. By definition everything we produced is a matter of public record. It is out there on the internet. You have the power to look at all the evidence from the court case, and you can watch YouTube on your computer. If you can find one piece of evidence to substantiate the charges against us, I will happily spend the next seven years in your prison and maybe we will even become friends. I tell you this because I know you will find nothing, but please – have a look for yourself and then we will discuss our conditions.'

•

'Zae'ir!' bellows the guard. 'Peter Greste, zae'ir!'

Visitors! It must be my mum and dad. I've been expecting them all morning, but I am still incredibly nervous. I have washed and shaved and put on my best prison blues early this morning, and spent the time since then pacing the cell, unable to settle. How will they feel? How are they coping with the stinking, stifling, gritty Cairo summer heat? What impact is the emotional strain of their son being in prison having on them? What support do they have? Who is there for them? Now I will find out.

I walk into the visitors area, a shabby, oven-like tin shed with a few plastic tables and chairs and a chipped one-way mirror embedded in the far wall. I doubt the guards are using it, though. They hover around the room like hawks looking for rabbits to dive on.

Mum and Dad are sitting in one corner with Andrew, and as I enter with a smile stapled to my face, they stand grimly. I walk to embrace them and tears start cascading down their cheeks. My own facade cracks open and we hold one another in a trio of sobbing. But as my brothers and I have already learned, a standard 45-minute visit slips by disarmingly fast. We pull ourselves together in five minutes, and spend the next fifteen minutes talking about how each of us is coping.

We move the conversation to the staggering international reaction to our verdict. The Australian foreign minister, Julie Bishop, led the condemnation with a particularly harsh news conference. The British foreign secretary followed suit, along with the UN and even the White House – President Obama was asked about it in a news conference.

When we check our watches again, we realise another fifteen minutes has vanished. We have just ten minutes left.

'What are we going to do about lawyers?' I ask. 'We've got to appeal, of course, but there is no way we are going back to the reprobates who ran the trial.'

It is a vexing problem. Do we stick with Al Jazeera and let them choose and pay for the lawyers? Or do we follow Fahmy's route to separate ourselves from the network and go it alone? And if we go it alone, how are we going to pay for lawyers? Egypt might be part of the developing world, but, as with getting good advice anywhere, a lengthy legal struggle is likely to cost hundreds of thousands of dollars. We simply don't have that kind of money.

'Whoever it is, they need to be taking instructions from us,' Andrew says. 'I'm not sure about Al Jazeera paying for it, though. I think it's dangerous to be too close to them.'

'I don't think it matters,' I reply. 'If we separate ourselves, it could wind up just confirming their conspiracy theory – that the network really is up to no good – and anyway, the case was so clearly baseless that I don't think they give a damn about who is representing us. We just need someone well connected, who knows how to mount a strong legal argument.'

My mother interrupts with a worried face. 'However we do this, we need to move quickly – but Ramadan is making things tough.'

My heart sinks. Of course! The holy month of Ramadan in the Islamic world is like stretching the gap between Christmas and New Year over four weeks. Everybody fasts through the heat of the day, and with no food or water between sunrise and sunset, people get notoriously cranky and uninterested in work. As a non-Muslim there is no obligation for me to join the fast, but because I am the only person in the prison in that position, it seems wrong to eat or drink while the others have to struggle through. Ramadan is taking its toll on me, and I understand why it is almost impossible to get things d—

'Time!' bellows a guard. 'Finish. Now.'

I hurriedly kiss my parents goodbye and wave to them as I am marched out the door back to the cell. It will be another two weeks before we see each other again.

•

'I have a strategy,' Fahmy tells me in a conspiratorial tone. I am not surprised. Fahmy always has a strategy.

'My family is working contacts at the Interior Ministry to get me transferred to a hospital for my shoulder. At the moment they are only talking of a few days, maybe a week, but once I am there I will try to hold on for as long as I can while I aim for a medical pardon. I reckon that will take about a month. And when that happens I will start writing my book. But don't worry – I won't publish anything until you guys are out.'

I am sceptical. He and his family have good contacts, but I honestly doubt they have the political clout to make any of that work. If we were just regular prisoners I might have more confidence in their ability to pull strings, but our case is so politically loaded that it won't happen without the support of some very powerful people.

But I am also hopeful. It has been almost two weeks since our conviction, and the stress of dealing with our own strategy for the appeal, combined with the stifling heat and the pressure of fasting through Ramadan, is straining relations among us. Fahmy has been fractious with his scheming and plotting, and it would be a relief to have him move on.

•

Guess what?

It has worked. Fahmy is leaving us, just as he promised. Two days after our conversation, a couple of guards call for him to pack his things, and he is gone. Just like that.

As he walks out the door, I feel as if someone has pushed in the valve of an overpressured tyre. I am both relieved and genuinely happy for him. He is on the course he has set for himself, and if he finally makes it out it will be good for all of us. I also hope the hospital will be relatively easy for him, though if he is confined to a room with a 24-hour guard outside, it will be a smaller, tighter, more cramped cage than the one we are in now.

It also means we won't have to tangle with his scheming. Instead, we can focus on supporting our families outside prison and looking after ourselves inside.

•

Once we settle in, I try to get back to the exercise-meditation-creative routine I established back in Limen. Oddly, it is harder here in the communal space. People struggling to deal with the stress of imprisonment and boredom create tension and friction far beyond the usual difficulties of dormitory life.

Major Sami has allowed books and writing material, and the embassy and my family take every opportunity to test the boundaries of what the prison will let in.

I start a diary. It is risky, of course. If it is found, and I have anything in there that is considered compromising (and it is hard to censor myself in a diary), I could find myself in real trouble. But I also have a compelling need to write and record what we are going through, to take refuge in my professional role as a journalist and storyteller, and I decide, perhaps foolishly, that it is worth the risk.

Erika has brought me a black hardback foolscap-sized notebook that is perfect for the job. The challenge is finding a place to stash it. I could hide the diary in plain sight along with all the other books and hope that if the guards find it they will assume that if it isn't hidden, it can't be a problem. Even if they do find it, there is a good chance they won't be able to read English or my scrappy handwriting (a teacher once told me it looked as if a spider had vomited its way across the page).

But that feels incredibly risky, so I begin searching for a hiding place. It needs to be discreet (obviously), but also somewhere I can easily access it. Under the mattress? That's always the first place the guards look whenever they search the cells. At the bottom of a bag of filthy laundry? That's the second place. Above the cistern in the toilet? It's too far away and the kind of place that someone else might try to hide something. It quickly becomes apparent that there are very few places that might work in this spartan environment.

Then I find it.

My bed is made of black metal, with a flat metal sheet at its head. Behind the sheet are two U-shaped bars to stop it from buckling. The bottom bar has its U facing upwards, while the top one faces down.

I have to stifle a whoop when I realise that the black book fits perfectly in between those slots and unless you physically pull the heavy metal bed away from the wall and have a good look, it is almost impossible to see or feel anything out of place.

•

After the end of Ramadan, Sami relents and allows us out of the cell and into the corridor. As convicted terrorists we are still forbidden from speaking to the other prisoners, but that is less of a problem for me than it is for Baher and the students.

And so we take up running again.

I estimate the corridor to be about 50 metres long, and although it is only about 3 metres wide, Baher and I realise we can still do a decent workout with tight turns at either end. It becomes a very long series of very long shuttle runs – fifteen exhausting, sweaty minutes to begin with, dodging any other loitering inmates, but as we get out each day we extend it to twenty, thirty, forty minutes, an hour.

It is hard, dull work, grinding up and down the same concrete hallway time and again, and each morning I step out it feels like a massive effort just to get started. But as I gradually get fitter, it becomes incrementally easier and eventually I find a groove like a stylus on a record album. One day, as the minutes tick by and I settle into a rhythm, I become a hypnotic metronome, swinging back and forth along the same path so often that I eventually leave a polished track in the concrete. And as I run into the groove, my mind begins to run free.

•

At times, the stress that I see my parents going through feels more burdensome than my own imprisonment. For me it is a psychological challenge, an exercise in maintaining mental control and equanimity. I am physically safe, I have water and nutrition and a dry bed to sleep in. I am in no serious danger beyond what my own mind might do, and I feel as though I have that more or less in hand.

But my parents are exhausted and strung out. The heat and grit of Cairo are grinding them down almost as effectively as the bureaucracy and stress of finding lawyers in a city that wants nothing to do with us. I can see it in their sleep-deprived eyes. They are visibly ageing with each visit, their foreheads creased with stress, their shoulders hunched with the weight of responsibility.

Every time my father comes through the layers of security, he feels it personally. It is as if he is himself being imprisoned. Each security gate, each search, each trek past an armed guard feels like not so much a humiliation as a psychological confinement, so that by the time he reaches the inner sanctum of the visitors area, he is feeling the burden of the injustice even more than I am.

I understand, of course. Having a son so deeply enmeshed in an Orwellian web of injustice is physically confronting and emotionally draining. I wish there was a way of lifting them, making them realise that I am genuinely okay and am going to get through this without major scars, no matter how long it takes.

'I'm fine,' I tell them time and again. And each time my mother looks at me with eyes that say, 'I know when you're lying, son.'

One day, they arrive walking a little more erect, with a glimmer of light in their eyes. 'We've done it,' my father says after we exchange greetings. 'We have found a lawyer. His name is Amr Eldib. We have been meeting a lot of dodgy characters in a lot of very smelly rooms, but this guy looks different.'

I grin and nod, as much at the relief of seeing them solve the problem as with the relief of at last having a lawyer.

'He seems to run a pretty professional practice, and although we only had a meeting that lasted about half an hour, he sounded as though he knows the case pretty well. He speaks reasonable English, which is good, and was very up-front about all the issues. He seems confident enough that he can get you through the appeal process, but he also had some difficult news.'

'Oh?'

'He reckons this won't be over in a hurry. It could take months to get the Court of Cassation to hear the appeal, and if they order a retrial it could be a year before that even begins. And then heaven only knows how long *that* process could take.'

Dad looks at me with a strained grimace.

'Well, let's just bite off one bit of this at a time,' I tell him. 'If we look that far in advance and start worrying about the years it might take to get out the other side, it will mess with all of our heads. Nothing happens without the appeal, though, so focus on that first.'

'There is one more thing,' Dad says. 'Al Jazeera is paying. We have struggled with this for so long that I don't know how to manage it without them. Amr has also said he is happy to take instructions from us, so we reckon we ought to sign him up and let Al Jazeera deal with the accounts.'

I heave a big sigh. I am dubious about the notion that Eldib will take money from one client and instructions from another, but the last thing I want is to add a massive financial burden to my family on top of everything else they're having to deal with.

I smile. 'Let's do this.'

•

Once we have signed the paperwork to formally lodge the appeal, there is nothing to do but wait. The Court of Cassation is Egypt's highest legal authority, and by all accounts the most independent (read 'least corrupted') judicial branch in the country. That is cold comfort given our experience so far, but we don't have much choice beyond letting the process take its course while our families, colleagues and governments keep up the pressure from the outside.

But I still need to soak up time.

We spend days trying to keep busy with exercise, backgammon and sleep, but it isn't enough. I make a deal with Shady, one of the students: I spend an hour each day teaching him English, and he spends an hour with me on Arabic.

'*Shibbaek,*' says Shady, pointing to the window. 'It means *window.*'

'*Baeb.* Door.' He pats his palm on the table – '*Sufra*' – and then taps the top of his chair. '*Kursi.*'

I repeat the words, 'Shibbaek, baeb, sufra, kursi.' But minutes later, they seem to have gone from my mind. No matter how hard I try, they just don't seem to stick. The language is so utterly foreign that I can't find ways of linking the sounds with their meaning. I know I ought to get my head around it given how much longer I might actually spend in prison, and intellectually I understand the importance of learning Arabic – the *need*, even – but in my quieter moments I realise that my heart just isn't in it.

Shady looks around for another word to give me. He points to a stack of stale flatbread in the corner. '*Chubz,*' he says. 'Bread,' and I heave a sigh.

'Bread. *Bread!* Of course.' I slap my hand against my head, and Shady looks at me as if I've gone mad. 'Chubz. Screw the bland stuff the prison gives us all the time. We can bake our own!'

'What about ingredients?' he asks. 'Have you thought of that? Where will you get flour or even, what you call it? *Chameera?* You know – the stuff to make it come up.'

'That's easy. You know how they bake bread here for the rest of the prison in the kitchens. I am sure we can get our hands on some of their flour. And chameera? I think you mean yeast. It is here all around us.'

Shady looks convinced that I have gone nuts.

'Wild yeast! The spores are in the air. And the way this place smells, I am pretty sure it is crawling with very active yeast.'

Arabic gets shoved to one side.

I have always wanted to bake sourdough bread, and once, when I had time on my hands back in Nairobi, I looked at recipes online. It is a simple enough process – you only need to get a dough of flour and water to start fermenting in the same way that fruit juice starts to fizz if it is left out too long. In time, yeast spores from the air settle on the dough and start eating the starches and converting them into carbon dioxide, which makes the dough rise. Once the starter culture is alive, you use half of it every few days to make a loaf, and replace that with fresh flour and water to keep the starter fed.

I have never tried it because it takes daily attention, and with constant trips away from home at short notice to cover news stories, I had enough trouble keeping food in the fridge from turning into green carpet, let alone giving a fussy sourdough culture the attention it needs. But here in prison, we have all the time in the world to experiment.

My mother brings in a recipe she has downloaded from the internet. It demands pineapple juice, of all things, presumably to give the starter culture some useful enzymes and the sugars it needs to entice yeast spores to come to the party. At least, that's my guess. Unexpectedly, the guards agree to let Mum give me a small container of juice.

The recipe says it will take between two and four days for the dough to get active and start fermenting enough to begin using it for real bread. It says you should let it go until it is completely bubbly before disturbing it. That afternoon I notice a bit of activity, but I dismiss it as the early stirrings of a more drawn-out process.

The next day it is bubbling enthusiastically in the warmth of the cell, and I can't wait for day two to come.

But then . . . nothing. The once-lively mix settles into a flat sludge. I give it a bit of a prod, half-expecting it to stir back into life like a sleeping dog.

Day three. Still nothing, apart from a slightly sinister smell.

By day four, the only life is a little green fuzz that has appeared on the edges. Surely that can't be a good sign. I wait.

On day five, when I peel back the cloth covering the plastic jar, the smell assaults my nose and the greenery has extended into a fully-fledged garden. Clearly something has gone wrong, but what?

It doesn't take long to realise the problem. The recipe is from an American website somewhere in New England, where even in summer temperatures only hover around the mid to high twenties. Here, in the sauna-like conditions of a prison cell in the Egyptian summer, with the heat climbing into the high thirties, the yeast spores are on steroids, munching through the starches in half the time it takes the more genteel American varieties.

My second attempt works swiftly and perfectly. When the loaves go into the oven, the smell of freshly baked bread fills the cell and for a while we are all transported to wherever we were when we first came across that warm, homely aroma.

When I finally pull the loaves out of the oven, I am bursting with pride as if they are newborn twins. I hold them aloft as I parade them around the cell with a grin. When we pull apart the big, brown pillows of fresh crusty bread, a cloud of nutty, yeasty steam fills the space. This thing we have created tastes extraordinary, but more than that, it *feels* nutritious – not just in its value for our bodies, but as an act of service to one another. Creating this simple living culture and turning it into something so remarkable feels like a spiritual process, honouring ourselves in our confinement.

It is also an act of defiance. For a few moments, we have managed to turn aside the grim prison austerity and make something beautiful and delicious – the antithesis of punishment.

Eventually the aroma wafts into the guards' area outside our door. When they ask what's going on with a hungry look in their eyes, I realise we might be onto something useful. We can't exactly *bribe* the guards, but I know they have to survive on the prison food too, and if we want something to keep them on side, this is a pretty good way of doing it. When we devour the fresh bread, I keep back half a loaf and offer it to the guards later with a conspiratorial nod and a wink.

•

I get better at bread. Occasionally we get fresh tomatoes from the prison, and we learn how to dry them out in the ovens. If I slice them up and add them to the dough, they make wonderful, rich tomato bread. Onions also occasionally make it through, and if I caramelise them with a bit of sugar and some cumin that my family has slipped in, it makes a fantastically flavoursome onion bread.

Getting spices in is no longer a major problem. I don't know what has happened, but the guards seem to be a little more forgiving about letting those little luxuries through the gates, and we are working hard to maintain good relations with them by sharing whatever comes out of the oven.

In the end, I realise that the guards are as much prisoners as we are. Their shifts are long and arduous, they eat the prison food along with the rest of us, and they spend their days in the same austere conditions. They are clearly underpaid – the shoes belonging to one of the guards, the good-natured Abdul-Saeed, have holes in their soles and tape holding their tops together. His shirt collar is threadbare and stained, and he smells as though he can't afford soap.

Some are arseholes, of course, but we soon learn that it is better for everyone if we avoid confrontations and treat all of them with humanity. It is a game of sorts, turning control of our relationships around so that *we* are the ones who decide who we make friends with rather than allowing them to dictate the terms.

On the night shift, they bring out mattresses and sleep on the tiled floor in conditions tougher than ours, locked in the corridor outside our cells. They may not have formal sentences, but with few skills of any use outside the prison, just like us they are trapped in the system.

•

Baher is beaming. No, it's more than that. He has a glow that seems impossible in this dungeon. He walks in with a bounce in his step and a joy that is infectious.

'I'm a dad again,' he says, swelling his chest. 'Haroun was born two days ago. Everything is just beautiful.'

We have been waiting for this moment for months. The ongoing confinement has meant separation for Baher from his wife and kids, which has been all the more painful since he learned of his wife's pregnancy. The baby was conceived a few weeks before our arrest, and now, nine months in, he is having a moment of joy tinged with bitterness at having to watch it from inside the cell.

Baher is an extraordinarily devoted family man. His wife and children live on the top floor of his parents' home in New Cairo, and his brother and sister-in-law occupy the lower floor. The idea of either of them moving out and living more independently is incomprehensible to all in the family. They share a closeness and a loyalty that I find extraordinary.

Baher asked the prosecutor for special permission to witness the birth – a caesarean section at the local hospital – but all he got in return was silence. So he asked my parents and Fahmy's mother and father to be at the hospital as 'members of our own extended family', as he wrote in a poignant open letter to his newborn son:

> *The moment you will arrive you will meet two great Australians, the parents of Peter Greste, who is in prison [with] me, as well as the great Egyptian family of Mohamed Fahmy my colleague. Together we are sharing this struggle; and together we will celebrate your birth. They are your family and their sons are your father's brothers.*[101]

Once the door to the cell swings closed behind him, Baher reaches inside his shirt with a grin. He puts his index finger to his lips to shush the question written in my eyes, and pulls out two fat Cuban cigars.

'Tonight we will have our own little celebration,' he whispers.

•

Erika is clearly animated when I meet her in Major Sami's office, and the moment his deputy has moved far enough away to be out of earshot, she gives me the news in hushed but excited tones.

'The foreign minister, Shoukry, has called Julie Bishop. In the conversation, he made an offer. He said they could make this problem – and by that we think he means your imprisonment – go away if you don't appeal.'

'Is that it? Was there anything more specific?'

'No. Just that.'

'No details? Did he say how or when they could make the problem go away? And can we be sure that he means getting us out of prison?'

Erika shakes her head silently.

I churn the news over for a few moments, trying to process what it means and how I should respond. It soon becomes clear, though, that there is only one way of dealing with this.

'I'm sorry, but without something solid and in writing, there is nothing we can do. I am not willing to give up my only legal route out of here on an unverified conversation between the two foreign ministers. We have to have something more confirmed and more solid than that. I will mention it to the others, but I doubt they will think differently. I hope you'll understand we are all finding it hard to trust the Egyptian government right now.'

Erika nods. 'That's how we feel, too.'

'Oh, and if they do come up with something like a deal, there is something else you need to know. I am not willing to do anything that implies we accept our guilt. If they offer a pardon in exchange for, say, me agreeing to blame Al Jazeera or my colleagues, they can forget it. I'll stay here.'

Erika nods once again.

•

One day, the newspapers report a lecture that President Sisi has apparently given to a group of media editors. Revealingly (and for us, deflatingly), he berated the media for its critical, cynical coverage of the government and demanded that the editors recognise that the country is in a time of crisis. He told them that Egypt needs to be unified if it is to overcome its challenges, and that critical reporting of the government is undermining the popular will and sapping this great nation of life, like ringbarking a tree.

The president said that the media must adopt what he calls 'crisis reporting' – being supportive and encouraging the country, rather than being questioning and divisive. It is for the good of all Egypt, he said.

This is the entirely bogus case of a dictator: demanding that reporters become propagandists and advocates rather than independent fact-checkers and questioners. In fact, at a time of crisis, the government needs even more rigorous oversight. As John Stuart Mill said, the only way to be sure you are taking the best course of action is to hold it up to scrutiny and test it against all the alternatives.

Of course, we turn these statements every which way in an attempt to read their significance for our case. If that is what he expects of journalists, we might as well settle in here for the long haul.

•

As I'm waiting for Major Sami to finish a phone call, his deputy opens up a conversation with me.

'You are getting fit, yes? This place is good for you, I think.'

'No. This place is not good but I refuse to let it beat me, so we do what we can.'

'Yes, but the air is good, no?'

'No, it is not good. It is dusty and dry and unhealthy. There are many places where it is better.'

'Okay – but you are here for a reason, I think. You are guilty of attacking our country.'

'No, I am not. There was nothing presented in court that showed I am guilty of anything.'

'Then why did the judge convict you and put you in prison?'

'I don't know. But what he said has no relationship with what I did or what was presented in court.'

'But you work for Al Jazeera, and this is a part of the Qatar government.'

'I don't know about the issues between Egypt and Qatar, but I am here because of what I am supposed to have done. And there is no evidence. Have a look for yourself and see what we did. There is not one false video. Not one. And no evidence we did anything with the Muslim Brotherhood that ordinary journalists wouldn't have done.'

'Okay, I believe you are a victim. Lots of people are victims, but these are difficult times for Egypt and you must accept.'

'Why must I accept? I have done nothing wrong. I am innocent. And if your courts keep imprisoning people who are not guilty, public trust collapses and law and order break down.'

'But your prime minister has accepted the reasons you are in prison.'

'What?'

'He met President Sisi [at the UN General Assembly] in New York and I think he agreed that the judge had reasons.'

He could be trying to mess with my head, but I don't think so. And while I have faith in Foreign Minister Julie Bishop, I am less confident in Prime Minister Tony Abbott.

'I don't see how that could be. My government has always said there is no evidence at all, so how can he accept this now?'

'I respect you. You are strong. You are a good man, and *inshallah* something will be worked out. But you must have patience.'

•

Our next target is the appeal. Like everything in the Egyptian judicial system, it is a slow process. The deadline is thirty days from the conviction, and our new lawyers are keen to use as much time as they can to put together a strong case. It is a small, manageable target that keeps us from obsessing about the years in prison that we have been sentenced to.

And so we idle the time away. We persist with the Arabic lessons, exercise and bread baking. I plough through books at a rate of one every two or three days and get very good at backgammon.

We know the pressure from outside is having an impact. Our conditions would be dramatically tougher without the vast and ongoing social-media outrage and the persistent calls for our freedom from diplomats and political leaders. The European Union gives standing instructions for its officials always to make 'What is happening to the Al Jazeera journalists you have in prison?' the first item on the agenda in any meeting with their Egyptian counterparts.

But diplomats and foreign ministry officials have no power over our incarceration. That rests with the president and the judiciary, and the president keeps insisting that the matter is out of his hands.

'Firstly, if I had been in office at the time [of the arrests], I would have wanted no further problems and would have asked them to leave the country,' he tells a German magazine. 'Secondly, our judiciary is independent. It is important that the Western world does not see itself as the only one with an independent judiciary.'[102]

That is perhaps more true than cynical observers might think.

The judiciary was established under President Mubarak, who used the Interior Ministry as his principal tool for projecting power within the country. He and his loyalists installed compliant judges and let them act 'independently'. Mubarak didn't intervene when he was in power, just as President Sisi doesn't now, because he didn't have to. Indeed, because Sisi's main centre of power is the Ministry of Defence, his capacity to influence the judicial system is even more remote.

'Not so much "independent" as "autonomous"' is the way one of Egypt's most seasoned political analysts, Hisham Hellyer, put it to me once. Hellyer compares Egypt's politics with 1920s New York, when rival Mafia dons controlled various sectors of the city.

'There was one who was more powerful than all the others – the *capo di tutt'i capi* or boss of bosses – who in theory could impose his will on the others, but couldn't do it without losing some of his power in the process. Egypt is like that. Sisi could intervene in the judiciary, but each time he does, it costs him political capital – so he has to choose his time and place very carefully.'[103]

It seems the time is not now. The Court of Cassation has our papers, but for the first time since our arrest, the case seems to have run out of steam. There is no movement, much less momentum. We have no clear date when we can expect a hearing for our appeal – under the law, the court has ninety days to set a date, but there is no guarantee it will even stick to that schedule.

•

The students call a meeting.

'We must do something dramatic, something hard,' says Sohaib. 'We have to do something that shows our supporters we are fighting from the inside just as they are campaigning for us from the outside. We have to prove that we are committed, and make the government give us freedom.'

'What exactly do you have in mind?' I ask.

'What about a hunger strike?' The others nod in agreement. Sohaib poses it as a question, but I can see immediately that they have already discussed it. They do not want a debate – this is about persuading Baher and me to be a part of their action.

'What is the point of it? What are you hoping to achieve?' I ask them.

'What do you mean?' Sohaib asks incredulously.

'Well, if we make a hunger strike, we have to have clear, achievable demands. We have to ask for something the authorities have the power to give us, and we have to hold the moral high ground. We also need some idea of how long it is going to go for. Are you prepared to sacrifice your health and possibly your life for this now?'

'We want our freedom. What could be more clear than that?'

'I understand that. I want out of prison too, and I agree that at some point we should consider a hunger strike, but I don't think now is the time. We are still within the legal time frame for an appeal, so if we do this, we will only look impatient, like we are demanding special treatment, and that will only lose us support. I know it is hard, but we have to wait for the Court of Cassation. If they miss the ninety days, then we can go on strike and demand that they examine our appeal. That is clear, reasonable and achievable. To demand our freedom is too much – the government couldn't grant that. It would make them look weak.'

'It worked for Abdullah al-Shami. Why shouldn't it work for us?'

Al-Shami was the Al Jazeera reporter who worked for the Arabic-language channel and spent 306 days in prison before the prosecutor general ordered his release on medical grounds.

'Al-Shami is different,' I say. 'He was being held without charge. The prosecutor was breaking the law by continuing to hold him, so he gave them a way out. We have been tried and convicted and now we have an opportunity to appeal, which we have taken. If we go on hunger strike now, it might even make the Court of Cassation less inclined to let us go because it will look like it is caving in to pressure.'

Baher has been sitting silently listening to the debate with his chin on his hand, giving nothing away. I am guessing – hoping – that he agrees with me. He sees me looking at him and says, 'So when do we strike? If we wait until the Court of Cassation has rejected our appeal, we will have lost our chance to put pressure on them. It will be too late.'

'But if we strike now, what are we complaining about?' I say.

'What do you mean? We are complaining about our sham of a trial. How can you not think that is worth striking about?'

I can hear the anger and frustration percolating in his voice. It is steeped with bile that I hadn't expected.

'I just think we need to be patient—'

Before I can continue, Khalid explodes with frustration. 'Patience? You are mad! We have been patient for nine months now! We have lost so much time, and for what? For those fools in the prosecutor's office to put us away just because they don't like what we think? We have to strike. If you are with us, then that is good. But if you are not, we will go without you.'

Khalid has done a hunger strike in the past, so he knows what is ahead of him. He still suffers from stomach ulcers as a result of the last strike, and although I begrudge his stubbornness, I can't help but admire his strength of will.

I let out a big sigh. 'So when do you want to start?'

'Why not tomorrow?'

People who have been through a hunger strike say it is better to ease your body into it rather than go cold turkey. Your body needs to shift its metabolism to get used to the idea of reduced nutrition and drawing on reserves of fat. Stopping food suddenly can apparently induce shock, making it incredibly difficult to cope with an empty stomach. They also say the first thirty-six to forty-eight hours are the worst, when hunger pangs can become overwhelming. Stomach cramps and dizziness are pretty common, but once you are over that initial threshold, it is supposed to get easier.

'We have to prepare for this,' I say. 'We need to start reducing our food intake so our bodies are ready for the strike. And we have to make sure we have released letters. When the prison finds out we are on strike, they will make sure we have no communication with anybody. They will probably separate us so we can't support each other. And if we can't tell anyone outside that we are on strike, what is the point?'

Sohaib and Khalid look unmoved.

'I think it's time for a vote,' says Shady. 'Who thinks we should go on a hunger strike?'

All four of them raise their hands.

The pressure feels enormous. I am a minority of one, and to ignore the group's vote will feel like a colossal betrayal. If I stay out of it, it will send a message of disunity and make it easier for the authorities to ignore our protest. And although it sounds unfair, the simple fact is that, as the white guy in the group, if I join the strike it will get vastly more attention in international media and therefore be much more likely to be successful.

I decided a while ago that under the right circumstances I will be willing to give up food in protest. It means placing your health, and possibly your life, on the line, but if the principle is important enough and there are no other options, I am prepared to do it. But I also know that now is not the right time, so I try to stall. I argue that we don't have enough information.

'Let's tell our families what we are thinking and get them to find out how the process is going. If there is any chance of the appeal being heard, I think we should wait until after that. And if not, we can give them a public letter announcing our strike. Our next visit is later this week, and they could come back with answers two weeks after that.'

The group reluctantly agrees to a pause.

•

The next few weeks are fraught with tension. We try to get on with life, but the issue of the hunger strike is a shadow always hovering above us. Baher becomes depressed and withdrawn and refuses to talk to me, spending much of each day lying flat on his bed. He has also gone back to smoking. He stopped after the conviction, determined to use prison for *something* positive, but now he has given up. Even in our relatively spacious cell the smoke chokes everyone, but complaints only make him angry and sullen. This downward spiral is dangerous, and I do not know how to turn him around.

I had hoped that Baher's wife might convince him to change his mind. The idea of Baher sacrificing his health or worse must be horrific to her, especially with a newborn baby to care for, but one day after a visit he simply shrugs. 'She says she will support me in whatever I choose to do. She is a good wife.'

Then, I notice Baher has radically reduced his eating. We usually try to eat together as a group, but instead he sits on his bed in silence, refusing to eat with the rest of us, and even then nothing more than a few mouthfuls.

'Dude, you've got to keep up your strength,' I implore. 'This hunger strike is madness. Think of your family.'

'I *am* thinking of them,' he retorts. 'I don't think of anything else. I have to do *something*. I can't take this waiting any longer. We have to fight back, and the hunger strike is the only way to do it. I want to make my wife and family proud, but if all we are doing is sitting in this cell eating and reading, how can we hold our heads up?'

To figure out what to do myself, I write a long, tortured letter to my own family, laying out the arguments for and against the hunger strike and finally explaining that while I am opposed to the idea in principle, I can't abandon the group solidarity.

I slip it to my uncle on the next visit; he is standing in as family proxy in Cairo while the rest of them are dealing with their jobs back in Australia. I know it is going to cause a lot of angst, but I hope they will understand the pressure I am under and agree to support us.

In preparation, I too begin to reduce my food intake.

On the first few days we skip lunches, and then we reduce our meal sizes. After five days, we stop eating our evening meals altogether, surviving on a few slices of bread for breakfast. The hunger pangs are sharp but manageable, but I am still desperately worried about how I and the others will cope when we stop food for good.

Then the doubts come creeping in.

What if the authorities don't give a damn? How far are we willing to take this? Will we literally have the stomach to stay on the hunger strike indefinitely? This will ultimately become a test of wills but, by definition, the greater test must be for us – the ones putting our lives on the line.

What of our families? They are suffering enough as it is, let alone having to cope with worrying about our health. And could news of the strike backfire? Could we be seen as impetuous and lose valuable public support as a result?

How will the authorities react? Will they simply ignore us, or will they try to force us to eat? Might they separate us and play mind games, telling us that the others are eating in a bid to break our own fasts?

What of the Australian government? And Al Jazeera?

Some of the answers come from Erika during her visit the following week. She passes me a note from my family, who unequivocally rejects the idea. It seems everyone is against it, from my parents to Al Jazeera. Even the ambassador, Ralph King, strongly advises (presumably with a nod from Canberra) that the time is wrong.

•

Baher has begun the hunger strike already.

He didn't tell anybody. He simply passed a note announcing the strike to one of the other prisoners who was due for a family visit, with instructions for it to be sent on to his wife. Then he refused to eat dinner, saying, 'I'm in training.'

It was only afterwards that he came to tell me he had already begun regardless of how anybody else feels about it.

I'm deeply disappointed. We have already talked about the need for a well-thought-out strategy if the strike is going to be effective. We all need to be on board, and we need to have a communications plan worked out. Going solo is only going to hurt our cause.

Khalid too has had a visit from his family, and their message was the same as the one from mine: 'Don't.'

The other crucial message from them was that in ten days to two weeks, we will get a hearing date from the Court of Cassation.

Our next meeting to discuss the strike is less strained.

'I just don't think I can take part. I don't believe it is the right thing to do at the moment,' I tell them when we convene after lockdown.

'It's okay,' says Shady. 'We understand. It would be better for us if we were together, but it is your choice. All we ask is that you help us write a letter to send out.'

'So you are still going to go on strike?' I ask. 'Even though it seems that there is progress outside?'

'Yes,' says Baher. 'I for one can't keep going like this. For my family I need to get out, and I don't know what else to do.'

The group remains unmoved by my arguments and determined to stop eating.

•

It is raining today – the first time I have seen beautiful, life-giving rain in six months. It comes down softly, filtering through the mesh covering the corridor and falling in a gentle mist. It casts an ethereal light into the prison – a diffuse yellow-green glow that feels somehow more forgiving than the direct sunlight that is the daily standard. I go for a walk in the rain, up and down the corridor, enjoying the feeling of the droplets falling on my head and shoulders.

We have had three visits today – one each for Shady, Sohaib and Baher – and I was hoping for some kind of mass intervention to push back against the strike plans. The families talk often together, but clearly they are as divided as we are. Only one of them has sent in food.

Baher has some more news. Big news. His wife, Jihan, had a visit from the American Embassy last Thursday to tell her of a deal. Washington has apparently tied the release of the Apache helicopters and related military supplies to our liberation. It is to be a straight swap: choppers for prisoners (us six, plus Alaa Abd El-Fattah and a female activist). Apparently the Egyptians have agreed.

As exciting as it is, I don't know what to make of the report. Is this the much-rumoured 'development' that others have been talking of for a while now? Or is it a desperate story that Baher's wife has invented to stop him from striking? It seems too much for the USA to place that kind of condition on an arms deal worth billions, and anyway, how will we know if it is true? Neither side is ever going to admit it – it could be that the process will simply inch towards our release without any obvious political interventions. We will never know.

'It might be true,' says Baher at the meeting to discuss the visit, and I raise my eyebrows at his apparent change of heart.

'I think we should wait a bit more before we strike,' he continues. 'I have told Jihan not to release the statement just yet. I say we give them two more weeks, and if there is any delay, we go back to Plan A.'

When we finally call a vote, all hands go up to suspend the strike.

In East Africa, rain is considered a blessing. Today, it feels that way in Egypt too.

•

Twelve days later, the breakthrough we have all been waiting for comes.

The news ripples in through the prison like a gust of wind across a still pond. I can't work out who first hears it, or how (and right now, I don't really care), but pretty soon everyone in the cell is talking excitedly.

'We've got the appeal,' says Baher, giving me a high-five, a hug and a grin I haven't seen for a very long time. 'January first – New Year's Day. It has to be wonderful news, no?'

For all my growing scepticism, it *is* wonderful news. It has felt as though we are treading water alone in a very big sea, and now suddenly someone has thrown us a lifebuoy. It doesn't save us, but it does give us something solid to hold onto. It gives us a chance to rest, and to believe that somewhere, someone recognises there is something that needs fixing.

•

I have an idea, and ask for a meeting with Major Sami. It is a bit crazy, and will force him onto the back foot, but that is half the point – to challenge him, to ask something of him that is utterly unthreatening and almost certainly not anticipated in any of the bureaucratic rule books that line his shelves. It is also the kind of thing that will do us all some good if I can pull it off.

Sami is distracted when I walk into his office. He has a pile of papers on his usually clear desk, and I can tell he is mildly irritated by the meeting.

'I'd like to grow some herbs,' I tell him.

Now I have his attention.

'In the courtyard outside the mosque,' I continue. 'It is sunny in there, and warm. I'd like you to let me fill a few plastic shopping bags with soil from the gardens so I can put them in the courtyard and grow herbs. You know – mint for tea, some coriander and chives. That sort of thing. All you need to do is let my family bring some seeds in, and let me get into the courtyard every day with the Muslim prisoners so I can water them. There is no security issue. I just want to grow something.'

He frowns, and I can see him mentally leafing through the regulations, looking for an excuse to say no.

Eventually, he waves me off with a grunt. 'I have work to do. This garden thing. Maybe. Maybe not.'

I walk out struggling to suppress a wry smile. I think I have him.

•

The ratchet moves forward another notch.

One of our cellmates has just brought in the text of a new decree from President Sisi that grants the president the power to deport foreign nationals who are in the judicial system.

Rumours of this law have been kicking around for a few weeks. It says that the president has the power to deport any foreign national within Egypt's judicial system to their country of origin, either to serve out their sentence if they have been convicted, or to complete the judicial process if they haven't. The embassy thinks I may be the only person in Egypt right now who could technically benefit from it. Fahmy is a dual national, with both Canadian and Egyptian citizenship, so his situation is a little fuzzier. Worryingly, it does nothing for Baher, who holds only Egyptian citizenship and therefore is much more vulnerable than those of us with foreign governments lobbying on our behalf.

Although it all seems encouraging, we have become too cynical to get excited. Now, the only thing that will mean anything at all is a key turning in the lock outside the cell, and a voice announcing that we are free to go.

When Andrew comes to visit, he and I have a lot to discuss.

Technically, no country can 'deport' a prisoner into another judicial system. Deportation simply means kicking someone out of a country's borders. There is no extradition treaty between Egypt and Australia, so the Australian government would need to make some special arrangement for me to go to jail there.

'Mate, they are not going to put you in prison back home,' Andrew says, rubbing his forehead. 'It would be political suicide. There would be massive protests. But I doubt Sisi will agree to let you go if it means you simply walk free. So I don't know how this is going to work, to be honest, but at least we can now make an application to get you sent home under the decree.'

'I'm sorry, but I can't do that,' I tell him.

He looks at me as if I've slapped him. 'What do you mean? Why the hell not?'

'Because I am currently a convicted terrorist. The decree only lets me apply to be sent to another prison. It means I also give up any legal way of clearing my name.'

'Well, another prison would be a damned sight better than this one, and you'd be much closer to home, too.'

'Maybe, but it would be an implicit acknowledgement that I am guilty of some kind of crime. I am simply not going to go there. Ever.'

I know Andrew is frustrated – my family wants this to be over as badly as I do, and in their view anything that gets us closer to an end is worth trying. But my fellow prisoners and I have stood on principle for so long that I don't think I can betray that.

'Can't we wait until after the appeal? If we do that, at least I will be back in prison whites as an accused person rather than a convict. That way, the question of prison goes off the table.'

'We'll see,' says Andrew.

18

THE FOURTH ESTATE

Everyone remembers where they were when they learned of the 9/11 attacks.

I was walking out of the shower in a hotel room in Lima, Peru, buttoning up my collared shirt and thinking about how to cover a summit of leaders from across the Americas that was about to open in a conference centre a few blocks away. I flicked the television to BBC World and stood transfixed, shirt half-buttoned, as I watched the live feed of the first tower ablaze and that sickening black column of smoke rising above Lower Manhattan. Then, with horror, I watched as the second plane slammed into the other tower.

As the story began to unfold and it became clear that this was not an accident but the most brutally spectacular act of mass murder in modern history, I realised, as did many others, that in that instant the world had changed.

The images are so familiar now, like the wallpaper of our collective memory, that it is easy to forget the impact they had at the time. It wasn't just the number of people who died in the Twin Towers and at the Pentagon, but the symbolic intent behind the method of attack and the choice of targets. It was a strike at the heart of American commerce, politics and the military, clearly meant to create outrage – an audacious, savage whack at the world's biggest hornets' nest, intended to stir it into a frenzied backlash.

It also raised huge questions about how we – the media – would respond to it, though at the time I and most of my colleagues barely gave that a second thought. The immediate worry was figuring out what to do next.

Once I had gathered my thoughts and my equipment in the hotel room, my most urgent task was to get the reactions of the leaders gathered in Lima. Most of the continents' presidents were there, but the United States was represented by the then secretary of state, Colin Powell.

Powell was ashen-faced when he appeared at the meeting. He made a brief statement calling for international support to help catch whoever was behind the attacks, and then left with questions trailing in his wake.

•

Radicals linked to Al Qaeda had tried to bring down the Twin Towers before. In 1993, activists parked a truck loaded with more than half a tonne of fertiliser fashioned into a bomb in the underground car park of the north tower, and detonated it. The bomb failed to bring down the tower, but it did kill six people and injure 1000 others. While the incident generated a lot of media attention at the time, it hardly moved the dial on public opinion or US foreign policy.

Then, in 1996, Al Qaeda issued its 'Declaration of War against the United States'. This was followed two years later, in February 1998, by a new communiqué called 'World Islamic Front for Jihad against Jews and Crusaders'. Again, despite what now seem to be two clear warnings, these statements barely registered with the media.

Al Qaeda's next attack was more successful at gaining headlines. Later in 1998, they hit the US embassies in Nairobi, Kenya and Dar es Salaam in neighbouring Tanzania, also with truck bombs. The twin attacks killed more than 200 people and injured more than 5000 others, but for all the graphic violence and the images of bloodied victims and rubble-strewn streets they generated, even those bombings are hardly remembered outside the cities where they took place.

Al Qaeda was clearly scaling up, learning the lesson that the Algerian political activist and revolutionary Abane Ramdane articulated in 1956 when he wondered if it was better to kill ten enemies in a remote gully 'when no one will talk of it' or 'a single man in Algiers, which will be noted the next day'.

The 9/11 attacks were undeniably successful at gaining global attention. They simply could not have been as successful as they were without the modern mass media broadcasting every grim second, live, on hundreds of millions of television screens around the world.

If visually spectacular attacks are designed to use the media as a megaphone to terrorise their target populations and force political change, they also throw up a dizzying array of ethical dilemmas for the media. How do you report on an assault like that, when the media itself is part of the strategy? Do you close down coverage altogether with either official censorship or self-censorship and avoid what Margaret Thatcher called 'the oxygen of publicity'? Is it better simply to charge ahead and report as usual, doing the attackers' bidding, and trust audiences to respond appropriately? Or is there a better way of covering terrorism that at least moderates some of the megaphone effect?

In the immediate wake of 9/11, most journalists and editors were too busy covering the rapidly unfolding events to have time or energy to examine those questions, and of the handful that did, even fewer were able to find satisfactory answers.

As the dust settled on the pile of rubble that used to be the Twin Towers, the US was swamped by a wave of patriotism and a sense of national unity and purpose that made it almost impossible to report in a way that wasn't implicitly nationalistic. Fox News took to showing an American flag and a bald eagle in the corner of its screen, preferring to become a champion of 'the American way of life' than to maintain a degree of editorial neutrality. In fact, a lot of journalists – not just those at Fox – suspended their usual scepticism, accepted the jingoism of the Bush administration, and treated those who questioned the War on Terror and its policies as traitors.

At the time, it seemed perfectly natural. The 9/11 attack was so emotive that to adopt the usual standards of 'balance' and try to understand the reasoning behind it would have made Western journalists look positively treacherous. The few outsiders who tried to look more deeply into the ideology that motivated the attackers were villified.

As the war progressed, it became clear that to cross the line in Afghanistan was suicidal, especially in the wake of the murders of my friends and colleagues in Surobi and Daniel Pearl in Pakistan. Like so many of us covering the conflict in 2001, I was bitterly angry at the Taliban, and through that red mist I struggled to see how we could ever understand why they continued to harbour and support Al Qaeda and Osama bin Laden.

In hindsight, though, it is clear that through the flapping of the stars-and-stripes and the revving of tank engines, the media became both blind and deaf to the stories it should have been chasing and the questions it should have been asking. Amid the jingoism and the outrage, the media lost its moral and ethical compass, with disastrous consequences.

The first failure concerns the way the media unquestioningly accepted the rhetoric of war. If it seems natural and unavoidable for the American government to have treated 9/11 as an act of war, consider how different things might have been if they had regarded it as a crime of mass murder. Instead of being led by the Pentagon in an attack on the state of Afghanistan and later on Iraq (allowing their opponents to cast it as a wider assault on conservative Islam), it could have been led by the Federal Bureau of Investigation in what might have turned out to be a far more narrowly focused mission to bring the *individuals* involved to justice. It possibly might have avoided what evolved into a much wider and more poorly defined 'war on terror'. It is all speculation, of course, but the point remains that by parroting the language of war, the media effectively closed down any alternative options.

For a clearer understanding of how language affects policy, it is worth going back to the Bush administration's attempts to sell the invasion of Iraq in 2003. Remember: the invasion was premised on the idea that Saddam Hussein was also somehow involved in terrorism, with an implied-but-never-stated connection to Al Qaeda, and that he had weapons of mass destruction. Recall too, how we all knew what those letters – WMD – stood for. The rehtorical shorthand was loaded with assumptions that Sadam Hussein posed a threat to both his own people and to the West, that the US knew things that the rest of us didn't, and that somehow the only appropriate response was military.

In retrospect, it is now abundantly clear that the Western media singularly failed in its duty to question and challenge those assumptions. With a few notable exceptions, most news organisations were seduced by the nationalist rhetoric, the 'classified briefings', the shaky 'evidence' of weapons of mass destruction, and the dubious ambitions to remake the Middle East. The consequence was a sense of unity and purpose that felt noble and invigorating at the time. But it also meant that the most powerful element of a functioning democracy – a vigorous public debate about the right thing to do – got smothered in folds of patriotic red, white and blue.

After the invasion, a few journalists joined the hunt for those elusive chemical weapons that Saddam Hussein was supposed to be hiding, until eventually it became clear that they simply didn't exist. But by then the utterly false idea that Saddam was in league with Al Qaeda had become so embedded in the minds of the American public that polls conducted in the years following the invasion consistently showed that between a third and half of Americans believed him to have been 'personally involved' with 9/11.[104]

More recently, in an article for *The Saturday Paper*, the President of Timor–Leste and Nobel Peace Prize laureate, José Ramos-Horta, warned of what he describes as the weaponisation of language. He writes about how one word in particular, 'security', has been stripped of its true meaning and distorted to mobilise public opinion for cynical political ends.

> With just a few keystrokes, governments, corporations and the media can dramatically shift public sentiment against democratic participants. A 'protester' becomes an 'extremist', an 'independent critic' an 'activist', a 'refugee' an 'illegal'.
>
> These powerful actors can similarly edit the national lexicon to influence public understanding of their own actions. I have seen firsthand how inequality and extreme wealth has been described as a manifestation of 'freedom'. How authoritarianism has been rebranded as 'social cohesion'.
>
> In some places, human rights violations, surveillance, political machismo and oppression no longer exist. To be clear, the actions are still very much there, they have just been rendered as nameless, necessary components of maintaining social order and, of course, 'security'…
>
> A noun once synonymous with peace, safety and harmony is now implicitly threatening. It accommodates the traditional discourse of war and conflict without the need to refer directly to them. 'Security' has been militarised and mobilised, somehow more verb than noun. 'Security' is something that can be inflicted on people in various ways: posturing, intimidation, withholding support, diplomatic silence or physical acts of hostility.
>
> All manner of domestic and international transgressions are now seemingly acts of 'security'.
>
> We are told these acts are necessary to deal with the ever-present *threats* lurking at the fringes of our lives – even if we can't see them – because those at the top are privy to information and intelligence that we are not.[105]

If Ramos-Horta's description sounds a bit Orwellian, that's because it is. In 1946, George Orwell wrote a classic essay called 'Politics and the English Language'. Orwell was writing as Europe emerged dazed and battered from the Second World War. He was concerned with the way the world had sleep-walked into the bloodiest conflict in human history and, like Ramos-Horta, he believed that the abuse of language was a significant part of the problem. In Orwell's view, the underlying meaning of politically loaded language had created a kind of social psychology that allowed governments on both sides to take their people to mass slaughter. He was talking about precisely the kinds of politically loaded phrases that crept into the coverage of Iraq ahead of the 2003 invasion. I also suspect Orwell and Ramos-Horta would find themselves in furious agreement.

A disciplined news organisation would shy away from repeating that kind of language because of the way it limits our thinking. Constantly repeating talk of 'the War on Terror' brings with it a vast array of cultural baggage – the kind of meaning that has been built up over centuries of conflicts and institutionalised myth-making around the notion of war. It comes with connotations of heroism, sacrifice and honourable struggle. It also implies the tools of war – tanks, army divisions, helicopter gunships, drone strikes, special forces, and so on – the kinds of national defence strategies that were designed for conflicts with other countries. It suggests that the right response – indeed, the *only* response – is a military one, that we make ourselves safer by attacking or invading another country. It makes politicians look strong and decisive, of course, but it isn't necessarily rational.

Recent history suggests that those tools have been pretty ineffective in dealing with the much messier, much more poorly defined struggle with terrorism and the horribly named 'non-state actors' such as Al Qaeda and Islamic State. It's hard to see how more drone strikes in Syria or Iraq might have stopped terrorist attacks in Paris or London. George W. Bush's notion that we 'should fight them over there so we don't have to fight them over here' now looks like a cheap slogan. There are plenty of sensible analyses of the invasion of Iraq that suggest it helped create the environment that allowed Islamic State to flourish, making both Iraqis and ourselves poorer and less safe than we were before the invasion.

If a country is trying to tackle a massively complex problem that has its roots in political, social and economic conditions, it makes sense to use the kind of language that allows people to think more widely. If the media avoids the language of war, it doesn't necessarily stop the government from using military means to deal with the problem, but it does open up the possibility of more subtle security tools, such as policing, intelligence, and economic and social policies.

News organisations inevitably have to quote politicians and analysts when they advocate for an invasion or condemn attackers as psychopaths. That is what reporters do. And yet too often in the coverage we've seen loaded words such as 'psychopath' find their way into copy. Those kinds of words imply that the attackers are beyond comprehension or somehow afflicted by madness. Undoubtedly some are: several studies have suggested that some chronically depressed people use extremist ideology to legitimise their own suicidal tendencies.[106] And yet that notion fails to explain why a host of radical Islamist organisations have managed to use their ideology to attract thousands of otherwise intelligent, sane individuals.

The rhetoric of 'terrorist-as-sociopath' gives us a way out of understanding how intelligent, well-educated people come to think it's a good idea to shoot up a rock concert or fly aircraft into New York skyscrapers. And if we don't understand it, if we flatten out the attackers into two-dimensional demons, we can never develop the kinds of economic, social and security policies that might be genuinely effective in stopping terrorism.

Even the word 'terrorist' is a problem. In its style guide, the BBC tells its journalists never to use the T-word in their reporting. It's fine to quote somebody else describing an attack as terrorism, but never for its journalists to use the descriptor themselves. That's because of the old cliché that 'one man's terrorist is another man's freedom fighter', and if reporting is to be genuinely independent, neutral and fair, journalists have to keep to that very difficult middle ground in the words they use.

The way the media tends to cover conflict emphasises its binary us-and-them nature. Western reporting of the Bataclan attack in Paris, for example, focused powerfully on the individuals involved, on the very personal and agonisingly human experience of those caught up in the violence. We knew the names of the victims; we felt their pain and empathised with all they went through.

But a few days before the Paris attacks there was another bombing, in Beirut. In the coverage of that incident, descriptions of the violence and anguish on the streets were secondary. Instead, headlines immediately diluted the massacres with qualifying adjectives that labelled the victims according to where they lived and their assumed politics. The *New York Times* announced, 'Deadly blasts hit Hezbollah stronghold in southern Beirut', while Reuters said, 'Two suicide bombers hit Hezbollah bastion in Lebanon'. The implication was that someone opposed to Hezbollah had attacked, and that the victims were Hezbollah members and supporters who were somehow part of the fight and therefore not necessarily innocent.

Buried deeper in the body of the stories from Paris you could find a token mention of France's military involvement in Syria. By contrast, in the writing about Beirut the military and geopolitical details were at the very heart of the stories – nearly every paragraph in the *New York Times* and Reuters stories examined Hezbollah's deployment in Syria. There were virtually no quotes from the victims, and the word 'terrorism' was rarely used.

It plays perfectly into the agenda of our political leaders. A bomb in Paris kills people we identify with and care about. We feel their pain and want to support them. We join their fight because we don't want those kinds of attacks in our own country. Yet we separate ourselves from a similar strike in the Middle East because we don't want to have to get involved.

In the days after the Paris attacks, French and Russian aircraft attacked what were routinely described as 'Islamic State positions'. The phrase sounds straightforward enough. It brings to mind a sandbagged command post defended by machine-gun nests, or a checkpoint manned by armed IS fighters, or perhaps an ammunition store full of weapons and supplies.

The targets might have been all those things – some of them probably were. But anyone who has worked in the region understands that they are far more likely to have been things like a house in the middle of a village where armed men had been seen going in and out; a mosque where IS gunmen gather for Friday prayers but that also acts as a community medical centre and a school; or, as has happened on at least one occasion, a petrol station where militants' pick-up trucks are filling up next to local farmers. Those attacks inevitably had civilian casualties and seriously damaged local infrastructure, hurting people who were caught up in the conflict simply because they had the misfortune to live in a region that IS had decided to occupy. Without any extra information, the phrase 'Islamic State positions' obscures more than it reveals.

Australian Defence Force aircraft were involved in the bombing campaign, and have acknowledged that they were involved in two incidents in 2014 that, according to some sources, resulted in 'credible claims' of civilian casualties. The ADF says the claims were not substantiated, but Airwars, an independent watchdog that monitors the results of air campaigns, says that of all the military forces involved, Australia is the least transparent, and that it is inconceivable that there have been no verifiable examples of civilian casualties.

Some dogged reporters ask what exactly is being hit in air strikes, but the vast bulk of the coverage in the Australian media tends to celebrate the technology involved and the heroism of the Australian soldiers and airmen. Again, this is not to judge the rights and wrongs of the military strategy. Anyone who has experienced war knows that there will always be civilian suffering, and that military planners have to be ready to accept civilian casualties if the public decides military action is the best approach to winning a war. But voters must be aware of what is being done in their names, and ask whether air strikes made in an angry attempt to appear tough and decisive and make us feel safer might actually create more problems, result in more insecurity, and encourage more suicide bombers than they actually eliminate.

Of course, politicians would love us to slavishly follow their slogans and platitudes, with all the baggage they carry. But journalists have a moral responsibility not to use that kind of language even if they are accused of being unpatriotic or somehow 'un-Australian'. In fact, it seems that the most patriotic thing the media can do in a time of national crisis is to be fiercely sceptical of politicians, to always question and challenge and doubt what we are told.

At the same time, adopting the language of war plays perfectly into the hands of Islamic State, who, as we have already seen, carefully calibrate their attacks to attract just that kind of coverage. Remember: in this world of instant communication on Twitter and Facebook, everything the militants do is designed to generate the kind of panicked, hyped-up coverage we've been delivering.

As I discovered in Egypt's prison system, a lot of radical Islamists who support Islamic State *want* a war. It's something that was well explained in a now-famous essay by Graeme Wood in *The Atlantic* magazine called 'What ISIS really wants'. Theirs is a millennial cult that sees the coming conflict as the final battle – the end of days. And so, by adopting the language and posture of war, we are not only failing to tackle the causes of the violence: we are feeding them. Maajid Nawaz, a British writer and former political prisoner in Egypt, has gone so far as to argue that by adopting the language of war, we are framing the problem in accordance with *their* world view. In an article in *The Australian*, he argued that instead of talking of the conflict as a war, it would be better to see it as a global Islamic insurgency. Recognising it that way would frame the way we reacted to it, and could avert a third world war from becoming a self-fulfilling prophecy.

Once again, this is not to suggest that a military approach is necessarily wrong. It's an option and must always remain so, and there are plenty of good arguments as to why using the military might be the right thing to do. What I am arguing is that the media has a duty to avoid blindly adopting the politically loaded rhetoric of our leaders. When we are under attack, it is the easiest thing in the world to adopt jingoistic language, to close ranks, to shun outsiders, to flatten the attackers into two-dimensional demons and ultimately fail to get to the bottom of the problem.

Our critics can and do accuse the media of being unpatriotic, and that makes it tough to hold to our professional standards. But if we don't, we abrogate the most basic responsibility to our democracy. That kind of blinkered language dangerously limits our thinking. It reduces public debate to nationalistic tub-thumping, making it harder to see alternatives, and we slip into groupthink – precisely the kind of psychology that led us to war in Iraq.

•

There is another reason for holding the line on standards, and it is a lesson learned, once again, from our Egypt experience.

It is almost certain that the Egyptian government and our critics across the region were scouring our professional records for past transgressions. If we had been loose with the truth at any point; if we had shown a particular bias, or expressed support for one side or another; if we had been sloppy with any of our reporting in the past, and allowed our own professional standards to slip, the Egyptian government and its supporters would have hailed it from the rooftops. The information would have made it into social media, and the hundreds of thousands of people who backed us in the #FreeAJStaff campaign would have started to wonder if there might be some truth in the allegations against us.

If there had been any doubt at all – any hint that perhaps we might have been, or inclined to do that kind of thing in the past – public confidence would have crumbled. And without public backing, the politicians and diplomats who worked so hard behind the scenes would have avoided getting so closely involved. And without that political pressure, things would have turned out very differently. I would not be here to write this book.

The point is not to boast about our own past, but to recognise the crucial importance of public trust and confidence in the media.

A survey published in 2024 confirmed what most Australian journalists already suspected – that trust in the media is at an all-time low. The Edleman Trust Barometer found that in Australia, only 39 percent of respondents had any faith in traditional news services.[107]

The results showed that people were shifting their faith towards the internet rather than traditional media as sources of truth.

The loss of confidence is most severe amongst those that Edelman describes as 'the mass population' (as opposed to 'the informed public'), and for the first time, people seem to trust online search engines more than they trust traditional media.

But the media can't survive without public trust. Certainly, the battles with government over media freedom won't be won without public support, just as we would in all probability still be in prison without it, and while there are countless new pressures that drive journalists towards a hunt, it is hard to see how the media can survive in any meaningful way if it can't claw back some level of trust.

That means keeping a clear distinction between comment and news – something that too many news organisations have been letting slip in the hunt for advertising revenue.

It means holding the line on the professional standards such as balance, accuracy and precise language that have been discussed here, even if it means losing some readers. Without that commitment to standards, trust will erode further and, ultimately, the media will slip into irrelevance.

•

There is one final lesson for the media to be drawn from Egypt, and that is the need for solidarity.

Journalists are a cranky, cantankerous lot. Argumentative and fiercely competitive by nature, they are almost impossible to organise, and yet throughout our detention, our professional colleagues abandoned the habits and instincts of a lifetime to line up behind us in an extraordinary way.

The wave began in Nairobi when the local press corps organised a 'zipped-lips' campaign, posting selfies with their mouths taped shut, and then marching on the Egyptian embassy early in 2014. A group of some of the world's most respected journalists wrote a joint letter to the interim president Adli Mansour, calling for our release.[108] The subject was constantly coming up in news conferences and interviews with Egyptian officials. Unexpectedly, in a world as competitive as the media's, Al Jazeera's direct rivals including CNN and the BBC joined in with on-air statements of support.

That unity of purpose was one of the main reasons why the Egyptian authorities found it so hard to make the allegations against us stick in the court of public opinion. Our own professionalism made it possible for our colleagues to stand behind us with confidence, but it also made it clear more widely that there was a line the industry as a whole was prepared to defend, and in the end, I sincerely doubt the campaign would have been successful without the industry's support.

It is incredibly hard to find that sense of unity when newsrooms everywhere are struggling in what often feels like a fight to the death with their rivals, but if the industry is to hold the line and defend attacks on media freedom, and if it is to ever win back public confidence, it needs to hold together in a way that we haven't seen since, well, the Egyptian authorities threw three Al Jazeera journalists in prison.

19

FREEDOM

1 FEBRUARY 2015

In prison, New Year's Eve doesn't feel like New Year's Eve. There are no fireworks, no party hats and definitely no champagne, and anyway, nobody feels that there is much to celebrate. When we wake to the first day of 2015, the weather is chilly and our unheated cell feels cold-steel grey.

But 1 January – 369 days into our ordeal – is the day of our appeal.

Six months ago, we might have held on to that fizzy, buzzy sense of hope that the court will overturn our conviction and possibly even order our release. In theory, it has the power to toss the whole embarrassing thing out and send us home, but by now we know better. Nothing changes until something has changed. The hearing is hugely important to us – perhaps our last, best hope of getting out of here – but we do not and must not hold on to hope.

The hearing will also take place without us. The Court of Cassation is like the High Court of Australia, with a bench of judges who take written submissions before listening to oral arguments from the lawyers. Their role is not to adjudicate on the judgement against us, but on complaints about technical violations of legal procedure in our trial. They judge the judges.

We know there is huge interest in the hearing. All the local papers are apparently previewing it, and we expect there will be a huge media scrum with a phalanx of diplomats and human-rights observers keeping watch. But when we wake, all we hear is the usual marching of guards outside the cell and movement of the first prison work shifts.

I don't expect any news will come until perhaps early afternoon – Egyptian judges are not known for being early risers – so I head out for my run.

It is a long one. It takes time for me to warm up, so I begin by shuffling up and down the corridor, more like a 65-year-old with arthritic hip problems than a fairly fit 49-year-old. By the time I am done, though, the stiffness has left me and my legs feel strong. I check my watch. An hour has passed.

I plan to bake more bread today, this time with some Latvian stoneground rye flour that Dad managed to get through the gates, and I have barely finished scraping dregs of dough off the bench when Sohaib saunters in with an unexpected sly grin on his face.

'What's up with you, dude?' I ask.

'We got it,' he replies simply.

'Got what?'

He looks at me as though I am the prison idiot.

'The appeal,' he says. 'Court of Cassation. They agree to make us accused again.'

We grab each other in a big, powerful embrace.

Baher rushes in. 'Have you heard—' he starts. 'Of course you have. We got it! We are back in prison whites!'

He does a little jig, his prison blues flapping loosely in time with his gyrating body. We high-five and once again he throws his arms around me, with an unexpected sense of commitment.

'Hey, brother. We might just get out of this shithole yet,' he grins.

•

And we might, but January is the longest month.

The newspapers – both local and international – are full of stories and analysis about our case. Crucially, the local coverage is either neutral or positive, portraying us as victims of an injustice rather than evil terrorist infiltrators. It is too much to suggest that public opinion is swinging in our favour – after all, I suspect the journalists writing those stories are sympathetic to our cause. But there seems to be a clear shift in mood, like a freshening breeze running through Cairo.

That breeze has no effect on the judicial system. Day after day we wait for the court to publish its findings – it has a month to do so and set a date for a retrial – but we can't control our impatience. We also keep hoping for a pardon or announcement that the charges have been dropped, but there's nothing. Even the Australian Embassy's regular contacts aren't returning calls or answering emails.

When day thirty passes with no news, it seems obvious to me that the government and judiciary are playing with us and have absolutely no intention of releasing us. All the rumours and speculation of deals are mere games, designed to give the appearance of progress without actually delivering anything.

We are now in clear blue legal and political water, with no apparent target to aim for. The highest court in the land has violated its own laws and there is no longer any obvious judicial path for us to take. The mood in the cells has turned very dark indeed, with Baher's mood the darkest of all.

When I wake on the morning of 1 February and pull my shoes on for my morning run, the frustration of the past month crystallises into one clear thought: now is the time for a hunger strike. Mike is due for a visit later today, and I will tell him we have to start making plans.

I pace up and down the corridor, following the path I have trodden a thousand times before. Up and back, along the grey concrete tube, time and again. Down to the guard's desk at one end. Turn. Back to the mosque gate. Turn. Down to the guard's desk. Turn . . .

As I run, the walls and doors melt into a viscous sameness. Concrete wallpaper. My mind starts to settle, and I slowly realise I am now perfectly comfortable with the idea of giving up food. The moment is right. The cause is right. And my commitment is right.

•

'Mr Peter.'

I hardly hear it.

'Mr Peter.' The voice penetrates my thoughts, but I am in no mood to respond.

'Mr Peter.'

It is one of the guards, and he steps out, flapping a hand to interrupt my run.

'You stop now. Major Sami – you see him.'

Sweat is dripping down my face, and my shirt is damp. I struggle to catch my breath.

'What? Now?'

'Yes. Now.'

'I'll go and change.' The prison has strict dress protocols about meetings with officers. No sweaty running clothes.

'No. You go, now.'

This is unusual. Very little happens in a rush in prison, apart from snap searches. And like snap searches, when something unexpected does happen, it is rarely good news.

Before I can tell the others I am going for a meeting, the guard ushers me out towards the central courtyard. Sami and his deputy are standing together, chatting easily.

'Hello, major. I am sorry but the guards didn't let me change.'

Sami brushes my apology away as if he is swatting a fly.

'What is the problem?' I ask.

'I have news,' he says. 'You are going.'

Suddenly I am alert, confused. 'Going? Where? You mean you are moving me to another prison?'

'No. You are going home. Back to Australia. The embassy is coming now. Maybe in half an hour. You had better get going and pack your things. Just make sure you don't tell the others anything. Tell them we are moving you, and you don't know where.'

'But what about the others? Are they leaving too? If I am going, surely they must be leaving too?'

'Don't ask questions,' Sami says. 'They will be fine. Now go. *Yalla.* Get moving.'

I return to the cell with my head spinning. I have heard the words, of course, and they have registered in my brain. I understand the enormity of their meaning, but somehow I don't feel it. My head realises that my 400-day ordeal is over, and I know I ought to be elated, joyous, happy, but somehow the words won't penetrate my gut. It is too quick, too sudden. I feel like a five-year-old who has never heard of Christmas suddenly waking on 25 December to discover a pile of presents at the end of his bed. With no warning, it is hard to process – hard even to believe that the presents are mine. And I don't want to get too excited lest someone smacks me on the wrist to say it is all a big mistake.

'What's wrong?' asks Baher, instantly aware that something unusual has happened.

'Come and sit with me for a moment.' I walk him to my bed, unable to look him in the eye. Suddenly I feel overwhelmed by guilt, ashamed of my whiteness, which seems to have been the key to the lock on the door after all, for me and not him. Why should I – the foreigner with no family to speak of – be the one to walk out of here now?

'I've just spoken to Sami. I . . . I'm going.'

Baher looks just as confused as I am.

'I'm heading home. They're releasing me, dude. The embassy is due here any minute now to take me out of this joint. I'm so sorry.'

'What the fuck!' His face erupts in a vast grin. 'That's awesome news! I am so happy for you. And don't for a second worry about us, man. Not a second. That's just beautiful!'

He wraps his arms around me in a bear hug, and the others start to notice something is up.

Soon everyone is celebrating. There is back-slapping and high-fives, and I know the joy is genuine. It is always the way whenever anybody walks out of here. The fact that one of us is freed means that any of us can be freed. And when someone leaves, that person gives the others a bit of their freedom in exchange.

The idea that someone we have come to care about and love in the cell can resume living is a gift more precious to those still inside than I have ever understood before. It is never a moment for jealousy, always one for rejoicing.

Together we shove my clothes and books into bags. I take care to bury my diaries in a pile of sweaty underwear, terrified that the guards might find them in one final farewell search.

'I'll fight for you guys. All of you,' I vow in one final big embrace.

'Now, fuck off out of here,' says Baher.

EPILOGUE

The experience of walking free was not how I'd imagined it would be. The joy of being out of prison came not as an explosion but as a growing realisation that the ordeal was truly over, for me at least. I understood it intellectually, of course. My brain registered the fact that I was out of the concrete box, but it took time for that understanding to seep into my bones.

After leaving the cell, I changed into civilian clothes the embassy had brought, and then the guards took me to a prison van and gestured for me to sit in the front alongside them rather than in the cage in the back. We drove like a racing driver, weaving dangerously through the traffic with the embassy vehicle as a chase car, before they offloaded me at the airport with nothing more than a handshake and a mumbled hope that it hadn't all been too bad.

There were no crowds to celebrate the moment of freedom, nobody with streamers and balloons, no wild party – just my brother Mike, the Australian ambassador, Ralph King, and a couple of goons from the Interior Ministry to make sure I got on the aircraft. Then, together Mike and I flew to Cyprus for a few days to decompress and take stock of what had just happened.

It was not a deportation – convicts are not deported to a Mediterranean beach break before heading home. Instead, it appeared that I had been released under the section of the decree that authorised the president to send any accused person to their country of origin 'to complete the judicial process'. And yet the Egyptian authorities provided no file of evidence to their Australian counterparts. There was nothing to suggest I had broken any law, either in Egypt or Australia, and so as far as the Australian government was concerned, there was no judicial process to complete. I was a free man.

•

It only felt like freedom when we touched down in Brisbane four days later, in the early hours of Thursday 5 February. I had expected that perhaps a handful of people would show up – after all, my release was already old news and it was a weeknight. I thought a few camera crews from the morning TV shows and perhaps one or two insomniac freelance photographers would be there. Instead, as I walked into the arrivals hall, I was met by a wall of faces, lights, cameras and microphones. Without thinking, I raised my hands aloft and punched the air, and my face split into a grin. Dotted among the sea of faces, I saw those of old friends from high school and scouts, and colleagues I hadn't seen for decades in the phalanx of journalists. Some were shouting and cheering; one had tears streaming down her face.

The sense of arrival – of having *arrived* – was both exhilarating and disorienting. I realised that our story had gathered a bit of attention, but struggled to comprehend just how much people had cared.

While I enjoyed the overwhelming sense of exhilaration, I also knew that Baher and Fahmy and the three students remained in prison with an uncertain future ahead of them.

Under orders from my family to avoid getting caught in an impromptu news conference ahead of a more formal one planned for the following day, I let the cameras gather and the hubbub settle and then made just a brief statement: 'I think that Egypt now has an opportunity to show that justice doesn't depend on your nationality . . . If it's right for me to be free, it's right for everyone else imprisoned in our case to be free as well.'

•

Over the next few weeks I gave countless interviews, all with the same message: Egypt had moved a step towards justice, but until it released all of us, the pressure would remain.

Then, on 12 February the retrial began. Instead of watching it through the bars of the cage in the courtroom, I did what my parents had done for each of the hearings in the original trial. I sat in their study, watching the case unfold on Twitter.

'What the hell?' my mother declared with uncharacteristic bluntness as the judge read out the rollcall of the accused. 'You've been named as a defendant again! There must be some mistake.'

There wasn't. I might have been removed from Egypt on the orders of the president, but as far as the judicial system was concerned, I should have been back there in court to face the charges.

Encouragingly, the judge ordered all of the defendants to be released on bail, and throughout the retrial they remained relatively free, committed only to checking in at a local police station once a day. But at each subsequent hearing, the judge repeated the same bizarre charade, calling out my name, apparently confused as to why I was not standing before him to defend myself.

The ordeal stretched over another six months, exhausting everyone involved. ('Ya rap,' tweeted Sherine Tadros, who was covering the case for Sky News. 'Here we go again.') Throughout it, I spoke to anybody who would listen. There were meetings at the United Nations with Ban Ki-moon and the US ambassador to the UN, Samantha Power; quiet conversations with diplomats from some of Egypt's closest allies in the Middle East; meetings in Washington, DC with State Department officials and with some of President Obama's closest advisers at the White House; meetings in London and Paris; meetings, meetings, meetings. At each one, my message was the same: if Egypt is allowed to convict any of us without consequences, it will send a clear green light to regimes around the world who might be contemplating their own media crackdowns.

Finally, on 29 August, the court convened one last time to hear the verdict: guilty. The sentence was three years for all of us. I was convicted *in absentia*, making me a fugitive from justice in the eyes of the Egyptian judiciary. It was depressing and infuriating, but hardly surprising.

Baher and Fahmy went back to prison, while I stepped up my campaigning. The priority was to keep as much pressure on the Egyptian government as we could, to overturn the convictions and have Baher and Fahmy and the students released. (The travel wasn't easy – as a convicted terrorist with an outstanding prison sentence to serve, there are a significant number of countries with extradition treaties with Egypt to be avoided.) But during that period, the more I thought and talked about what had happened to us and its implications for journalism more broadly, the more I realised the wider significance of what we were going through.

•

24 SEPTEMBER 2015

I head to the ABC studios in Ultimo to take part in *The Chaser's Media Circus*, a popular satirical television program looking at the news with tongue firmly in cheek. It is light relief from the relentless round of otherwise dry, heavy conversations of the past eight months, and I am looking forward to a bit of comedy.

The show is recorded in front of a live studio audience and broadcast the following day. I field the expected jokes about being a convicted terrorist, including a segment devoted to finding a route around the world that I could take without crossing a country that has an extradition treaty with Egypt.

We get to the end of the show with a quickfire round of puns, and just as the host, Craig Reucassel, thanks the guests and the audience and the applause dies away, one of the producers hands Craig a phone.

His eyebrows rise as he passes it to me. On the screen is a single tweet: 'Mohamed Fahmy has been pardoned'.

I am speechless. The cameras are still rolling and the audience is waiting to hear what the fuss is about. There is a pregnant pause as I struggle to make sense of the message. It is only one tweet, and after all that we have been through I can scarcely believe the excruciatingly brief, insubstantial, unsourced line. As I am struggling to figure out how to respond, Craig solves the problem for me.

'We've just had some late breaking news here,' he announces, looking over my shoulder. 'Mohamed Fahmy has been pardoned in Egypt.'

The studio erupts with cheering and clapping, and amid the applause, I find my voice: 'If he's got a pardon, it means – and God, I hope it means – that Baher is out too.' My throat suddenly cracks with emotion and I apologise to the audience. 'We've been fighting for the past eight months for this, and I mean, Christ, I'm sorry . . .'

The audience once again bursts into applause, and I punch the air with both fists in triumph.

A few minutes later, the rest of the news follows. Both Fahmy and Baher have been pardoned, along with two of the students. The third student, Khaled, is returned to prison for trying to smuggle out a letter criticizing the government.

The pardon does not extend to me – it seems it had nothing to do with justice and everything to do with relieving the intense international pressure, but that hardly matters. What counts is the fact that Fahmy and Baher are clear. Within hours, they are taken to an anonymous police station in Cairo and, still dressed in their prison blues, dumped on the street to find their own way home.

After almost two years of arrest, imprisonment and trial, it is over.

POSTSCRIPT

2025

When I wrote this book in 2017, two years after finally walking out of prison, I was worried it would quickly slip out of date. Although the narrative of the war on journalism that I charted in these pages was clear and undeniable, as the tragic days of 9/11 slipped further into the past, I wondered whether the world would also grow up and discard that crippling War-on-Terror rhetoric. I assumed that, like overused clichés, the words would lose their power, and we would tire of hollow phrases like 'death-cult' and 'terrorist ideology'. I believed journalism would find its feet once again, and the world would come to regard reporters as part of the solution rather than the problem. In short, I suspected this story might lose its relevance.

I was wrong.

As I write this postscript almost exactly a decade after my colleagues and I were convicted in that cavernous Egyptian courtroom, near record numbers of journalists are behind bars. The New York-based Committee to Protect Journalists (CPJ) has a graph that tracks the figures of imprisoned reporters since 1992. It looks a bit like a camel's back, rising from the tail to a modest hump through the mid-1990s, before dipping to the camel's neck later in the decade when as many as ninety-two journalists were imprisoned. From 2002 it starts to sweep upwards, climbing steadily with only a few statistically insignificant blips until 2022, at which time 367 journalists had been locked up. It is still not clear if we have reached the head. (Those figures are conservative. Other press freedom groups have far higher numbers.)

The CPJ also analyses the charges that authorities have been using to detain journalists. About two-thirds are in prison for what the organisation loosely describes as 'anti-state charges'. By 'anti-state', the CPJ means things such as treason, sedition, breaches of national security and – yes – terrorism. These charges broadly confirm that governments still see journalism as a threat to the state, rather than as something essential to it.

•

Israel presents itself as the only true democracy in the Middle East. As evidence, it points to its democratically elected parliament, the Knesset, its independent judiciary and its tolerance of a free media. It rightly points out that those things are not all available in other Middle East states.

However, since the horrific attack on Israel on 7 October 2023 by militant group Hamas, it is hard to see Israel's treatment of journalists struggling to report on events in the West Bank and Gaza Strip as 'press freedom' in action.

Apart from the number of journalists imprisoned globally, the CPJ has also been counting those who have been killed and injured in the war between Hamas and Israel. Through the first 100 days of fighting, an average of almost one dead journalist was recorded each day. By the first anniversary of the start of the war, the rate of killings had slowed considerably; the total had reached 128 but the CPJ still describes the conflict as the bloodiest for the media since they started gathering data. As with the figures for journalists imprisoned, the CPJ errs on the side of caution in deciding who to include in its statistics, so the numbers are probably higher than reported.

The victims have mostly been Palestinian journalists and media workers killed during Israel's attacks on Gaza, but they include four

Israelis, whom Hamas murdered in its initial cross-border raid, and one Beirut-based videographer killed in south Lebanon. He died in shelling that also injured six other journalists.[109] Witnesses said the artillery fire came from Israel and hit the media throng, who had been travelling in clearly marked vehicles and body armour.

It is worth pausing for a moment to remember these are not merely numbers. Each of the victims has a name, relatives, loved ones and a story. The committee has a grim list of all those who have been killed or injured, or who are missing.[110]

The dead include Palestinian journalists working for international news services (Israel has refused to let foreign journalists into Gaza despite repeated requests), and others who work for local news outlets. Many have died in air strikes on their homes, some alongside their children and families. Others appear to have been targeted specifically *because* they were journalists.[111]

Wael Dahdouh is the Gaza Bureau Chief for Al Jazeera's Arabic service. He is an extraordinarily brave, dedicated journalist who has covered the Gaza Strip for years. Like most civilians, he and his family were forced to flee from their homes in Gaza City when Israel began bombing. They found what they believed to be a degree of safety in the Palestinian Nuseirat refugee camp further to the south. But, on 25 October 2023, two weeks after the initial Hamas raid, Wael was out reporting on the fighting when a bomb struck the home his family was sheltering in. His wife, fifteen-year-old son, seven-year-old daughter and grandson all died in the attack.

Soon after the bombing, he appeared in a heart-wrenching live broadcast, propping himself against the hospital wall to hide his tears before counting off the members of his own family who had just perished.

Some have accused Israel of aiming at the house because they knew it was where Wael lived, but there is still no evidence to suggest it was anything other than one more tragedy in a place littered with unspeakable loss.

Just two months later, Wael and his cameraman, Samer Abudaqa, went to Khan Younis to film the aftermath of the nightly Israeli strikes on a UN school sheltering displaced people in the centre of the city. They were in the school when another Israeli drone reportedly fired a missile at it. Both were injured, and Samer later died of his wounds.

Motivations for that attack seem more ambiguous. Was it aimed at civilians sheltering in the building? At Hamas militants that Israeli authorities claimed were also there? Or at the journalists covering the story? Soon after, the CPJ called for an independent investigation into what it described as a 'pattern of attacks on Al Jazeera journalists and their families'.[112]

Then, in January 2024, Wael's eldest son, Hamza, was driving with two other journalists along a road outside Rafah. Hamza, twenty-seven, also worked for Al Jazeera as a cameraman. He and his colleagues had just finished filming a report in Nasr City on the aftermath of an overnight Israeli airstrike. They'd used a drone to gather aerial shots of the scene but, as they were leaving, another drone launched a missile at their car. The explosion killed Hamza, freelance journalist Mustafa Thuraya and their driver, Qusai Salem. It also seriously wounded a third journalist, Hazem Rajab, who was travelling in the back seat.

In a statement, the Israel Defence Force (IDF) acknowledged the attack but said that Hamza and Mustafa were travelling in the car with 'a terrorist who operated an aircraft in a way that put IDF forces at risk'.

It is possible that it was a genuine case of mistaken identity – that perhaps an Israeli spy drone had seen theirs and assumed they were Hamas agents scoping out the scene for a strike of their own. But the journalists had been wearing body armour clearly marked 'PRESS', they had been carrying all the equipment of legitimate journalists, and there was no evidence that IDF troops were in the area.

These deaths are much harder to dismiss as 'collateral damage'.

UN Human Rights Council experts later expressed alarm at 'disturbing reports' of attacks against journalists wearing press insignia and said it 'seemingly indicates a "deliberate strategy" by Israeli forces to obstruct the media and silence critical reporting.'[113] The Paris-based Reporters sans Frontièrs (RSF), or Reporters Without Borders, has gone even further, bluntly declaring, 'Israel must stop targeting Palestinian journalists'.

It is hard enough for anyone outside Gaza to begin to comprehend the sheer scale of destruction and human misery they have had to endure. Watching from the outside, we are fed a numbing stream of figures about the numbers of dead, the movements of refugees, and images of flattened buildings and bedraggled civilians. We are overloaded with facts but get very little comprehension.

Palestinian journalists on the ground – in posts on Instagram and X – are providing vital insights. They are presenting what the *New York Times* poignantly described as 'pinholes in the murk'. In a feature article, the newspaper went on to say: 'With every passing week, however, the light dims as those documenting the war leave, quit or die. Reporting from Gaza has come to seem pointlessly risky to some local journalists, who despair of moving the rest of the world to act.'[114]

•

Roughly 3000 kilometres away, the story for reporters is similarly stark. On the third floor of a non-descript old office building in the Latvian capital, Sabine Sile-Eglite bustles about like a mother hen. Her pet Dachshund, Lulu, wriggles under her arm as she pops on the kettle in the Media Hub Riga. It's a medium-sized room, decorated more like a family kitchen than an office. There is a small blackboard with birthdays and upcoming events scrawled in chalk, and photographs of people with grinning faces are strung across another wall – happy snaps of friends fooling around. Perhaps the only thing out of place is a blood pressure monitor sitting on a shelf above the tea and honey.

The Media Hub Riga is a refuge, a safe house and workspace that, through the first three years of the war in Ukraine, sheltered hundreds of journalists exiled from across the former Soviet Union. Stress management is something they pay close attention to here.

Soon after Russia launched its invasion in 2022, Sabine set up the Hub for those independent journalists who refused to parrot the Kremlin's war propaganda, or who challenged its orthodoxy. At the time, she was running the media studies program at the Riga campus of the Stockholm School of Economics. She was more concerned with student grades than protecting exiled reporters. But then she got a call from Mikhail Danilovic.

The then thirty-eight-year-old had just fled from his home in Perm near the Ural Mountains. He was a journalist for *Perm News* – a free, independent paper with a history of critical reporting – and as a result he'd been marked as a threat to the state. As a member of the LGBTQIA+ community in increasingly militant and stridently conservative Russia, Mikhail knew he and his partner had no future there. In the months after the war began, the Russian authorities started locking up critical journalists and rounding up men of fighting age. Armed only with a phone number that a Czech media freedom group had given him, Mikhail and his partner slipped over the border and called Sabine. They needed help to find somewhere to wash their clothes, rest and work out their futures.

Mikhail was the first of many. The Latvian authorities began issuing emergency visas to hundreds of Russian journalists, and Sabine soon set up a co-working space with desks, computers, sound-recording studios – and that kitchen – for the exiles. She gave up her academic job and started working full-time running the Hub, helping new arrivals find accommodation, open bank accounts, organise phone contracts and get their lives back on track. Some, like Mikhail and his partner, arrived with only a hastily packed bag, while many of them needed to find schools for their kids and psychotherapists for themselves.

While the Media Hub Riga offers shelter, it also serves a wider political purpose. The journalists operating there still report on Russia, using the space to produce the kind of work that has become impossible at home. Mikhail set up *The New Tab*, an online publication that hires more than a dozen freelance reporters working discretely across Russia to write long-form stories about social and political issues. Other exiles have set up online TV stations, produce podcasts, newsletters and in-depth reporting projects. Their work might not dramatically alter the shape of Russian politics, but collectively it offers their readers and audiences a glimpse into the kind of journalism they could be getting at home.

In its 2024 World Press Freedom Index, RSF placed Russia at position 162 of the 180 countries in its rankings, and says that since the invasion of Ukraine, 'almost all independent media have been banned, blocked and/or declared "foreign agents" or "undesirable organisations". All others are subject to military censorship.' RSF goes on to point out:

> all privately owned independent TV channels are banned from the air, except for cable entertainment channels. Many western media such as *Euronews*, *France 24* and the *BBC* are no longer accessible in the country, without an announcement of any legal, administrative or judicial decision. The media regulator, Roskomnadzor, has censored most independent news sites, and the most popular ones, such as *Meduza* and TV Rain, have been declared 'undesirable organisations', which means that mentioning them or quoting them can lead to criminal proceedings. The remaining media are owned by the state or by Kremlin allies.

•

It would be easy to dismiss the attacks on journalism in Russia or the Gaza Strip as outliers, unique examples that don't reflect what is playing out in the rest of the world. But RSF is blunt about the reasons for what it regards as a global trend:

> Press freedom around the world is being threatened by the very people who should be its guarantors – political authorities … This finding is based on the fact that, of the five indicators used to compile the ranking, it is the political indicator that has fallen most.

RSF's researchers observed the biggest political impacts in Eastern Europe, Asia (including in the former Soviet republics in Central Asia), the Middle East and North Africa.

> In Eastern Europe and Central Asia, media censorship has intensified in a spectacular mimicry of Russian repressive methods, especially in Belarus (down 10 to 167th), Georgia (103rd), Kyrgyzstan (120th) and Azerbaijan (down 13 to 164th).

As of 2024, China remained the world's most prolific jailer of journalists, with forty-four behind bars. Almost all of them were Uighurs imprisoned on national security charges for covering the ongoing unrest in the province of Xinjiang. Myanmar was a close second with forty-three journalists in prison, almost all of whom were detained as a part of the government's crackdown on critics in its civil war. Then there were the usual suspects: Belarus (twenty-eight), Vietnam (nineteen) and Iran (seventeen). Unexpectedly, Israel tied in fifth place, also with seventeen journalists behind bars. All were Palestinians, detained under military law in the West Bank.

And what of press freedom in Australia?

In 2017, when this book was first published, we were among the top-ranking countries on the World Press Freedom Index in nineteenth spot. Then, in 2019, Australian Federal Police (AFP) officers conducted a raid on journalists from two news organisations on consecutive days.

The first was News Corp's then political correspondent Annika Smethurst. The police were looking for the source to a story about how the government was considering a top-secret proposal to expand the powers of Australian Signals Directorate (ASD). The ASD is the extraordinarily capable spy agency tasked with eavesdropping on the electronic communications of the nation's adversaries. The government wanted to let the ASD use its technology on domestic communications, and Annika's source clearly believed that information should be in the public domain.

The next day, police visited the Sydney headquarters of the ABC. This time they were looking for the source to the infamous 'Afghan Files' in which the ABC published secret military field reports with evidence that Australian special forces had murdered unarmed civilians in Afghanistan.

Five years after these raids on the media, Australia has plunged twenty places in RSF's rankings. In its analysis, RSF blamed two big issues. First, as I outlined in Chapter 14, 'The Fearful Country', Parliament continued to pass severe national security laws with remarkable enthusiasm. (The sixty-six new security laws that Professor George Williams counted between 2001 and 2016 had blown out to almost one hundred by mid-2024.)

But RSF also pointed to one other crucial factor: Australia is the world's only liberal democracy without any constitutional protection of press freedom (or, indeed, *any* human rights). We have no equivalent of the US First Amendment, no constitutional restraint that says Parliament can't pass laws that unnecessarily restrict journalists from doing their jobs. There is nothing that says the courts must interpret existing laws in ways that are consistent with media freedom. All we have is a set of conventions and a hopelessly ineffective 'implied right of political communication'.

The High Court of Australia settled on that phrase in a case from 1992. In *Australian Capital Television Pty Ltd v the Commonwealth*, the court decided that because we have a system of representative government – and that system can't work without free political communication – the right to media freedom can be inferred in the constitution. But an implied right is hardly a solid foundation for protecting one of the most fundamental elements of any democracy.

It explains a lot of the problems within the Australian media industry. We may have all the trappings – the bells and whistles of a noisy media – that make us look like a democracy, but essentially the system works on trust and convention, and as the 2019 AFP raids showed, it is not as robust as most of us imagine.

In 2020, the powerful Parliamentary Joint Committee on Intelligence and Security published the results of its inquiry into the raids and acknowledged, '… the prevailing argument to this inquiry from non-government stakeholders is that the balance in legislation and culture within the Australian Government has tipped away from transparency and engagement to excessive and unnecessary secrecy'.

This is not to suggest that Australia is about to become an authoritarian state like Egypt. But we are just as vulnerable to that slide away from democratic freedoms as any other country, perhaps more so because of the way our constitution is written. Our democratic institutions are strong, and our journalists are still producing some extraordinary work. But these things must not be taken for granted. Otherwise, we run the risk of following the direction of travel outlined in this book.

ENDNOTES

1 Human Rights Watch Report, Pakistan's Support for the Taliban, July 2001. The report quotes a retired senior Pakistani military officer who claimed that up to 30 per cent of Taliban fighting strength was made up of Pakistanis serving in units organised by Pakistani political parties. https://www.hrw.org/reports/2001/afghan2/Afghan0701-02.htm#P350_92934

2 'Text: Bush address to Congress', BBC News, 21 September 2001. http://news.bbc.co.uk/2/hi/americas/1555641.stm

3 'Attacks on the Press 2001: Afghanistan', Committee to Protect Journalists, 26 March 2002. The page includes a comprehensive list of attacks on the press by all the main groups, including the Taliban, Northern Alliance and US forces. https://cpj.org/2002/03/attacks-on-the-press-2001-afghanistan.php

4 Andrea Koppel and Elise Labott, 'US pressures Qatar to restrain TV outlet', CNN, 3 October 2011. http://edition.cnn.com/2001/WORLD/meast/10/03/ret.us.qatar/

5 'CPJ asks Pentagon to explain Al-Jazeera bombing', Committee to Protect Journalists, 31 January 2002. https://cpj.org/2002/01/cpj-asks-pentagon-to-explain-aljazeera-bombing-2.php

6 Matt Wells, 'How smart was this bomb?', *The Guardian*, 19 November 2001. https://www.theguardian.com/media/2001/nov/19/mondaymediasection.afghanistan

7 Matt Wells, 'Al-Jazeera accuses US of bombing its Kabul office', *The Guardian*, 17 November 2001. https://www.theguardian.com/media/2001/nov/17/warinafghanistan2001.afghanistan

8 Michael Ware, 'Journalism matters: A high price paid for the truth', *The Courier-Mail*, 19 August 2014. http://www.couriermail.com.au/news/queensland/journalism-matters-a-high-price-paid-for-the-truth/news-story/978517f7b87d81e2c1748e6ae9aa7dae

9 'Journalists' bodies recovered', *The Guardian*, 20 November 2001. https://www.theguardian.com/media/2001/nov/20/pressandpublishing.broadcasting

10 As an example, see http://online.wsj.com/public/resources/documents/pearl060200.htm. In this story, Pearl unpacks the way Islamic conservatives in Iran tried to coopt once-forbidden pop music to influence young people. It is a subtle, nuanced story that uses the Iranian music industry to guide readers to a deeper understanding of a regime that is otherwise often caricatured in Western media. It is also typical of the approach that Pearl took to his reporting.

11 'Reporter Daniel Pearl is dead, killed by his captors in Pakistan', *Wall Street Journal*,

24 February 2002. http://www.wsj.com/articles/SB1014311357552611480

12 Details of Daniel Pearl's kidnapping and murder come from the most comprehensive publicly available investigation into the case, *The Pearl Project: The Truth Left Behind.* http://www.icij.org/sites/icij/files/thepearlproject.pdf

13 'Reporter Daniel Pearl is dead, killed by his captors in Pakistan', *Wall Street Journal,* 24 February 2002. http://www.wsj.com/articles/SB1014311357552611480

14 *The Pearl Project: The Truth Left Behind.* http://www.icij.org/sites/icij/files/thepearlproject.pdf

15 Jeffrey Gettleman, 'The most dangerous place in the world', *Foreign Policy,* 30 September 2009. http://foreignpolicy.com/2009/09/30/the-most-dangerous-place-in-the-world/

16 'Aden Hashi Ayro: Militant Islamist leader in Somalia' (obituary), *Independent,* 2 May 2008. http://www.independent.co.uk/news/obituaries/aden-hashi-ayro-militant-islamist-leader-in-somalia-820385.html

17 Eric Schmidt and Jeffrey Gettleman, 'Qaeda leader reported killed in Somalia', *New York Times,* 2 May 2008. http://www.nytimes.com/2008/05/02/world/africa/02somalia.html?_r=0

18 Committee to Protect Journalists, 'Duniya Muhyadin Nur' (obituary). https://cpj.org/killed/2005/duniya-muhyadin-nur.php

19 Committee to Protect Journalists, 'Martin Adler' (obituary). https://cpj.org/killed/2006/martin-adler.php

20 Committee to Protect Journalists, '62 journalists killed in Somalia/Motive confirmed'. https://cpj.org/killed/africa/somalia/

21 Committee to Protect Journalists, 'Getting away with murder'. https://www.cpj.org/reports/2015/10/impunity-index-getting-away-with-murder.php

22 Julian Robinson, 'Trussed to a post then shot by firing squad: Terrorist who murdered five journalists is executed in Somalia', *Daily Mail,* 11 April 2016. http://www.dailymail.co.uk/news/article-3533626/Trussed-post-shot-firing-squad-Terrorist-murdered-five-journalists-executed-Somalia.html

23 All the details of arrests and detentions in this chapter are taken from the NUSOJ annual report for 2015. http://www.nusoj.org/wp-content/uploads/2016/01/Nusoj-Report_Jan-2015_v3.pdf

24 'The story of Ravel's *Boléro*', Classic FM. http://www.classicfm.com/composers/ravel/guides/story-maurice-ravels-bolero/#ZQcfXj3DjmbeEofx.97

25 Ibid.

26 'Egypt court confirms Morsi's death penalty in jailbreak case', *Daily Sabah,* 16 June 2015. http://www.dailysabah.com/mideast/2015/06/16/egypt-court-confirms-morsis-death-penalty-in-jailbreak-case

27 'Court upholds verdict sacking Morsi's PM Qandil, sentencing him to prison', *Ahram Online,* 3 July 2013. http://english.ahram.org.eg/NewsContent/1/64/75629/Egypt/Politics-/Court-upholds-verdict-sacking-Morsis-PM-Qandil;-se.aspx

28 Zachary Laub, 'Egypt's Muslim Brotherhood', Council on Foreign Relations. http://www.cfr.org/egypt/egypts-muslim-brotherhood/p23991

29 'US pressures Qatar to restrain TV outlet', CNN, 3 October 2001. http://edition.cnn.com/2001/WORLD/meast/10/03/ret.us.qatar/

30 Warren Richey, 'Arab TV network plays key, disputed role in Afghan war', *Christian Science Monitor*, 15 October 2001. http://www.csmonitor.com/2001/1015/p1s3-wosc.html

31 Ian Richardson, 'The Arabic TV "monster"', Preddon Lee Limited, April 1997. http://www.preddonlee.com/arabic.html

32 Gary C. Gambill, 'Qatar's Al-Jazeera TV: The power of free speech', *Middle East Intelligence Bulletin*, vol. 2, no. 5, 2000. https://www.meforum.org/meib/articles/0006_me2.htm

33 'TV station defends Bin Laden coverage', BBC News, 10 October 2001. http://news.bbc.co.uk/2/hi/middle_east/1591361.stm

34 Faisal Bodi, 'Al-Jazeera tells the truth about war', *The Guardian*, 28 March 2003. https://www.theguardian.com/world/2003/mar/28/iraq.television

35 Joel Campagna and Rhonda Roumani, 'Permission to fire?', CPJ, 27 May 2003. https://cpj.org/reports/2003/05/palestine-hotel.php

36 Sami al-Hajj, 'Remembering Guantanamo', Al Jazeera, 11 January 2016. http://www.aljazeera.com/indepth/features/2016/01/sami-al-hajj-remembering-guantanamo-160106182602246.html

37 'Call for Sami Al-Haj's release from Guantanamo after lawyer provides new information', Reporters Without Borders, 19 April 2006. https://web.archive.org/web/20160304082135/http://en.rsf.org/article.php3?id_article=17217

38 Sebastian Rotella, 'Al Jazeera reporter arrested in terror case', *Los Angeles Times*, 6 September 2003. http://articles.latimes.com/2003/sep/06/world/fg-jazeera6/2

39 Giles Tremlett, 'When a reporter got too close to the story', *The Guardian*, 3 October 2005. https://www.theguardian.com/media/2005/oct/03/mondaymediasection.broadcasting

40 Paul Farhi, 'Al Jazeera faces criticism in Egypt over its coverage of Muslim Brotherhood', *Washington Post*, 5 January 2014. https://www.washingtonpost.com/lifestyle/style/al-jazeera-faces-criticism-in-egypt-over-its-coverage-of-muslim-brotherhood/2014/01/05/04a397f4-74b3-11e3-9389-09ef9944065e_story.html?utm_term=.91486001c90d

41 Steven Sotloff, 'The other 9/11: Libyan guards recount what happened in Benghazi', *Time*, 21 October 2012. http://world.time.com/2012/10/21/the-other-911-libyan-guards-recount-what-happened-in-benghazi/

42 Peter Gelling, 'American journalist likely being held by Syrian government', Salon.com, 4 May 2013. http://www.salon.com/2013/05/03/american_journalist_likely_being_held_by_syrian_government_partner/

43 Michael Martinez, Gul Tuysuz and Karl Penhaul, 'Fixer recounts how ISIS abducted him and Steven Sotloff', CNN, 16 September 2016. http://edition.cnn.com/2014/09/16/world/steven-sotloff-fixer-isis-interview/

44 Omer Benjakob, 'Steven had Israel in his blood, says close family friend', ynetnews.com, 3 September 2014. http://www.ynetnews.com/articles/0,7340,L-4567179,00.html

45 Chelsea J. Carter and Ashley Fantz, 'ISIS video shows beheading of American journalist Steven Sotloff', CNN, 9 September 2014. http://edition.cnn.com/2014/09/02/world/meast/isis-american-journalist-sotloff/index.html

46 'Journalist Michael Ware explains the origins of Islamic State', Conversations with Richard Fidler, ABC, 21 August 2014. http://www.abc.net.au/local/stories/2014/08/21/4071673.htm?site=conversations

47 Greg Miller and Souad Mekhennet, 'Inside the Islamic State's propaganda machine', *Washington Post*, 20 November 2015. https://www.washingtonpost.com/world/national-security/inside-the-islamic-states-propaganda-machine/2015/11/20/051e997a-8ce6-11e5-acff-673ae92ddd2b_story.html

48 Charlie Winter, *Documenting the Virtual 'Caliphate'*, Quilliam, October 2015.

49 'Video of British hostage John Cantlie released', BBC News, 18 September 2014. http://www.bbc.com/news/uk-29258201

50 'Egypt: Rab'a killings likely crimes against humanity', Human Rights Watch, 12 August 2014. https://www.hrw.org/news/2014/08/12/egypt-raba-killings-likely-crimes-against-humanity

51 Ibid.

52 David Kenner, 'Egypt to media: Don't you dare distort our War on Terror', *Foreign Policy*, 18 August 2013. http://foreignpolicy.com/2013/08/18/egypt-to-media-dont-you-dare-distort-our-war-on-terror/

53 Alissa J. Rubin, 'Allies fear Trump is eroding America's moral authority', *New York Times*, 10 March 2017. https://www.nytimes.com/2017/03/10/world/europe/in-trumps-america-a-toned-down-voice-for-human-rights.html?_r=0

54 'Top secret America', *Washington Post*, July–December 2010. http://projects.washingtonpost.com/top-secret-america

55 Howard Kurtz, 'Media's failure on Iraq still stings', CNN, 11 March 2013. http://edition.cnn.com/2013/03/11/opinion/kurtz-iraq-media-failure/

56 Barton Gellman, 'Iraq's arsenal was only on paper', *Washington Post*, 7 January, 2004. http://www.washingtonpost.com/wp-dyn/content/article/2004/01/07/AR2005040204936.html

57 Seymour Hersh, 'Torture at Abu Ghraib', *New Yorker*, 10 May, 2004. http://www.newyorker.com/magazine/2004/05/10/torture-at-abu-ghraib

58 James Risen, 'State of War: The Secret History of the CIA and the Bush Administration', Free Press, 24 October, 2006

59 Leonard Downie Jr. 'The Obama Administration and the Press', *Committee to Protect Journalists Reports*, 23 October, 2013. https://cpj.org/reports/2013/10/obama-and-the-press-us-leaks-surveillance-post-911.php

60 Gary Pruitt, 'AP letter to Eric Holder on seizure of phone records', *USA Today*, 13 May 2013. http://www.usatoday.com/story/news/2013/05/13/doj-seizes-ap-phone-records/2156819/

61 James Risen, 'If Donald Trump Targets Journalists, Thank Obama', *New York Times*, 30 December, 2016. https://www.nytimes.com/2016/12/30/opinion/sunday/if-donald-trump-targets-journalists-thank-obama.htm

62 Jesselyn Cook, 'Donald Trump's "media bashing" is already hurting America's Press Freedom ranking', *Huffington Post*, 26 April 2017. http://www.huffingtonpost.com/entry/donald-trumps-media-bashing-is-already-hurting-americas-press-freedom-ranking_us_5900a036e4b0026db1dcf0dd

63 Ryan Teague Beckwith, 'Read a transcript of President Trump's CPAC speech', *Time*, 24 February, 2017. http://time.com/4682023/cpac-donald-trump-speech-transcript/

64 John Lee Anderson, 'The Dictator', *The New Yorker*, 19 October, 1998. http://www.newyorker.com/magazine/1998/10/19/the-dictator-2

65 Alan Rappeport, 'Donald Trump threatens to sue *The Times* over article on unwanted advances', *New York Times*, 13 October 2016. https://www.nytimes.com/2016/10/14/us/politics/donald-trump-lawsuit-threat.html

66 Callum Borchers, 'White House blocks CNN, New York Times from press briefing hours after Trump slams media', *Washington Post*, 24 February 2017. https://www.washingtonpost.com/news/the-fix/wp/2017/02/24/white-house-blocks-cnn-new-york-times-from-press-briefing-hours-after-trump-slams-media/?utm_term=.836198316d79

67 Adrian Carrasquillo, 'Trump administration keeps news orgs out of closed press briefing', *BuzzFeed News*, 25 February 2017. https://www.buzzfeed.com/adriancarrasquillo/trump-administration-keeps-major-news-orgs-out-of-closed-pre?utm_term=.qde3ABZob#.owLRPJQZl

68 Erin McPike, 'Transcript: Independent Journal Review's sit-down interview with Secretary of State Rex Tillerson, *Independent Journal Review*, March 2017. http://ijr.com/2017/03/827413-transcript-independent-journal-reviews-sit-interview-secretary-state-rex-tillerson/

69 German Lopez, 'Trump keeps lying about his Electoral College victory', *Vox*, 16 February 2017. https://www.vox.com/policy-and-politics/2017/2/16/14639058/trump-electoral-college-win

70 Charles J. Sykes, 'Why nobody cares the president is lying', *New York Times*, 4 February 2017, https://nyti.ms/2k86bRr

71 Committee to Protect Journalists, 'CPJ Chairman says Trump is threat to press freedom', *CPJ*, 13 October, 2016. https://cpj.org/2016/10/cpj-chairman-says-trump-is-threat-to-press-freedom.php

72 Editorial comment, 'Trump's "War with the Media"', *Zambian Observer*, 3 February, 2017. http://www.zambianobserver.com/the-mast-editorial-comment-for-03022017-trumps-war-with-the-media/

73 David Cole, 'We kill people based on metadata', *New York Review of Books*, 10 May 2014. http://www.nybooks.com/daily/2014/05/10/we-kill-people-based-metadata/

74 'Data retention v media freedom' (transcript), *Media Watch*, 2 March 2015. http://www.abc.net.au/mediawatch/transcripts/s4189859.htm

75 Paul Farrell, interview with the author, 3 February 2017.

76 'Open letter on the Border Force Act: "We challenge the department to prosecute"', *The Guardian*, 1 July 2015. https://www.theguardian.com/australia-news/2015/jul/01/open-letter-on-the-border-force-act-we-challenge-the-department-to-prosecute

77 David Marr and Oliver Laughland, 'Australia's detention regime sets out to make asylum seekers suffer, says chief immigration psychiatrist', *The Guardian*, 5 August

2014. https://www.theguardian.com/world/2014/aug/05/-sp-australias-detention-regime-sets-out-to-make-asylum-seekers-suffer-says-chief-immigration-psychiatrist

78 Daniel Hurst, 'George Brandis dismisses fears spy laws will lead to government cover-ups', *The Guardian*, 1 October 2014. https://www.theguardian.com/australia-news/2014/oct/01/george-brandis-dismisses-fears-spy-laws-will-lead-to-government-cover-ups

79 Margaret Stone, interview with the author, 8 February 2017.

80 'Senior intelligence officer Andrew Wilkie resigns in protest' (transcript), ABC *AM*, 12 March 2003. http://www.abc.net.au/am/content/s804540.htm

81 He was still prepared to go to prison. Wilkie said he even gave a friend a key to his house in case he was ever arrested.

82 Email from Andrew Wilkie to the author, 9 February 2017.

83 Brett Walker, interview with the author, 8 February 2017.

84 Michael Martinez, Dominique Debucquoy-Dodley and Ray Sanchez, 'Vignettes: More about the 17 killed in French terror attacks', CNN, 11 January 2015. http://edition.cnn.com/2015/01/10/world/france-paris-who-were-terror-victims/

85 Harriet Alexander, 'Inside Charlie Hebdo attack: "We all thought it was a joke"', *The Telegraph*, 9 January 2015. http://www.telegraph.co.uk/news/worldnews/europe/france/11334812/Inside-Charlie-Hebdo-attack-We-all-thought-it-was-a-joke.html

86 'Charlie Hebdo: Gun attack on French magazine kills 12', BBC News, 7 January 2015. http://www.bbc.com/news/world-europe-30710883

87 Dan Bilefsky and Maïa de la Baume, 'Terrorists strike Charlie Hebdo newspaper in Paris, leaving 12 dead', *New York Times*, 7 January 2015. http://www.nytimes.com/2015/01/08/world/europe/charlie-hebdo-paris-shooting.html?_r=0

88 Raziye Akkoc and Rob Crilly, 'Unity rally for Paris shootings: As it happened', *The Telegraph*, 11 January 2015. http://www.telegraph.co.uk/news/worldnews/europe/france/11329976/Paris-Charlie-Hebdo-attack-live.html

89 Gérard Biard, interview with the author, 24 November 2016.

90 Anjem Choudary, 'People know the consequences: Opposing view', *USA Today*, 8 January 2015. http://www.usatoday.com/story/opinion/2015/01/07/islam-allah-muslims-shariah-anjem-choudary-editorials-debates/21417461/

91 'PEN receives letter from members about Charlie Hebdo award', PEN America, 5 May 2015. https://pen.org/blog/pen-receives-letter-members-about-charlie-hebdo-award

92 'Paris attacks: Joint statement of the ministers of interior', Embassy of France in London, 11 January 2015. http://www.ambafrance-uk.org/Charlie-Hebdo-joint-statement-of

93 John Stuart Mill, *On Liberty*, Chapter 2. https://ebooks.adelaide.edu.au/m/mill/john_stuart/m645o/chapter2.html

94 Code pénal, Article 421-2-5, Legifrance, 13 November 2014. https://www.legifrance.gouv.fr/affichCodeArticle.do?cidTexte=LEGITEXT000006070719&idArticle=LEGIARTI000029755573

95 'Paris attacks: Dieudonné held as France tackles hate speech', BBC News, 14 January 2015. http://www.bbc.com/news/world-europe-30811401

96 'IS claims Paris attacks, warns operation is "first of the storm"', Site Intelligence Group, 14 November 2015. https://ent.siteintelgroup.com/Statements/is-claims-paris-attacks-warns-operation-is-first-of-the-storm.html

97 'French president sets out response to Paris terror attacks', Embassy of France in London, 16 November 2015. http://www.ambafrance-uk.org/French-President-sets-out-response-to-Paris-terror-attacks

98 Yorric Kermarrec, interview with the author, 5 November 2016.

99 'UN rights experts urge France to protect fundamental freedoms while countering terrorism', Office of the High Commissioner, UN Human Rights, 19 January 2016. http://www.ohchr.org/EN/NewsEvents/Pages/DisplayNews.aspx?LangID=E&NewsID=16966

100 *Dabiq*, Issue 7, 12 February 2015 (accessed via Clarion Project). http://media.clarionproject.org/files/islamic-state/islamic-state-dabiq-magazine-issue-7-from-hypocrisy-to-apostasy.pdf

101 'Egyptian jail causes Al Jazeera journalist to miss birth of son', Al Jazeera Media Network, 28 August 2014. http://pr.aljazeera.com/post/95991439840/egyptian-jail-causes-al-jazeera-journalist-to-miss

102 Dieter Bednarz and Klaus Brinkbäumer, 'Interview with Egyptian President Sisi: "Extremists offend the image of God"', *Der Spiegel Online*, 9 February 2015. http://www.spiegel.de/international/world/islamic-state-egyptian-president-sisi-calls-for-help-in-is-fight-a-1017434.html

103 Hisham Hellyer, interview with the author, 10 August, 2016.

104 Linda Feldmann, 'The impact of Bush linking 9/11 and Iraq', *Christian Science Monitor*, 14 March 2003. https://www.csmonitor.com/2003/0314/p02s01-woiq.html

105 Jose Ramos-Horta, 'The Real Meaning of Security', *The Saturday Paper*, 19 October 2024. https://www.thesaturdaypaper.com.au/comment/topic/2024/10/19/the-real-meaning-security#mtr

106 Paul Kix, 'The truth about suicide bombers', *Boston Globe*, 5 December 2010. http://archive.boston.com/bostonglobe/ideas/articles/2010/12/05/the_truth_about_suicide_bombers/

107 Edelman, *2024 Edelman Trust Barometer*, 26 March 2024. http://www.edelman.com/trust/2024/trust-barometer

108 Mary Louise Gumuchian, 'International media demand that Egypt release detained journalists', *CNN*, 13 January 2014. http://edition.cnn.com/2014/01/13/world/meast/egypt-al-jazeera-journalists/index.html

109 Reuters, 'Rueters journalist killed in missile fire from direction of Israel', *Reuters*, 14 October 2023. https://www.reuters.com/world/middle-east/reuters-videographer-killed-southern-lebanon-2023-10-13/

110 CPJ Alerts, 'Journalist Casulaties in the Israel-Gaza War', Committee to Protect Journalists, 28 October 2024. https://cpj.org/2024/09/journalist-casualties-in-the-israel-gaza-conflict/

111 Harry Davies, Mainisha Ganguly, David Pegg, Hoda Osman, Yuval Abraham and Bethan McKernan, '"The Grey Zone": How IDF views some journalists in Gaza as legitimate targets', *The Guardian*, 25 June 2024. https://www.theguardian.com/world/article/2024/jun/25/grey-zone-how-hamas-linked-journalists-legitimate-targets

112 CPJ Alerts, 'Al-Jazeera cameraperson Samer Abu Daqqa killed, corrsepondent Wael Al Dahdouh injured in drone attack in Khan Yunis', Committee to Protect Journalists, 15 December 2023. https://cpj.org/2023/12/al-jazeera-cameraperson-samer-abu-daqqa-killed-correspondent-wael-al-dahdouh-injured-in-drone-attack-in-khan-yunis/

113 United Nations Human Rights, 'Gaza: UN rights experts condemn "killing and silencing" of journalists', *UN News*, 1 February 2024. https://news.un.org/en/story/2024/02/1146132

114 Trent on War, 'The War the World Can't See', *The New York Times*, 30 January 2024. https://www.nytimes.com/2024/01/30/world/middleeast/gaza-war-palestinian-journalists.html

ACKNOWLEDGEMENTS

For reasons of coherence, a book's cover generally lists only one author, but it is rarely the product of that person alone. Like most things worth doing, this book would have been impossible without the support and collaboration of a small army of individuals and organisations.

My agent, Alex Adsett, has been a driving force behind this latest edition, which would never have happened without the leap of faith from Madonna Duffy at UQP. A huge thank you also to my editor, Jacqueline Blanchard, whose endless patience and attention to detail helped polished an otherwise dusty manuscript.

And if it hasn't already been obvious, I owe a huge debt of gratitude to the army of people who joined the campaign to free Fahmy, Baher and myself. There were those at the Australian and Latvian Embassies, lawyers Chris Flynn from Gilbert+Tobin and Chris Ward, media campaign guru Peter Wilkinson, and one of my oldest and dearest friends, Heidi Ross, who organised news conferences on her mobile phone at the same time as designing the website for her new business. Then there were the hundreds of friends and colleagues who wrote, asked difficult questions and zipped their lips at countless news conferences and demonstrations, and the millions more who joined the social media campaign.

Above all though, I will always be grateful to my family – my parents Juris and Lois Greste, my brothers, Andrew and Mike, and their long-suffering wives, Kylie and Nikki, for their patience, grit and determination to get me out of prison. More than anybody else, this project belongs to them.